AN INTRODUCTION TO

The Apocrypha

BRUCE M. METZGER

†

NEW YORK · OXFORD UNIVERSITY PRESS

Copyright © 1957 by Oxford University Press, Inc.
Library of Congress Catalogue Card Number: 57-11636
First published as an Oxford University Press paperback, 1977

Quotations from the Revised Standard Version
of the Bible and of the Apocrypha, copyrighted
1946, 1952, and 1957 by the Division of Christian
Education of the National Council of Churches,
are used by permission.

10 9 8 7

Printed in the United States of America

To

My Father and Mother

PREFACE

To MANY people the word 'Apocrypha' has a mysterious and intriguing sound. They vaguely remember having heard the word applied to what were alleged to be 'the lost books of the Bible.' Articles in Sunday supplements of newspapers speak of them as books that were 'excluded' from the Scriptures, usually with the implication that they were unfairly excluded. It is not surprising, therefore, that the term 'Apocrypha' carries with it a certain fascination that is born, it must be confessed, more of ignorance than of knowledge. On the other hand, those who have ventured to read sample passages of these Apocryphal books, perhaps in the large 'family Bible' where grandmother used to keep a record of births, marriages, and deaths, have often been still more mystified, partly because of the unfamiliar subject matter and partly because of the archaic phraseology characteristic of most earlier English translations of the Apocrypha.

It is the purpose of the present volume to supply in nontechnical language a concise yet comprehensive account of this body of literature. The Introduction is devoted to a brief history of the process of differentiation between the canonical and Apocryphal writings of the Old Testament. In the main part of the volume each of the books of the Apocrypha forms the subject matter of a separate chapter, in which, after a statement of what is generally agreed among scholars as to its authorship, date of composition, original language, and the like, a condensation of the book is provided, with quotations of significant portions giving the reader a sample of the author's style. These summaries are furnished with chapter and verse references so that one may know exactly where to turn for the fuller account. At the close of each digest there is a discussion of the importance of that book, or of a noteworthy part of it, in the history of the Synagogue and/or of the Church. The three concluding chapters deal with allusions to the Apocrypha in the New Testament, the history of the Apocrypha in the Christian Church, and aspects of the influence of the Apocrypha on the culture of the Western world in general.

The books of the Apocrypha provide today's reader with important information regarding the life and thought of the Jewish people during a significant period of their history, namely the period just prior to the emergence of Christianity. By becoming acquainted with these books, therefore, one will be better able to understand the political, cultural, ethical, and religious background of the contemporaries of Jesus Christ. One will also be enabled to appreciate something of the manifold influence of the Apocrypha upon such diverse figures as poets, artists, hymn-writers, dramatists, composers, and even explorers —notably Christopher Columbus, who was encouraged to undertake his voyages by a passage from II Esdras (see below, pp. 232 ff.).

Perhaps it will be helpful to offer a suggestion to readers who may be making their first acquaintance with the books of the Apocrypha. Those who have had little or no previous knowledge of this body of literature will probably find it less confusing if they start with the chapters which deal with the books of Tobit, Judith, Susanna, the Wisdom of Solomon, and Ecclesiasticus. Probably the most difficult of all the Apocryphal books for the modern reader to understand and appreciate is II Esdras.

Grateful acknowledgment is made of the permission granted by the Division of Christian Education of the National Council of the Churches of Christ in the U.S.A. to quote from the Revised Standard Version of the Bible, copyright 1946 and 1952, and from the Revised Standard Version of the Apocrypha, copyright 1957. Many courtesies were shown the author when he consulted rare and early Bibles (some of which are mentioned in Chapter XVII below) in the possession of the American Bible Society, New York, the Newberry Library of Chicago, the State Library of Pennsylvania at Harrisburg, and the libraries of Yale Divinity School, the University of Chicago, and Princeton Theological Seminary.

As a member of the Standard Bible Committee which was commissioned to translate the books of the Apocrypha, the author feels deeply indebted to the other members of the committee for the intellectual stimulus and the pleasant camaraderie which he enjoyed while working with them. It is to my wife, however, that I owe the chief inspiration and encouragement throughout the preparation of this volume.

BRUCE M. METZGER

Princeton Theological Seminary

CONTENTS

CONTENTS

An Introduction to the Apocrypha

INTRODUCTION

A. *The Meaning and Use of the Term 'Apocrypha'*

ONE OF THE DIFFICULTIES IN EXPLAINING THE MEANING AND USE OF THE WORD 'APOCRYPHA' ARISES FROM THE CIRCUMSTANCE THAT THIS term has signified different things to different people throughout the centuries. As commonly defined, and as used generally in this volume, it refers to a nucleus of fourteen or fifteen documents, written during the last two centuries before Christ and the first century of the Christian era. The following are the titles of these books as given in the Revised Standard Version (1957):

1. The First Book of Esdras
2. The Second Book of Esdras
3. Tobit
4. Judith
5. The Additions to the Book of Esther
6. The Wisdom of Solomon
7. Ecclesiasticus, or the Wisdom of Jesus the Son of Sirach
8. Baruch
9. The Letter of Jeremiah

10. The Prayer of Azariah and the Song of the Three Young Men
11. Susanna
12. Bel and the Dragon
13. The Prayer of Manasseh
14. The First Book of the Maccabees
15. The Second Book of the Maccabees

In most of the previous English editions of the Apocrypha the Letter of Jeremiah is incorporated into the book of Baruch, which stands immediately before it, as the final chapter of that book. In these editions, therefore, there are fourteen books of the Apocrypha.

An idea of the length of the Apocrypha, in comparison with the thirty-nine books of the Old Testament and the twenty-seven books of the New Testament, may be gained from the following statistics, which are based on the King James Version:

	CHAPTERS	VERSES	WORDS
Old Testament	929	23,214	592,439
New Testament	260	7,959	181,253
Apocrypha	183	6,081	152,185

The books of the Apocrypha belong to varied literary genres, which include historical, romantic, didactic, devotional, and apocalyptic types. I Esdras, I Maccabees, and, to a less extent, II Maccabees belong to the historical genre. Ostensibly historical but actually quite imaginative are the books of Tobit, Judith, Susanna, and Bel and the Dragon, which may be called moralistic novels. Of a serious and didactic nature are two treatises on wisdom, one circulating under the title of the Wisdom of Solomon and the other commonly called Ecclesiasticus (abbreviated Ecclus.). The Prayer of Manasseh takes its place with devotional literature of a relatively high order. Finally, II Esdras, a book which attempts to unveil the future, is a specimen of the type of literature known as apocalyptic, similar in intent to the last six chapters of Daniel in the Old Testament and the Book of Revelation in the New Testament.

Etymologically, the word *apocrypha* is of Greek derivation and signifies books that are 'hidden away.' (Like the word *data* it is plural number; the singular is *apocryphon*.) From the point of view of those who approved of these books, they were 'hidden' or withdrawn from common use because they were regarded as containing mysterious or esoteric lore, too profound to be communicated to any except the initiated. From another point of view, however, it was held that such books deserved to be 'hidden' because they were spurious or heretical. Thus, the term has had an honorable significance as well as a derogatory one, depending upon those who made use of the word.

As was hinted in the opening paragraph, besides the fourteen or fifteen books of the Apocrypha in the narrower sense of the word, there are other books which also are classified as apocryphal. During the early centuries of the Christian Church various Gnostic and Jewish sects produced dozens of Gospels, Acts, Epistles, and Apocalypses in competition with those of our New Testament. (For a brief account of some of these New Testament Apocrypha, see Appendix II below, pp. 249ff.) The Apocryphal books, however, which are dealt with at length in this handbook belong to the category of Old Testament Apocrypha. In addition to those which are enumerated above, a score or more of other apocryphal writings of Jewish or, occasionally, Christian authorship, dating approximately from the same period, were accorded a certain measure of respect among various groups of Jews and Christians. Thus, the book of Jude in the New Testament quotes (verse 14) a passage from the book of Enoch (1:4). This latter book, as well as others, such as the Psalms of Solomon, the books of Adam and Eve, the Martyrdom of Isaiah, and the Testaments of the Twelve Patriarchs, belongs to what are usually called Pseudepigrapha, or writings which circulated under false titles.[1] This term, however, is far from being satisfactory, for it is applied arbitrarily to only certain Apocryphal books and not to others which are equally deserving of the name.

Still another difficulty of definition emerges when one compares Protestant usage with Roman Catholic usage. In 1546 the Roman Church officially declared Tobit, Judith, Wisdom, Ecclesiasticus, Baruch, I and II Maccabees, and certain supplementary parts of Esther and Daniel to be inspired and on a par with the books of the Old Testament, among which these are interspersed. Some Catholic scholars have designated these disputed books as deuterocanonical, meaning thereby canonical books that are of a later date than the others, which are termed protocanonical. It is usual among Roman Catholics to apply the term *Apocrypha* to the books which others commonly designate as pseudepigrapha.

From what has been said thus far it will be seen that the definition and indeed the limits of the Apocrypha are both confused and confusing. To some it may appear strange that there could ever have been any doubt as to whether a given book was or was not part of the Bible. But the recognition of the canon of the Old Testament and of the New Testament is the result of a long process that went through many stages, and at critical junctures of many of those stages we lack the information which is necessary if a full picture is to be formed. Furthermore, at certain stages there is conflicting testimony as to whether a given book should

---

1. The most complete collection of these in English is the monumental two-volume work edited by R. H. Charles, *The Apocrypha and Pseudepigrapha of the Old Testament* (Oxford, 1913). More comprehensive than Charles is the German translation by Paul Riessler, *Altjüdisches Schrifttum auserhalb der Bibel* (Augsburg, 1928).

or should not be regarded as inspired. The criteria for discriminating between canonical and Apocryphal documents may appear to be less than satisfactory, and at times the application of these criteria may seem to have been almost haphazard. Nevertheless, in the winnowing process, which extended over centuries, a certain degree of unanimity has been attained despite a marginal residuum of controversy. The chief stages of that process, in the case of the Old Testament, are the following.

B. *The Growth of the Hebrew Canon*

The books of the Hebrew Bible fall into three divisions, the Law, the Prophets, and the Writings. The canonical status of books within each of these parts came to be recognized during successive centuries. It is generally agreed that the five books of Moses, or 'The Law,' were regarded as fully authoritative by about the time of the return of the Jews from Babylon under Ezra (in the fifth century B.C.). The second section of the Hebrew Scriptures, called 'The Prophets,' includes the 'Former Prophets' (represented by the four books, Joshua, Judges, Samuel, and Kings) and the 'Latter Prophets' (represented by the four books, Isaiah, Jeremiah, Ezekiel, and the Twelve Minor Prophets). The steps by which these came to be acknowledged as authoritative are hidden in the mists of history. It is generally thought, however, that by the time of the high priesthood of Simon II (219–199 B.C.) they were considered to be Scripture, occupying a rank after 'The Law' and above all other books. The books in the third division of the Jewish canon, 'The Writings,' were the last as a group to be recognized as authoritative.

Sometimes called the Hagiographa, these miscellaneous books
comprise the books of Psalms, Proverbs, Job, the Song of Songs,
Ruth, Lamentations, Ecclesiastes, Esther, Daniel, Ezra, Nehemiah, and Chronicles. Several of these books had undoubtedly
begun to be recognized as authoritative as early as parts of the
prophetic collection. At the close of the first Christian century
they had come to be so highly regarded among the Jewish people
in general that the Jewish Assembly or Council held at Jamnia
(A.D. 90) made an official pronouncement of canonicity, recognizing all of the books now in each part of the threefold division
of the Hebrew Bible. Though the right of several books
(namely, Ezekiel, Proverbs, Song of Solomon, Ecclesiastes, and
Esther) to remain in the canon was discussed by Rabbinical
scholars at this time (and even later), such debates are thought
to have been largely academic. The Hebrew canon had been
determined by long and approved usage of the books, and the
Assembly at Jamnia merely ratified what the most spiritually
sensitive souls in Judaism had been accustomed to regard as holy
Scripture.

During the long period of the writing of the Old Testament,
other books by Jewish writers were also produced. Some of
these are mentioned in the canonical Scriptures. For example,
the book of Jashar is favorably referred to in Josh. 10:13 and II
Sam. 1:18, and a quotation from the book of the Wars of the
Lord appears in Num. 21:14f. In II Chron. 33:18f. the reader
who wishes to learn more of the exploits of Manasseh is told to
consult the Chronicles of the Kings of Israel as well as the
Chronicle of the Seers. None of these documents is known to
exist today. Probably not only were they not regarded as canonical, but were so little esteemed as not to be recopied in subsequent generations. On the other hand, obviously what are now
called the Apocryphal and pseudepigraphic books were con-

INTRODUCTION 9

sidered to be worthy of recopying for transmission to posterity.
Furthermore, certain of these writings, composed in Hebrew or
Aramaic, were translated into Greek and, with those originally
composed in Greek, began to circulate in that language along
with the Greek version of the canonical books of the Old Testament, commonly called the Septuagint. How far some of them
were accorded a degree of authority in certain Jewish circles
cannot now be accurately determined. Undoubtedly there was
an interval during which their religious value was being ap-
praised, along with that of some of the later books now included
in the third division of the Hebrew canon.

The standards of judgment which led to the approval of some
books and the rejection of others are unknown to us today. At a
later date the theory was elaborated by the Rabbis that inspiration belonged to the prophetic office, which began with Moses
and ended in the time of Alexander the Great. Therefore books
which were obviously of later origin could not be regarded as
canonical. The fact that this theory does not fit all of the cases
(for example, the present form of the Book of Daniel appears to
be later than Ecclesiasticus) does not mean that in general most
Jews would not have felt its force. From all that is known or can
be inferred, the process of canonization was complex and subtle.
Like the growth of a tree, which passes imperceptibly from the
stage of a sapling that can be transplanted to the stage when it is
impossible to remove it, except by felling, so the appreciation of
the canonicity of Biblical books also grew imperceptibly. If one
could have interrogated Jewish communities, at worship in the
synagogue and at study in the schools, they would doubtless
have declared that in certain books they somehow heard the
Word of God speaking to them, while in other books this was
not so. The spiritual sensitivity of generations of Jews was finally ratified by the official action of subsequent councils. In the

nature of the case, however, there can be no human authority outside of and higher than the canonical books themselves which could confer upon them the essential quality of being the Word of God. In some undefined manner, certain books imposed themselves upon the Jewish community as the inspired oracles of God. Thus, from this point of view, the process of canonization was the progressive recognition and acknowledgment of the limits of the canon.

I

The First Book of Esdras

THE BOOK WHICH STANDS FIRST AMONG THE APOC-
RYPHA DIFFERS FROM THE OTHER APOCRYPHAL
BOOKS IN THAT IT IS, EXCEPT FOR ONE PORTION,
merely a divergent account of events which are related in several canonical books of the Old Testament. None of the other
Apocryphal books is so intimately connected with the Old
Testament. Beginning somewhat abruptly with a description of
the great Passover held by King Josiah at Jerusalem, I Esdras
reproduces the substance of II Chronicles 35:1–36:23, the whole
of the canonical Book of Ezra, and the Book of Nehemiah
7:73–8:12, breaking off in the middle of a sentence after an
account of the public reading of the Law by Ezra. It thus includes portions of Israel's history from about 621 B.C., before
the captivity in Babylon, to about 444 B.C., when the Jewish
people had been restored to their native land.

What the relation is between I Esdras and the canonical narratives has perplexed scholars of many generations. There are
three possible solutions: Ezra-Nehemiah may have been derived

from I Esdras; or I Esdras may be a modification of Ezra-Nehemiah; or both forms may derive from a common original. Of these possibilities, it appears that the last solves the greatest number of problems. For one thing, the form of the Greek in which I Esdras is written is much smoother and more idiomatic than the literalistic and wooden rendering characteristic of the Septuagint Greek version of the canonical Ezra-Nehemiah, which slavishly follows a Hebrew original. On the other hand, I Esdras is not a translation of the existing Masoretic text of Ezra-Nehemiah, but represents another form of the Hebrew and/or Aramaic original, substantially identical with the Masoretic text. In one respect the literary sequence of material in the Apocryphal account appears to be superior to that of the two books of Ezra and Nehemiah. Between the latter there is a gap of twelve years; but I Esdras rearranges the material so as to make what is said in Neh. 8 follow immediately after the end of Ezra, and thus the Ezra narrative is continued without the break occasioned by the insertion of Neh. 1:1–7:72a. The continuity of narrative, however, is achieved at the expense of the total omission of the material in the first part of Nehemiah. As regards the historical sequence of events as recorded in I Esdras, the list of repetitions, errors, and inconsistencies in the book is a long one. Why Flavius Josephus, the Jewish historian in the first century of our era, preferred to use I Esdras and not the canonical Ezra-Nehemiah as his authority for the history of the period is a perplexing question. Perhaps he was attracted by the superior Greek style of the Apocryphal work.

The date of the composition of I Esdras is difficult to determine. Josephus's use of the book in compiling his own history provides a limit of time in one direction. The majority of scholars find reason to think that it was written sometime during the previous two centuries, that is, sometime after about 150 B.C.

Slight hints involving what appears to be an Egyptian coloration of the narrative at several places suggest that it was composed by a Jew in Egypt. From the circumstance that both the beginning and the conclusion are abrupt one gains the impression that the book today is but a torso, a fragment of what was once in more complete form. Whether it is an extract from a larger work, or whether the original manuscript was accidentally damaged, cannot be answered.

The narrative begins, as was mentioned above, with an account of the celebration of the Passover in the eighteenth year of the reign of Josiah (1:1–24). Then there follow the events subsequent to Josiah's death at the battle of Megiddo (1:25–33): Jeconiah [Jehoahaz], who was the people's choice, ruled only three months when he was deposed by the king of Egypt, Pharaoh Necho, who put Jehoiakim in his place; Nebuchadnezzar carried Jehoiakim captive to Babylonia; Jehoiachin, after reigning for three months and ten days, was likewise taken captive to Babylonia; Jedekiah was set on the throne by Nebuchadnezzar, but because he too was wicked, God sent Nebuchadnezzar to destroy Jerusalem and to bring the people into exile for seventy years (1:34–58; this first chapter corresponds more or less closely to II Chron. 35:1–36:21).

After seventy years had passed, according to a prophecy of Jeremiah (25:11f.), Cyrus, king of Persia, issued an edict permitting the exiled Jews to return and rebuild the Temple at Jerusalem. He also brought out from his temple of idols all the holy vessels of the Lord (5,469 of them) which Nebuchadnezzar had taken from the Jewish Temple when he despoiled it, and Cyrus gave them to Sheshbazzar, the governor of Judea, to carry back to Jerusalem (2:1–15; corresponding to II Chron. 36:22–23 and the canonical Book of Ezra 1:1–11). Sometime later, in response to an adverse report from certain Samaritan leaders who protested against the rebuilding of the walls of Jerusalem and of the Temple, King Artaxerxes I forbade the work to proceed. Thus the construction of the Temple was interrupted until the second year of Darius I (2:16-30; compare the canonical Book of Ezra 4:7-24, though it makes no mention of the rebuilding of the Temple. Furthermore, the historical sequence in I Esdras is chaotic, for the second year of Darius I is 520 B.C., whereas the dates of Artaxerxes I are 465-425 B.C.).

The next section (3:1-5:6), which tells how it came about that Darius authorized the resumption of the work of rebuilding, is a dramatic interlude quite unlike anything in the canonical Scriptures. Perhaps it was chiefly because of this interesting portion that I Esdras was preserved at all. The subject matter is an old favorite: a contest of wits is held in the presence of a king who bestows a reward to the one adjudged the winner.

The tale begins by recalling that King Darius had given a great banquet for the nobles of his vast empire, which extended from India to Ethiopia. Later that night three young soldiers of Darius's body-guard were whiling away the monotonous hours by debating what was the strongest thing in the world. They seemed to take for granted that the successful one would be richly rewarded by the king. Each wrote down his statement on a slip of paper, and these were sealed and placed under the king's pillow. The first wrote, 'Wine is strongest'; the second wrote, 'The king is strongest'; the third wrote, 'Women are strongest, but truth is victor over all things.'

After the king awoke he summoned all the state officials into the council chamber so that they too might hear the guardsmen defend their propositions. The first sought to establish the truth of his sentence by showing that the power of wine is uniform over all men, for 'it leads astray the minds of all who drink it. It makes equal the mind of the king and the orphan, of the slave and the free, of the poor and the rich. . . . It makes all hearts feel rich, forgets kings and satraps, and makes every one talk in millions. When men drink they forget to be friendly with friends and brothers, and before long they draw their swords. And when they recover from the wine, they do not remember what they have done. Gentlemen, is not wine the strongest, since it forces men to do these things?' (3:18–24).

The second guardsman discoursed upon the unlimited power of the king over his subjects. Though only one man, many obey his every command, civil and military alike. After enumerating the royal prerogatives, he brought his presentation to a climax with the question, 'Gentlemen, why is not the king the strongest, since he is to be obeyed in this fashion?' (4:12).

Then the third, who, it is added parenthetically, was Zerubbabel, spoke at great length. He admitted that the king is great and wine is strong, but argued that, 'Women gave birth to the king and to every people that rules over sea and land . . . and women brought up the very men who plant the vineyards from which comes wine. . . . Men cannot exist without women. If men gather gold and silver or any other beautiful thing, and then see a woman lovely in appearance and beauty, they let all these things go, and gape at her, and all would prefer her to gold or silver or any other beautiful thing. . . . A man takes his sword, and goes out to travel and rob and steal and to sail the sea and rivers; he faces lions, and he walks in darkness, and when he steals and robs and plunders, he brings it back to the woman he loves' (4:14–16, 17–19, 23–24).

Then, while the king and the nobles looked at one another, the same contestant started the second part of his oration. Taking what appears to be an unfair advantage, he began to discourse upon another topic, that of truth. With true Oriental oratory he argued that though the earth is vast, and the heavens high, and the sun swift in its course, yet earth and heaven and all their works magnify truth. He concluded with the peroration: 'All men approve her deeds, and there is nothing unrighteous in her judgment. To her belongs the strength and the kingship and the power and the majesty of all the ages. Blessed be the God of Truth!' At this all the people applauded, and exclaimed, 'Great is truth, and strongest of all!' (4:39–41).

The upshot was that Darius declared that Zerubbabel had won the contest, and prepared to give him anything he asked. The youth seized the opportunity to remind the king of a vow he had made at his accession, to restore the Jews to their land and to rebuild their Temple. Then Darius issued an edict grant-ing permission to the Jews of his dominion to return, with grants of money and many privileges. The section concludes with a description of the caravan of Jews departing from Babylonia, with a partial list of the names of the leading men who were in charge of it (5:1–6).

This Tale of the Three Guardsmen, which has counterparts in the folklore of the Near East, has obviously been adapted to the special interests of the author of I Esdras. For him, a loyal Jew, nothing could be stronger than the eternal truth of God. The episode of the guardsmen therefore serves him not only as a vehicle for moralizing, but also as a pseudo-historical account of how kings of an alien world-power became disposed to look with favor upon the Jewish exiles. The pregnant phrase, 'Great is truth, and strongest of all!' (4:41), has had its own part to play in the history of subsequent Christian exegesis, as will be indicated later in this chapter.

The book of I Esdras continues with a register of the Jewish exiles who returned with Zerubbabel (5:7–43; compare Ezra 2:1–67 and Neh. 7:6–69). Back in Jerusalem they erected the altar of burnt-offerings upon its former site, and observed the Feast of Booths as well as the other stated festivals (5:44–53; compare Ezra 3:1–7). After obtaining cedar logs from Lebanon and making other preparations for rebuilding the Temple, they laid its foundations amid mingled joy and sorrow (5:54–65; compare Ezra 3:8–13). The construction work, however, was hindered by the plots and demagoguery of the Samaritans, whose hypocritical offer to co-operate in the rebuilding had been rejected by the Jews. 'And they were kept from building for two years, until the reign of Darius' (5:73; compare Ezra 4:1–5, 24). At that time, however, through the activity of the prophets Haggai and Zechariah, the work was resumed despite a crafty attempt made by the local rulers to interfere, and at length the Temple was finished 'in the sixth year of King Darius' (7:5, that is, 516 B.C.) and was solemnly dedicated (6:1–7:15; compare Ezra 5:1–6:22).

More than a century later, 'in the seventh year of Artaxerxes' (about 397 B.C.), Ezra, the scribe, prepared to journey from Babylonia to Jerusalem with another company of returning exiles. The King bestowed on him a royal commission in writing which granted him various privileges and immunities as well as extensive authority in Jerusalem (8:1–67; compare Ezra 7:1–8:36).

It will be observed that the author records three different occasions when Jewish exiles returned to Jerusalem—one in 538 B.C. or soon after, headed by Sheshbazzar; one in 520 B.C., headed by Zerubbabel; one in 397 B.C., headed by Ezra. Curiously enough each caravan is said to bring back the long-lost sacred vessels which Nebuchadnezzar had plundered from the Temple (2:12; 4:44, 57; 8:60).

Having arrived at Jerusalem, Ezra was horrified to learn that the Jewish people, including priests and leaders, had been intermarrying with non-Israelites (8:68–96; compare Ezra 9:1–10:5). A national assembly was then called to hear an address and exhortation by Ezra. So sternly did he rebuke the multitude that in repentance they agreed to divorce all wives of an alien race. Then Ezra and others compiled a list of priests, Levites, and laymen who repudiated their foreign wives and children born of them (9:1–37; compare Ezra 10:6–44).

The final episode of the book recounts how, after the national repentance and purging of non-Israelitish elements, the people requested Ezra to read to them the Law of Moses. A great congregation assembled at the east side of the Temple, and from a specially constructed wooden pulpit Ezra read from morning to midday. Thirteen Levites assisted him in expounding the significance of the Law, and the Jews turned from mourning to rejoicing. Then the people went their way to celebrate and to send presents to the needy (9:38–55; compare Nehemiah 7:73–8:13a).

It will have been observed more than once in the synopsis just given that the author of I Esdras leaves much to be desired from a historical point of view. Not only does he contradict other sources, but he is involved in internal inconsistencies. In view of these serious deficiencies the most charitable verdict which one can pass is that the writer aimed more at inculcating a moral lesson than at recounting an accurate chronicle of events.

The chief interest of this book of historical fiction centers in the Tale of the Three Guardsmen, and the most famous line is the cry of approval which was raised by those who heard the exposition of the third guardsman (4:41). This text, whether in its Latin form in the Vulgate ('Magna est veritas, et praevalet') or in the Elizabethan English of the King James Version ('Great is Truth, and mighty above all things'), has justly attained the rank of an immortal proverb. What is of special interest here is the use made of these words by theologians in the early Church. Thus, Augustine comments that, since Christ is the Truth, it may be that in this passage referring to the greatness of Truth, 'Esdras is to be understood as prophesying of Christ' (*City of God*, XVIII, 36). Somewhat earlier than Augustine, another Church Father, in an impassioned argument against heretical error, connected this peroration on the importance and value of truth with 'the truth which Christ showed us in his Gospel, when he said, "I am the Truth" ' (Cyprian, *Letter* 73, 9, referring to John 14:6).

II

The Second Book of Esdras

THE BOOK KNOWN GENERALLY AS II ESDRAS BELONGS
TO A TYPE OF LITERATURE WHICH SEEMS STRANGE
AND EVEN BIZARRE TO MODERN READERS. LIKE
the Book of Revelation in the New Testament, this treatise is
an apocalypse. Apocalyptic literature undertakes to reveal the
future (the Greek word *apocalypsis* means 'a revealing'). But
the revelation of the future is not told in a straightforward, prosaic manner. It is told by means of what is often an elaborate
system of symbols—symbols such as wild beasts with several
heads and many horns, composite creatures made up of the head
of one kind of animal and the body of another, the falling of
stars and gigantic hailstones upon earth, the turning of the sea
into blood, and many similar features. Much of this literary
method seems fantastic to us, particularly because in some cases
the key to the interpretation of such symbols has been lost. At
the same time, it should be pointed out that we moderns are well
acquainted with the use of animals as symbols. Newspaper car-
toonists in many countries use, for example, a bear to represent

Russia and a lion to represent Great Britain. In the United
States, who would not immediately know the significance of a
political cartoon picturing a donkey and an elephant having a
tug of war, each trying to defeat the other? In a similar way,
among writers of ancient apocalypses there was an established
system of symbolism which, for the initiated, conveyed a religious message in a more dynamic and forceful way than any
purely conventional literary style could do.

The problems connected with the composition and transmission of II Esdras are extremely complicated. The central portion, consisting of chapters 3 to 14, purports to record seven
revelations granted to Ezra in Babylon, several of which took
the form of visions. The author of these chapters was an unknown Jew who probably wrote in Aramaic about the end of
the first Christian century. Subsequently his book was translated into Greek. Near the middle of the next century an unknown Christian author added in Greek an introductory section, which is now chapters 1 and 2. About the middle of the
following century another unknown Christian author appended chapters 15 and 16, also in Greek. The original Aramaic
text of chapters 3 to 14 has perished. Almost all of the Greek
has also been lost, except for three verses of chapter 15 which
turned up a few years ago in Egypt on a leaf from a parchment
manuscript dating from the fourth century (Papyrus Oxy-
rhynchus, VII, 1010). From the Aramaic or Greek form of
chapters 3 to 14 several early translations were made into various other languages, namely Syriac, Coptic, Ethiopic, Arabic
(two independent versions), Armenian, and Georgian. In the
West the entire book circulated in several Old Latin versions.
A later form of the Latin text is printed as an appendix to the
New Testament in the official Roman Catholic Vulgate Bible,
in which it is called the Fourth Book of Esdras.

The last stage of the complicated history of this book is perhaps the most interesting and dramatic; it involves the discovery of a lengthy section (amounting to no less than seventy verses) which had been lost from chapter 7, and which was thenceforth incorporated by the English revisers of the Apocrypha in 1895. For many years the text of the Latin version of II Esdras was based on manuscripts which presented chapter 7 in a form which made it clear that a passage was missing between verses 35 and 36. Though other ancient versions (Syriac, Ethiopic, Arabic, and Armenian) contained a long addition at this place, most scholars were hesitant about accepting it as genuine. When, however, in 1874 Robert L. Bensly of Cambridge University discovered a ninth-century manuscript in the public library of Amiens containing the lost Latin text, it was recognized that now the equivalent of a chapter must be added to the Apocrypha. In modern English translations this previously missing section is numbered 7:36-105, while the rest of chapter 7 in the King James Version (7:36-70) is now given the additional enumeration 7:106-140. It is probable that the lost section was deliberately cut out of an ancestor of most extant Latin manuscripts, because of dogmatic reasons, for the passage contains an emphatic denial of the value of prayers for the dead (verse 105).

What Bensly did not know, however, and what ordinarily is overlooked in histories of the transmission of the Bible, is the fact that long before the English Revised Version of 1895 included this lost section, Bibles had been published in Westphalia and in Pennsylvania which contained the missing portion. In 1726-42 a German mystic by the name of Johann H. Haug published in eight folio volumes an edition of the Bible at Berleburg; his version was a rigorous revision of Luther's translation, based on the original texts with comparison of the

English and French translations. Haug also included a translation of various books of the Apocrypha (of both the Old and
the New Testament), the pseudepigrapha, and several post-
apostolic writings. What is of importance here is that the lost
section in II Esdras 7 was restored from an Arabic manuscript
in the Bodleian Library at Oxford. The first Bible published in
America in a European language[1] was a reprint of the thirty-
fourth edition of Luther's German Bible. It was issued in 1743
by an enterprising and philanthropic printer, Christoph Sauer,
at Germantown, a suburb of Philadelphia. Because Luther's
edition of the Apocrypha lacked I and II Esdras (he did not
consider them to be worthy of translating), Sauer added these
books, along with the less well-known apocryphal book of III
Maccabees, all of them taken from the Berleberg Bible. Thus,
Bibles were published on both sides of the Atlantic which contained the missing section of II Esdras more than one hundred
and fifty years before it appeared in the English Revised Version
of 1895.

A summary of this composite book is as follows. After an
elaborate genealogy of the reputed author, where he is at
pains to make it clear that he can boast of a priestly descent from
Aaron (1:1-3), Ezra is commanded by the Lord to denounce
the people of Israel for their sins, committed in the face of continued exhibitions of divine grace and mercy (1:4-27). In a passage in which clear echoes of New Testament phraseology betray its author as being a Christian (see especially 1:30 and
Matt. 23:37), the Lord announces that he will scatter Israel
among the nations and will choose in their place Gentile nations

---

1. The first Bible published in America was John Eliot's translation of the
Scripture into the language used by the Algonquian Indians (Cambridge,
Massachusetts, 1663).

(1:28-40), who 'though they do not see me with bodily eyes, yet with the spirit they will believe the things I have said' (1:37; compare Jesus' words to Thomas, John 20:29). The second chapter, which reiterates this message of woe to faithless Israel, contains an account of Ezra's vision of the risen saints (who are doubtless Christian martyrs) standing on Mount Sion, 'a great multitude, which I could not number' (2:42). They are crowned and receive palms (symbolizing victory) from a young man of great stature in their midst. An angel informs Ezra that this is 'the Son of God, whom they confessed in the world,' and then bids him, 'Go, tell my people how great and many are the wonders of the Lord God which you have seen' (1:47f.).

After this introduction, the Ezra-Apocalypse proper begins. In the first vision (3:1-5:20) Ezra bewails the fate of his people in Exile and ponders the problem of evil. He seeks an answer to the question why God, who did not remove from man the evil impulse transmitted by Adam to his descendents, allowed the Gentiles to destroy Jerusalem for its sins (3:1-36). In reply the angel Uriel bids him recognize that he cannot understand even the simplest things that are involved in his own daily life; how then can he hope to understand the ways of the Most High (4:1-11)? Man belongs to the earth; his vision is bounded by the finite; therefore it is vain for him to seek to comprehend what is heavenly and infinite (4:12-21). Ezra protests that he has no wish to peer into what is of no concern of his, but only to learn 'why the people whom you loved have been given to godless tribes, and the law of our fathers has been made of no effect and the written covenants no longer exist?' (4:23). In a rather unsatisfactory reply the angel tells him that the righteous will understand and be vindicated in the age to come. In response to Ezra's impatient question of how soon the future age will come, the answer is given that once the predestined number of the righteous has been completed the end of the age will most assuredly arrive, and nothing—not even man's sins—can at that time delay its consummation (4:33-43). In response to further queries as to the signs which will precede the end of the present world-order, the angel elaborates upon traditional signs mentioned in both Old and New Testaments (5:1-13).

In the second vision (5:21-6:34), which involves some repetition of Ezra's basic complaint that God has been unfair to Israel (5:21-40), a new problem is raised regarding the lot of those who die before the present age has passed away (5:41). The reply, which is couched in high-sounding phrases, is intended to provide assurance that their lot will be similar to that of those living at the inauguration of the new age (5:42-55). This vision closes, like the previous one, with a detailed list of the signs of the last times (6:7-34).

The third vision (6:35-9:25) is lengthy, not to say tediously wordy. A fast of seven days is followed by an address of Ezra to God (6:35-59) and the return of the angel Uriel (7:1-17). This time the main topic of discussion is the small number of those who will be saved (7:17-25), and the chief revelation is a long description of the final judgment and the future state of the righteous and the wicked (7:26-[131]). The details include the promise that God's Messiah will reign in his kingdom four hundred years; after this he and all humankind will die, and primeval silence will prevail for seven days; finally will come the Resurrection and the Day of Judgment (7:28-35). Ezra is saddened by the knowledge that the joys of the world to come will be the lot of so few, while the torments will be for so many. By means of a parable he is taught that the worth of the few is far greater than that of the many, and that therefore God takes pleasure in the saved and will not grieve over the many who perish (7:[45-74]). When Ezra inquires about the state of the departed, a detailed reply is given, contrasting Gehenna and Paradise (7:[75-131]). The compassion of Ezra for the lost exceeds that attributed by the author to God himself, and he makes intercession at great length in behalf of the mass of mankind who, as sinners, will be doomed (7:[132-140]). But his prayer is in vain; he is told bluntly, 'Many have been created, but few shall be saved' (8:3). In perplexity and despair Ezra once again makes intercession to God in behalf of sinners (8:4-36).[2] The heavenly messenger reproaches Ezra for seeming to love the creature more than the Creator (8:37-62). Then, in reply to his query as to when the end of the age will come, the angel discloses some of the signs which will herald the approach of the Day of Judgment (8:63-9:25).

In the fourth vision (9:26-10:59), which is preceded by Ezra's moving lament over his people (9:29-37), he sees a woman in deep mourning for the death of her only son—a son who, born after she had been barren for thirty years, died on the very day of his wedding (9:38-10:4). Ezra chides her for her concern with herself, reminding her of the far greater calamity which has befallen Zion (10:5-24). While he is speaking, she suddenly becomes transfigured and then vanishes, and in the place where she was he beholds a great and splendid city (10:-25-28). Uriel now returns to him and explains that this woman represented heavenly Zion (10:29-29).

The fifth vision (11:1-12:39) is an elaborate allegory involving an eagle rising from the sea. It has three heads, twelve wings, and eight other smaller wings (11:1-35). A roaring lion comes out of the wood and denounces the eagle for its tyranny and cruel oppressions (11:36-46). While the lion is speaking, by

2. This beautiful prayer, in liturgical structure, also occurs as the 'Confessio Esdrae' among the *Cantica* in manuscripts of the Latin Vulgate.

degrees the wings and heads of the eagle disappear, and finally the body of the eagle is burned (12:1-3). In answer to his prayer for an explanation of the meaning of the vision, Ezra is told that the eagle represents the fourth kingdom which appeared in a vision to Daniel (Dan. 7:7-8:23); the heads and wings are various rulers of the Roman Empire; and the lion is the Messiah whom the Most High has reserved for the end of days to punish the evil-doers and deliver the remnant of God's people (12:-4-34). Following this disclosure, Ezra is told to write in a book all that he has seen in his dream-vision (12:35-39). While waiting for further visions, he encourages his countrymen by assuring them that 'the Most High has you in remembrance, and the Mighty One has never forgotten you in your struggle' (12:47).

In the sixth vision (13:1-58) a wondrous man rises from a storm-tossed sea. Everything trembles at his look; whoever hears his voice is consumed by fire (13:1-4). After annihilating all his enemies (13:5-11), this same man gathers a peaceful multitude to himself; some come willingly, others have to be brought by force (13:12-20). Ezra then awakes and prays for an interpretation of the vision. He is told that the man from the sea is the pre-existent Messiah; those who came to fight against him are the Gentiles; and the peaceable multitude symbolizes the ten 'lost' tribes of Israel who had been taken away captive by Shalmaneser, the Assyrian king (13:21–56).

In the seventh and last vision (14:1-48), which differs somewhat from the other visions of this book, Ezra, while sitting under an oak, is addressed from a bush by the voice of God. He is informed that he is shortly to be taken up from among men, and that the end of the age is near (14:1-18). Ezra pleads for the people who will be left without teacher or law (14:19-22), and he is commanded to procure a great quantity of writing materials and five scribes who can write rapidly. The next day he receives a wonderful drink in a cup, by which he is inspired to dictate continuously for forty days 'to the five men, and by turns they wrote what was dictated, in characters which they did not know' (14:42). In this manner ninety-four books are produced. God commands Ezra to publish twenty-four of them (these are the books of the Hebrew Old Testament), but to keep the seventy others hidden, reserved for the wise among the Jews (these esoteric books are probably various apocalyptic writings).

At this point in the Oriental versions the book comes to an end (14:48), concluding with a short postscript giving the year, according to the Era of Creation, when these events took place, and closing with the announcement that 'Ezra was caught up, and taken to the place of those who are like him' (14:48 margin).

Some of the Latin manuscripts, as was stated above, continue with a kind of appendix, comprising chapters 15 and 16. (These manuscripts naturally omit the reference to Ezra's assumption to heaven, mentioned in the Oriental versions at the end of chapter 14.) Here Ezra is assured that the cruel nation—Rome is meant—will no longer tyrannize over God's people, but will soon suffer destruction (15:1-27). He is granted a vision of terrible wars in Syria, in which punishment is meted out to the wicked (15:28-63). Further denunciations are added against Babylon, Asia, Egypt, and Syria; and their punishment is described in dismal detail (16:1-39). Next, God's people are warned as to what is coming upon the earth owing to the wickedness of men; it will be a hard time even for the righteous (16:40-51). In a rather disjointed section, the righteous are encouraged by the promise that soon iniquity will be removed from the earth, yet no sinner is to say that he has not sinned, for God knows the thoughts of men. The power and the wisdom of God are described, and men are exhorted to fear him, the judge of all (16:52-67).

Finally, the chosen people are told they need not be afraid, for God is their guide; it is only those overwhelmed by their sins against whom woe has been pronounced (16:68-78).

Such is a summary of this, the most difficult book in the Apocrypha for the modern reader to understand and appreciate. There is a certain element in the literary form which is tiresome and almost trivial. We do not care nowadays for such elaborate and fantastic symbolism. At the same time it must be acknowledged that a real vein of poetry runs throughout the book. Whether the writer is lamenting the sorrows of Jerusalem, or describing the wonders of God's handiwork in creation, or denouncing the wickedness of Rome (under the image of 'Babylon'), one feels the power of effective expression.

Furthermore, though the succession of unusual and often confusing visions may leave the reader bewildered, behind the apocalyptic forms there is obviously a deep religious concern. The author wrestles with one of the most perplexing of all problems, the question of God's justice in dealing with his people. It is difficult for us to realize how tremendous were the implications which the fall of Jerusalem in the year 70 had for thoughtful Jews of the time. For the Jew who was to live on in the world as a witness to the past, what a terrible strain upon his faith in God's Providence it must have been! In spite of the essentially pessimistic outlook of II Esdras, the author's strong religious faith often enables him to rise above the fires of adversity to the very highest spiritual levels. His agonizing is both honorable and pathetic as he seeks 'to justify the ways of God to man.'

III

Tobit

ONE OF THE MOST WIDELY READ BOOKS OF PIOUS
FICTION AMONG ANCIENT JEWS IS THE COLORFUL
TALE OF TOBIT. COMPOSED BY A DEVOUT JEW ABOUT
190–170 B.C., this short book was intended to provide religious
and moral instruction in the form of an adventure story. The
chief lesson which it conveys is that God in his mysterious
providence, though permitting various calamities to befall those
who are righteous, at the same time exercises a special care over
them in the midst of their sufferings and grants them a happy
ending to all their trials.

The popularity and charm of the book are attested by the
multiplicity of forms in which it circulated. It has come down
to us in three recensions or editions of the Greek text, as well as
in several versions, such as Latin (two versions), Syriac (two
versions), Hebrew (four versions), and Ethiopic. Recently
fragments of the book in Hebrew and Aramaic were discovered
in caves at Qumran near the Dead Sea. What their relation is to
the versions already known has not yet been ascertained.

Tobit is represented as a Jew of Galilee, living in the eighth century before Christ. Despite the idolatrous practices of his countrymen in the Northern Kingdom, he maintained a stead-fast faith and practice. He often went on pilgrimages to Jerusalem to observe the appointed festivals, taking three-tenths of his income to distribute there (1:1-9).

Along with the rest of the people of Israel, Tobit, his wife, Anna, and their son, Tobias, were taken as captives to Nineveh during the reign of Shalmaneser (about 721 B.C.; see II Kings 18:9-11). Though all his relatives neglected to observe the Jewish dietary laws, Tobit was careful to eat only kosher food. As a result God gave him favor in the sight of Shalmaneser, who made him his purchasing agent. On one of his trips to Media, Tobit left ten talents of silver in trust with a friend of his in Rages, named Gabael. After the accession of another king, Sennacherib, Tobit's fortunes took a turn for the worse. Yet he continued to perform acts of charity to fellow-Jews, and was especially zealous in honoring the dead by burying those of his people who had been the victims of the cruelty of the king. When an informer brought this to the ears of Sennacherib, Tobit left home in fear for his life, and all his property was confiscated (1:10-20).

Within fifty days, however, Sennacherib was assassinated by his sons (see II Kings 19:37 and Isa. 37:38); his successor, Esar-haddon, appointed Ahikar, Tobit's nephew, to be the royal cupbearer, the keeper of the signet ring, and the chief administrator in charge of accounts. Through Ahikar's influence at the court, Tobit was permitted to return to Nineveh (1:21-22).

Tobit's first concern after returning was the continuance of his good works. He sent his son to invite destitute Israelites to dinner in celebration of the feast of Pentecost. The boy came back with the news that he had found one of their race lying dead, strangled, in the market place. Immediately rising from the table, Tobit went out to remove the body to a place of shelter until sunset. Having returned he washed himself and ate his food in sorrow, recalling the words of the prophet Amos,

Your feasts shall be turned into mourning,
and all your festivities into lamentation (cf. Amos 8:10).

Despite his neighbors' mockeries, after sunset Tobit buried the corpse, and, being then in a state of ritual impurity, slept outside his house, by the wall of the courtyard. While taking his rest there, poor Tobit, through no fault of his own, suffered a curious accident: droppings from sparrows on the wall fell into his eyes and blinded him. Not being able now to provide for his family, Tobit was forced to depend upon the earnings of his wife as a dressmaker. Owing to a misunderstanding they quarreled, and Tobit in his anguish prayed to God to release him from his sufferings by death itself (2:1-3:6).

Meanwhile it happened that far away at Ecbatana in Media, Tobit's pious kinswoman Sarah, the only daughter of Raguel, also prayed for death as a relief from her humiliation and sufferings. The unhappy girl had been married seven times, but each of her husbands had died before the marriage could be consummated. Sarah's maids taunted her that she had strangled her husbands; actually they had been murdered by a foul demon, Asmodeus, who had fallen in love with her. In her grief Sarah contemplated hanging herself, but refrained, thinking of her father's disgrace. So, like Tobit, she too prayed God to let her die. God graciously heard the prayer of both, and sent his angel Raphael (meaning 'God heals') to help them (3:7-17).

In the meantime Tobit, believing that the hour of death was at hand, gave final instructions to his son, Tobias. In a notable section of ethical exhortation (chapter 4) Tobit admonishes his son, 'Remember the Lord our God all your days, my son, and refuse to sin or to transgress his commandments.' In particular he lays emphasis upon the virtues of generosity in giving alms, love of the brethren, fair dealing with employees, and self-discipline in all conduct. Here also is to be found in negative form the Golden Rule, 'What you hate, do not do to anyone' (4:15). Finally, after explaining about the ten talents of silver he had left in trust with Gabael, Tobit concluded his paternal admonitions: 'Do not be afraid, my son, because we have become poor. You have great wealth if you fear God and refrain from every sin and do what is pleasing in his sight' (4:21).

Thereupon preparations were made for Tobias to go to Media in order to secure the ten talents of silver. Needing a traveling companion and guide for the journey, the lad found a certain Azarias to go with him. Azarias is the angel Raphael in disguise, but Tobias did not know it. After the old man had satisfied himself of the trustworthiness of his son's companion and had agreed to pay him a drachma a day and his expenses, the two set out for Rages, taking Tobias's dog with them (5:1–21).

At evening they came to the Tigris river and prepared to camp there overnight. While Tobias was washing in the river, a great fish attacked him, but he seized it and threw it up to land. On the advice of the angel, he cut open the fish and removed its heart and liver and gall. He put these away safely, for his companion informed him that a smoke made from the heart and liver would drive away a demon or an evil spirit that was molesting anyone, and that ointment made from the gall was a powerful medicine for his father's peculiar type of blindness (6:1-8).

As they approached the city where Sarah dwelt, the angel disclosed to Tobias that she was destined to be his bride, for as her kinsman he alone had the right to take her. Quite understandably, Tobias was not very happy over the privilege offered to him, for he had heard of the fate of her seven previous husbands; but Azarias assured him that the demon would flee from the smoke of the heart and liver of the fish, never to return (6:9-17).

The travelers reached Ecbatana in due course, and were received with true Eastern courtesy by Raguel, Edna his wife, and Sarah. Tobias lost no time in making his proposal of marriage. He refused to be daunted when Raguel conscientiously explained to him what had happened to his daughter's previous husbands. The father was so pessimistic of the outcome that, while the mother prepared her daughter for the wedding, he dug a grave for Tobias!

The fortunate bridegroom followed exactly the angel's prescription of immunity, and when the demon smelled the odor of the burning entrails of the fish, he fled to the remotest parts of Egypt, where the angel bound him. This deliverance called forth two beautiful and touching prayers, one from Tobias and one from Raguel. The wedding festivities were prolonged for two weeks (8:1-21), in the midst of which Tobias sent Azarias on to Rages to get Tobit's money from Gabael. When he had returned with it, and after the days of feasting were over, Raguel divided his property with his son-in-law, and Tobias and his wife set out with Azarias for his father's house.

Meanwhile the scene shifts back to Nineveh, where Tobit and his wife have become alarmed over Tobias's prolonged absence and almost despair of seeing him again (9:1-10:14). His mother, the narrative says with touching pathos, 'went out every day to the road by which they had left; she ate nothing in the daytime, and throughout the nights she never stopped mourning for her son Tobias' (10:7). The reader, of course, knows the outcome of Tobias's journey and is able to anticipate the happiness which the parents will soon experience.

Having come now to the vicinity of Nineveh, Azarias and Tobias, at the former's suggestion, went ahead of the rest of the caravan, bringing the gall of the fish and being accompanied by the dog. Soon the mother's arms were around her son's neck. Seeing his blind father come stumbling toward him, Tobias with one hand saved him from falling and with the other applied the fish's gall to his eyes. At once Tobit received his sight again (11:1-15). He blessed God for his mercies, and welcomed his daughter-in-law. Family ties being reunited, they celebrated Tobias's marriage for seven days with great festivity (11:16-19).

When Tobit and Tobias attempted to remunerate the guide most handsomely, to whom their present happiness was chiefly due, he revealed that he was not a mortal servant, but Raphael, 'one of the seven angels who present the prayers of the saints and enter into the presence of the glory of the Holy One' (12:-15). After admonishing them to pray and give alms, he ascended to heaven. Whereupon Tobit expressed his gratitude by composing a psalm of thanksgiving (13:1-18).

The book closes with Tobit's last words to his son in which he advised Tobias to leave Nineveh because it was to be destroyed in accordance with the prophecy of Jonah. The dutiful son, after providing what is said to have been a magnificent funeral for his aged father, returned to live in Ecbatana with Raguel his father-in-law. The book ends, as all such stories do, on a tranquil note: Tobias 'grew old with honor, and he gave his father-in-law and mother-in-law magnificent funerals. He inherited their property and that of his father Tobit. He died in Ecbatana at the age of a hundred and twenty-seven years. But before he died he heard of the destruction of Nineveh, which Nebuchadnezzar and Ahasuerus captured. Before his death he rejoiced over Nineveh' (14:13-15).

Though the story is entirely unhistorical, it is nevertheless a valuable historical source for our knowledge of Jewish piety and family life in the second century before Christ. The air of simple goodness and heartfelt devotion which pervades this book reflects the highest religious affections among the Jews of the Dispersion. Though there are doubtless symptoms of a tendency to emphasize a formal righteousness of works, yet the works are depicted as springing from a living faith. Furthermore, nowhere else is there preserved so complete and beautiful a picture of the domestic life of the Jews after the return from the Babylonian Exile. Almost every family relationship is touched upon with natural grace and affection: husband and wife, parent and child, kinsmen, near or distant, master and servant, are presented in the most varied action, and always with life-like power. Even the boy's dog goes along with Tobias on his journey (5:16 and 11:4)—a delightful touch which is without parallel in Scripture and seems more natural to the West than to the East, where the Jews generally regarded dogs as useless and unclean beasts. It is no wonder that many Church Fathers had the highest praise for this book, and that Martin Luther pronounced it 'a truly beautiful, wholesome, and profitable fiction, the work of a gifted poet . . . A book useful and good for us Christians to read' ('Preface to the Book of Tobit,' Luther's translation of the Bible, ed. 1534). The famous Danish philosopher and theologian of the past century, Kierkegaard, dwelt at length upon this story at the close of his book, *Fear and Trembling*, concentrating his attention upon the character and pathetic situation of Sarah, whom he regarded as the heroine of the book.

Among the doctrinal and practical themes of the book which receive special emphasis, the following deserve fuller notice. God is represented as a transcendental deity who hears men's prayers through angelic mediation (12:12). The power and majesty of God are indicated by such appellations as King of Heaven (13:7, 11), the Great King (13:15), the Everlasting King (13:6, 10). He is the Holy One (12:12, 15), surrounded by glory (12:15). At the same time he is merciful (3:2) and like a father (13:4), who will restore his people after they have been led into captivity (14:5). There is even a hint that Gentiles will some day acknowledge the majesty of Israel's God (13:11).

It is chiefly with reference to angels and demons that the book of Tobit takes its place as a valuable source of our knowledge of the development of doctrine. As is well known, the Old Testament has relatively little to say about angels, and even less about demons. On the other hand, in the New Testament the presence and activity of both angels and demons are everywhere taken for granted. The contrast between the two Testaments is less sharp when one takes into account the intertestamental literature written during and just after the Exile in Babylonia and Persia, when the Old Testament rudiments of these beliefs were expanded in many directions. The book of Tobit reflects both the legitimate development of this subject as well as the admixture of many speculations derived from folklore and magic (for example, the view that a demon can be exorcized by means of a disagreeable odor).

It is in the practical sphere, however, that our author's religious outlook and moral outlook find their fullest expression. The person of Tobit is held up as a model for the author's contemporaries. As a precursor of the Pharisees and of orthodox Jews through the centuries, the hero of this story bases his life upon what came to be called 'the three pillars of Judaism,' namely prayer, almsgiving, and fasting (12:8). Though fasting (2:4) has not yet reached the culmination of its later development, the necessity of giving alms is stressed again and again. It is a

virtue to be practised by the rich (1:16) and the poor alike
(11:14). No less an authority than the angel Raphael is made
responsible for the dictum, 'Almsgiving delivers from death,
and it will purge away every sin' (12:9). The repeated acts of
charity on the part of Tobit reinforce this teaching by providing examples of its practice. Particular stress is laid upon the
duty of giving decent burial to the dead.[1]

The tendency to an excessive emphasis upon externals is bal-
anced in part by the frequent reference to heartfelt prayer to
God, which hallows the whole conduct of life (4:19, 6:17, 8:5-
8, etc.). Particularly instructive is the care which the author
obviously took with the form and contents of Tobit's (3:1-6)
and Sarah's (3:11-15) prayers. Each begins with an invocation
and an act of adoration, followed by the specific supplication
and a lengthy retrospective explanation. Since the same struc-
tural arrangement also characterizes Tobias's prayer (8:5-7),
it is likely that such was the typical form in which Jewish prayers were cast in the author's day.

Morality and lofty standards are inculcated in all areas of life.
For example, Tobias is exhorted to show piety toward his parents, to feed the hungry, to cloth the naked, not to drink wine
to excess, to seek advice from the wise, and, in short, to refrain
from doing to anyone else what is displeasing to himself (see
4:12-19).

In view of the happy combination of such generally high religious and ethical teaching with an appealing story involving
travel, love, adventure, conflict, and a happy ending, it is not

1. The reader of the New Testament may ask what prompted Joseph of
Arimathea to take down the body of Jesus from the Cross, wrap it in a linen
shroud, and lay him in a tomb (Matt. 27:57-60; Mark 15:43-46; Luke 23:50-
53). Was it at least partly because he knew the story of Tobit with its emphasis upon the decent and pious disposition of the bodies of fellow-Jews who
had been murdered by their oppressors (Tobit 1:17-18; 2:3-5, 7-9)?

difficult to understand why the book of Tobit held a position in Jewish households similar to that once held by Bunyan's *Pilgrim's Progress* in our own.

In the history of Christianity the influence of the book of Tobit has been felt chiefly in wedding ceremonies. The Latin version of Tobit, which was followed by the earliest English translators, describes how Tobias and Sarah gave the first three nights after their marriage to prayer, postponing their wedlock until the fourth (6:21-22 in the Vulgate). During the Middle Ages this was considered to be the ideal for Christians, and was followed, for example, at the marriage of Louis IX of France and his queen in 1234 (this Louis, who had led the Sixth and Seventh Crusades, was canonized as St. Louis later in the thirteenth century by Pope Boniface VIII). In England the pre-Reformation order of matrimony in the ritual which was adopted in 1085 for use in the diocese of Salisbury and which by the middle of the thirteenth century had come to be widely used throughout Britain, mentions Tobias and Sarah as a model pair, and concludes with the blessing of the bridal chamber and the marriage bed by the priest, in the words, 'Keep thy servants who rest in this bed from all phantoms and apparitions of demons'—an obvious reference to Asmodeus who had haunted Sarah and murdered her husbands. The marriage service in the first edition of the Book of Common Prayer, issued in 1549, contains the following prayer in which the minister petitions God: 'As thou diddest sende thy Aungell Raphaell to Thobie, and Sara, the daughter of Raguel, to their great comfort: so vouchsafe to sende thy blessinge vpon these thy seruantes.' In the United States the Old Order Amish (members of this group, which originated among the Swiss Brethren during the Reformation, are found today chiefly in Pennsylvania, Ohio, and Indiana) have traditionally made this Apocryphal book the basis of the wedding sermon. A manuscript *Amish Minister's Manual* directs that, in addition to expounding passages of the Old and New Testaments, the minister shall relate the story of Tobit. Its value is set forth as follows. 'Even though this is an Apocryphal book and is not counted among the books of Holy Scripture, still it presents a beautiful lesson which strengthens the pious and God-fearing in the faith, especially as regards marriage, and in all trials and troubles it leads one in the hope that God will bring things to a joyful end.' [2]

2. John Umble, 'An Amish Minister's Manual,' *Mennonite Quarterly Review*, Vol. xv (1941), p. 101.

IV

Judith

ONE OF THE BEST EXAMPLES OF EARLY JEWISH
STORY-TELLING IN A SETTING OF WARFARE IS
THE BOOK OF JUDITH. THE ANONYMOUS AUTHOR
was probably a Palestinian Jew who wrote during the strenuous
years following the Maccabean revolt, perhaps about the middle
of the second century before Christ. Living evidently at a time
of national emergency when the Jewish religion and independence were at stake, he wished both to encourage his people in
resisting their enemies and to inculcate a strict observance of the
Law of God. His book, which teaches that for the Jews patriot-
ism and religion are one, reflects the belief that God will defend
his people if they observe his Law; otherwise he will allow their
foes to prevail. The heroine of this stirring tale is a Jewess who
combines the most scrupulous observance of the Law of Moses
with a grim and cunning bravery in the face of great personal
danger.

The book of Judith falls into two distinct parts. The first describes the war of the Assyrians against the Jews (chapters 1-7);

the second relates the deliverance wrought by Judith (chapters 8-16).

Hostilities broke out between the Assyrians and the Medes, who were supported by many neighboring peoples (1:1-6). Nebuchadnezzar, who is said to have ruled over the Assyrians in the city of Nineveh, called the Western nations to form a coalition with him against his enemies, but they refused to assist him (1:7-11). Angry and vowing to take revenge on them (including the Jews), Nebuchadnezzar marched against Arphaxad, king of the Medes. The latter was defeated and Nebuchadnezzar returned to Nineveh where he celebrated his victory for four months (1:12-16).

After recuperating his military strength, Nebuchadnezzar decided to destroy all the Western nations that had flouted his request, and sent his commander-in-chief, Holofernes, to go with a great army against them. With 120,000 foot soldiers and 12,000 cavalry, as well as innumerable contingents from other nations, Holofernes ravaged all the lands in his progress westward (2:1-28). The cities on the seacoast of the Mediterranean (including Tyre, Sidon, Jamnia, Azotus, and Ascalon) in their fear sent messengers to Holofernes offering unconditional surrender. Occupying their territories, the Assyrians demolished all the local shrines and gods, demanding that the subjugated peoples should henceforth worship Nebuchadnezzar alone as god (3:1-10).

In the meantime, the people of Israel in Judea, who are said to have recently returned from their Babylonian captivity, heard of Holofernes's atrocities and, being fearful of his despoiling their Temple, determined to block his advance against Jerusalem. They mobilized forces and provisions at strategic passes in the hills to the north of Jerusalem. At the command of Joakim the high priest and of the Sanhedrin in session at Jerusalem, they also made supplication to God with great fervor; they fasted, put on sackcloth, and prayed earnestly for divine favor (4:1–15).

Enraged at their audacity in preparing to fight against him, Holofernes made inquiries among the chiefs of Moab and Ammon who this people was—the only nation in the West that had dared to defy him (5:1-4). Achior, the leader of the Ammonites, summarized for him the history of Israel from the time of Abraham to the Jews' return from exile and the rebuilding of the Temple. He concluded his recital with the observation that no power could vanquish them unless they sinned against their God (5:5-21). Indignant and angry at these words, which implied the superiority of the Jewish forces, Holofernes ordered Achior to be bound and abandoned in the vicinity of the Jewish camp, so that he might be destroyed along with the nation which he had declared to be invincible (5:22-6:9). Typical of Assyrian malice and pride are his concluding words: 'You will not die until you perish along with them. If you really hope in your heart that they will not be taken, do not look downcast! I have spoken and none of my words shall fail' (6:8-9).

Achior was taken to the foot of the hill on which the Jewish city of Bethulia stood. Then the men of the city found him and took him before the city magistrates, to whom he related the boastful threats of Holofernes. He was treated kindly by Uzziah, the chief ruler of the city; and all that night the Jews continued to call upon the God of Israel for help (6:10-21).

The next day Holofernes moved his whole army to the valley by Bethulia, filling the inhabitants with terror. He decided not to attack the city, but to cut off the water supply and to lay siege to it until famine would force the Jews to surrender (7:1-18.)

After a siege of thirty-four days the famishing inhabitants of the beleaguered city began to lose heart and called upon the elders to surrender to the Assyrians. In desperation Uzziah pleaded with them to hold out for five more days, saying, 'By that time the Lord our God will show us his mercy, for he will not forsake us utterly' (7:30). Nevertheless, he agreed to capitulate to the enemy should help not be forthcoming within that time (7:19-32).

At this critical point the heroine of the story is introduced (8:1). Judith, whose name means 'a Jewess,' was a wealthy widow whose great beauty was matched only by her deep piety. Having heard of the decision made by Uzziah, she summoned him with the other elders to her home and indignantly upbraided them for attempting to force the hand of God. Her speech is too long to be quoted here in full, but the following extract will illustrate its tone and temper: 'Who are you,' she expostulated, 'that have put God to the test this day, and are setting yourselves up in the place of God? ... You cannot plumb the depths of the human heart, nor find out what a man is thinking; how do you expect to search out God, who made all these things, and find out his mind or comprehend his thought? No, my brethren, do not provoke the Lord our God to anger. For if he does not choose to help us within these five days, he has power to protect us within any time he pleases, or even to destroy us in the presence of our enemies. Do not try to bind the purposes of the Lord our God; for God is not like man, to be threatened, or like a human being, to be worn down by pleading. ... Now therefore, my brethren, let us set an example to our brethren, for their lives depend upon us, and the sanctuary and the temple and the altar rest upon us. In spite of everything let us give thanks to the Lord our God, who is putting us to the test as he did our forefathers' (8:12, 14-16, 24-25).

Moved by these stirring words, the elders acknowledged

their lack of faith and begged her to pray to God for rain, that the cisterns might be filled and the people obtain relief from thirst. But Judith replied that she had formed a plan of her own to defeat the enemy, and that within the five days the Lord would deliver Israel by her hand (8:28-36).

The whole of the next chapter is taken up with Judith's prayer to God in preparation for her perilous undertaking. She implored divine help in defeating the proud Assyrians, praying, 'Break their strength by thy might, and bring down their power in thy anger; for they intend to defile thy sanctuary, and to pollute the tabernacle where thy glorious name rests. . . . Give to me, a widow, the strength to do what I plan. By the deceit of my lips strike down the slave with the prince and the prince with his servant. . . . And cause thy whole nation and every tribe to know and understand that thou art God, the God of all power and might, and that there is no other who protects the people of Israel but thou alone!' (9:8, 9-10, 14).

Her prayer finished, Judith dressed herself in her finest clothes, and adorned her person with jewelry, perfume, and cosmetics, 'and made herself very beautiful, to entice the eyes of all men who might see her' (10:4). Packing a bag with some kosher food and taking her maid with her, she left the city and went down into the valley toward the camp of the enemy. Stopped by the Assyrian patrol, she stated that she was a Jewess who was fleeing from her people in order to escape the imminent fall of the city, and that she would show Holofernes how he might capture all the hill country without the loss of a single man (10:11-13).

Hearing these words and admiring her beauty, the sentries arranged to usher her into the tent of their general. Brought into the presence of Holofernes, she prostrated herself and made obeisance to him. Holofernes assured her that she had nothing to fear, and encouraged her to tell her mission (10:14-11:4). She began by beguiling him with persuasive words, some of which carry a *double entendre*; for example, 'If you follow out the words of your maid-servant, God will accomplish something through you' (11:6), and 'God has sent me to accomplish with you things that will astonish the whole world' (11:16). Confirming the principle which Achior had stated, namely that the Jews could not be defeated unless they had sinned, she informed Holofernes that owing to the rigors of the siege the Jews were now on the point of bringing down the wrath of God upon them by eating unclean food as well as sacrificial animals, the first fruits, and the tithes which had been consecrated for the Temple. She, being deeply religious, had been scandalized —so she avers—by the sin which her people intended to commit, and therefore had fled from their midst. She suggested that she remain with Holofernes except to return to the valley each night where she would pray to God, who would disclose to her when the people had committed their sins. Then, she promised, she would come and tell him so that he might lead his whole army in an easy conquest of all Judea (11:11-19).

Needless to say, Holofernes was greatly pleased with these arrangements, and ordered his servants to supply her with some of his own food and wine. She remonstrated, however, explaining that she must conform to the Jewish dietary laws and therefore would eat only the provisions she had brought with her. When Holofernes expressed concern how he could secure more food for her when her present supply became exhausted, she assured him, with another *double entendre*, that 'your servant will not use up the things I have with me before the Lord carries out by my hand what he has determined to do' (12:4).

On the fourth night after her arrival, Holofernes, who was captivated by Judith's charms, arranged a banquet in her honor and sent his chief eunuch, Bagoas, to invite her. Accepting the invitation, Judith decked herself in her finery, and reclined at Holofernes's table on soft fleeces, partaking of her own kosher food and drink (12:10-20). The feast lasted long; the general, almost stupefied with wine, dismissed all his servants, and so Judith was left alone with the enemy of her people. All her plans had been directed toward this moment. With a silent prayer for strength she came close to his couch where he was lying intoxicated and, seizing his sword, took hold of his hair and, after another prayer, struck his neck twice with all her might, severing his head from his body. Now all that remained to be done was to put the head in the bag in which she carried her food, and to go out calmly, as on the previous nights, into the darkness beyond the borders of the camp (13:1-10).

When she drew near to Bethulia, Judith called out to the watchmen at the gates, 'Open, open the gate! God, our God, is still with us, to show his power in Israel, and his strength against our enemies, even as he has done this day!' (13:11). There was unbounded joy in the city when they learned what Judith had done. Displaying the bloody trophy, Judith frankly acknowledged, 'It was my face that tricked him to his destruction, and yet he committed no act of sin with me, to defile and shame me' (13:16). Then Uzziah and all the people gave thanks to God and called down a blessing on Judith for her daring exploit (13:-17-20).

Judith arranged for the Jews to make an attack on the morrow (14:1-4), and summoned Achior the Ammonite. After he had been shown the head of the great Holofernes and was told what had happened, he became a convert to Judaism (14:5-10).

In the morning the Jews hung the head of Holofernes on the wall of the city, and all their warriors rushed out boldly to attack the Assyrian encampment. The enemy, panic-stricken when they discovered the murder of their general, fled in utter confusion and terror. The Jews of all Palestine fell upon them, slaughtering and pursuing them beyond Damascus. The rest of the people of Bethulia fell upon the Assyrian camp and plundered it for thirty days, greatly enriching themselves (14:11–15:7).

Then the High Priest Joakim and the members of the Sanhedrin came from Jerusalem to honor Judith for her bravery, and all the people joined in praising her in song and dance (15:8–13). The heroine burst forth in a hymn of praise and thanksgiving to the God of their salvation (16:1–17), whereupon all of them went up to Jersualem to worship the Lord with sacrifices and feasting for three months (16:18–20). Here Judith dedicated as a gift to the Lord all the dishes of Holofernes as well as the canopy from his bed-chamber where he had been slain.

The book closes with a short account of Judith's return to Bethulia where, despite many proposals to marriage, she remained loyal to her deceased husband. Becoming more and more famous, she died finally at the age of one hundred and five years, was buried beside her husband, and was mourned seven days throughout the house of Israel (16:21–25).

One of the first questions that naturally rises regarding this book is whether it is historical. The consensus, at least among Protestant and Jewish scholars, is that the story is sheer fiction. Apart from exaggerations in numbers (1:4, 16; 2:5, 15; 7:2, 17), such as are found even in acknowledged historical works of the time, the book teems with chronological, historical, and geographical improbabilities and downright errors. For example, Holofernes moves an immense army about three hundred miles in three days (2:21). The opening words of the book, when taken with 2:1ff. and 4:2f., involve the most astonishing historical nonsense, for the author places Nebuchadnezzar's reign over the Assyrians (in reality he was king of Babylon) at Nineveh (which fell seven years before his accession!) at a time when the Jews had only recently returned from the captivity (actually at this time they were suffering further deportations)! Nebuchadnezzar did not make war on Media (1:7), nor capture Ecbatana (1:14). It is passing strange that Bethulia, a city of such strategic importance, is otherwise unknown. The rebuilding of the Temple (4:13) is dated, by a glaring anachronism, about a century too early. Moreover, the Jewish state is represented as being under the government of a high priest and a kind of Sanhedrin (6:6–14; 15:8), which is compatible only with a post-exilic date several hundred years after the book's presumed historical setting.

These difficulties in taking the book as history led Martin Luther to describe it as 'a religious fiction or poem, written by a holy and ingenious man, who depicts therein the victory of the Jewish people over all their enemies, which God at all times most wonderfully vouchsafes. . . . Judith is the Jewish people, represented as a chaste and holy widow, which is always the character of God's people. Holofernes is the heathen, the godless or unchristian lord of all ages, while the city of Bethulia denotes a virgin [the Hebrew word *bethulah* does in fact mean 'a virgin'], indicating that the believing Jews of those days were "the pure virgins" ' ('Preface to the Book of Judith,' Luther's translation of the Bible, 1534).Without going to these lengths of allegorizing the story, most scholars today regard the book of Judith as a piece of fiction written with a certain historical flavor so as to enhance the dramatic effect. As a quasi-historical novel, the book displays a high degree of excellence in storytelling. The scenes depicted are realistic and follow one another in logical sequence. Unnecessary details are avoided. The reader feels a certain fascination as he is drawn closer and closer to the climax. Judith's motive in coming to Holofernes seems to be represented at first as the act of a traitress, and yet her deep piety convinces the reader that this cannot be. The outcome is cleverly concealed from the reader who comes to the book for the first time, yet instances of *double entendre* provide a piquancy that rewards subsequent rereading.

As compared with the story of Tobit, which inculcates such virtues as gentleness and kindliness, the plot of this book is strenuous, not to say fierce and almost vindictive. The name of the heroine was doubtless chosen to suggest her as a counterpart to that doughty warrior, Judas Maccabeus. She stands in the tradition of other intrepid women—from Jael, by whose treachery the tyrannical Sisera met his death when she drove a tent pin into his temple (Judges 4:4–22; 5:2–31), to Charlotte Corday, who, having forced her way into the home of Jean-Paul Marat, the most bloodthirsty of the French Terrorists, stabbed him to death in his bath. Candor demands that we acknowledge that certain aspects of the grim story of Judith are far from being exemplary. At the same time we remember that it was written in a time of war to inspire a people who were fighting desperately for their religion as well as for their independence.

The religious emphasis in the story is of the rigidly orthodox type: the observance of the Mosaic Law is the supreme test of piety. In fact, the book affords a valuable source for the study of early Pharisaism and its punctiliousness in going beyond the written Mosaic code. Thus, Judith not only strictly observed the dietary laws, but she fasted continually (8:6) even though the Old Testament prescribes fasting for only one day in the year, the Day of Atonement. She kept not only the Pentateuchal feasts of the Sabbath and New Moon, but also the eves of them (8:16), as required by post-exilic teaching. Like the later Pharisees and Essenes, she performed her ablutions, even under difficulties (12:7), and scrupulously avoided ritual pollution (12:9).

As a tract for the times we may well believe that the book of Judith accomplished much in revitalizing flagging courage and reviving faltering devotion. The popularity of the story is attested by its existence in three slightly different Greek editions, two Latin versions, a Syriac version, as well as several later Hebrew forms. In view of this evidence of the book's wide circulation, it is perhaps surprising that Josephus makes no mention of its contents. The first writer to refer to Judith (he calls her 'the blessed Judith') is the Christian author, Clement of Rome. Writing at the end of the first century he speaks of her and of Esther as examples of 'women who were strengthened through the grace of God to perform many a manly deed' ([First] Epistle to the Corinthians, 55:3). During the early Middle Ages events which the book records were incorporated into the liturgy for the Jewish festival of Hanukkah (the feast commemorating the Dedication of the Temple; see below, pp. 136f.). In subsequent centuries Judith and her deed of prowess were celebrated by literally hundreds of poets, painters, and dramatists.

V

The Additions to the Book of Esther

WHAT NOW APPEARS IN THE APOCRYPHA AS A
SEPARATE BOOK, ENTITLED IN THE KING JAMES
VERSION 'THE REST OF THE CHAPTERS OF THE
Book of Esther which are found neither in the Hebrew nor in
the Chaldee,' has bewildered many readers. When read consecutively these chapters are incomprehensible. If one knows,
however, the vicissitudes through which the material has passed,
it is possible to bring order out of the present chaotic state of
the chapters. Briefly, what has happened is the following.

Sometime in the second or first century before Christ a certain Lysimachus (11:1) translated the Hebrew text of the Book
of Esther in the Old Testament into Greek. At six different
places in the Greek narrative he or someone else added substantial episodes not in the Hebrew, totalling one hundred and seven
verses. The elaborated form of the book subsequently passed
from Greek into an Old Latin version. Later, when Jerome,
who had been commissioned by Pope Damasus at the close of
the fourth century to prepare a standard Latin version of the

Bible, came to the Book of Esther he translated the Hebrew form of the book as it stands. Then, having gathered together the several additions found in Latin copies, he added them at the close of his rendering of the Hebrew, attaching notes to indicate where each addition belonged within the canonical book. But in the course of the subsequent transmission of Jerome's Vulgate, in manuscript form, careless scribes would frequently omit these explanatory notes, resulting in a meaningless amalgam of separate portions. The final confusing step came in the Middle Ages when Stephen Langton, archbishop of Canterbury (died 1228), having divided the Latin Bible into chapters to facilitate its citation, numbered the chapters of the canonical and the apocryphal material of Esther consecutively as though all of the latter material formed a direct continuation of the former. Luther's Bible and the early English versions follow this absurd chapter numeration. Thus it happens that what is now printed as one book in the Apocrypha is made up of fragments formerly dispersed throughout the canonical Book of Esther. Obviously, therefore, when they are read apart from the Book of Esther they make no sense at all. In the following synopsis these Apocryphal additions are considered in their proper sequence within the framework of the canonical Esther. Brief summaries of the latter book are enclosed within square brackets.

Addition A (11:2-12:6)

In the second year of the reign of Artaxerxes the Great, Mordecai, a Jewish courtier in the Persian city of Susa, had a

THE ADDITIONS TO THE BOOK OF ESTHER 57

dream. In this dream, which foreshadows the action of the story, he saw two great dragons, both ready to fight and roaring terribly. At their roaring every nation prepared to fight against the Jews, who cried unto God for help. 'And from their cry, as though from a tiny spring, there came a great river, with abundant water; light came, and the sun rose, and the lowly were exalted and consumed those held in honor' (11:11).

After Mordecai awoke he overheard two eunuchs, named Gabatha and Tharra, plotting to assassinate the king. Reporting this to Artaxerxes, who executed the plotters, Mordecai was rewarded for his loyalty by being elevated to a position of service in the court. Haman, however, who was presumably in league with the conspirators, determined to ruin Mordecai and his people (12:1-6).

[At this point the Hebrew Book of Esther in the Old Testament begins. The king, Ahasuerus, entertained all the dignitaries of the Persian Empire at a great feast. On the last day he ordered that Queen Vashti be brought 'in order to show the peoples and the princes her beauty; for she was fair to behold' (1:11). She, however, refused to come, and so he divorced her lest her wifely insubordination set a bad example in his kingdom. In the search for a new queen, Mordecai's ward, Esther, was chosen by the king, and became queen. She concealed her Jewish religion and nationality. Mordecai discovered that two eunuchs were plotting the assassination of the king, and the plotters were executed. Haman, a pompous vizier, was offended when Mordecai refused to bow down before him, and resolved to destroy the Jews. He poisoned the king's mind against them, and the king issued an edict authorizing their destruction (Esther 1:1-3:13).]

Addition B (13:1-7)

This Addition purports to be a copy of the edict sent by the king to the governors of the provinces commanding the massacre of the Jews.

[In consternation, the Jews everywhere mourned bitterly, and Mordecai sent word to Esther to appeal to the king and save her people: 'Who knows whether you have not come to the kingdom for such a time as this?' Esther finally agreed: 'I will go to the king, though it is against the law; and if I perish, I perish' (Esther 3:14–4:17).]

Addition C (13:8-14:19)

This rather lengthy Addition contains the prayers of Mordecai and Esther beseeching God for help in their predicament. Beginning with an ascription of praise to God who rules all and whom none can resist, Mordecai continued: 'Thou knowest, O Lord, that it was not in insolence or pride or for any love of glory that I did this, and refused to bow down to this proud Haman. For I would have been willing to kiss the soles of his feet, to save Israel! But I did this, that I might not set the glory of man above the glory of God, and I will not bow down to any one but to thee, who art my Lord. . . . And now, O Lord God and King, God of Abraham, spare thy people' (13:12–15).

Preparatory to her prayer, Esther took off her splendid apparel and put on the clothes of distress and mourning. She began her supplication by recalling how in the past God ever performed what he had promised; she then referred to the threat of the enemy to annihilate the Jewish people. There follows the most impressive part of her prayer: 'Give me courage, O King of the gods and Master of all dominion! Put eloquent speech in my mouth before the lion, and turn his heart to hate the man who is fighting against us, so that there may be an end of him and those who agree with him. But save us by thy hand, and help me, who am alone and have no helper but thee, O Lord' (14:12–14).

Addition D (15:1-16)

This is an elaboration of the Hebrew Esther 5:1-2, which two verses are omitted in the Greek form of the book. It tells of how Esther, in fine attire and filled with fear, ventured to come before the king seated on his royal throne. At first he became angry at her intrusion, and she fainted away in terror. 'Then God changed the spirit of the king to gentleness, and in alarm he sprang from his throne and took her in his arms until she came to herself' (15:8). He then granted her permission to present to him her petition.

[Esther deferred her real request, and merely invited the king and Haman to a banquet. The king is reminded that Mordecai's warning had saved his life, and asked Haman to suggest how a faithful subject should be honored. Imagining that the king was planning to honor him, Haman suggested that elaborate public recognition be accorded such a person. To his utter chagrin the king bade him to carry out his recommendations for Mordecai the Jew.

At a second banquet for the king and Haman, Esther exposed Haman's plot to destroy her and her people. In anger the king ordered Haman's execution on the gallows which he had originally erected for Mordecai's destruction. At Esther's request the king also revoked the bloody decree which Haman had devised against the Jews (Esther 5:3-8:12).]

‥‥‥

Addition E (16:1-24)

‥‥‥

This Addition supplies the full text of the counter-edict revoking the earlier edict (given in Addition B). In florid and rhetorical language, it recites the treasonable plotting of Haman. The Jews, however, 'who were consigned to annihilation by this thrice accursed man, are not evil-doers but are governed by most righteous laws and are sons of the Most High, the most mighty living God, who has directed the kingdom for us and for our fathers in the most excellent order. . . . Therefore post a copy of this letter publicly in every place, and permit the Jews to live under their own laws' (16:15-16, 19). Cities which did not act in accordance with the edict were to be utterly destroyed.

[The canonical Book of Esther concludes with an account of the revenge which the Jews took upon their enemies, and the institution of an annual feast, called Purim, to commemorate their deliverance (9:1-10:3).]

Addition F (10:4-11:1)

This Addition supplies the interpretation of Mordecai's dream, recorded in Addition A with which the expanded form of the book opens. He recognized now the hand of God in directing the triumph of the Jews. The two dragons in his dream represented Mordecai and Haman. The tiny spring which became a river was Esther. Thus God's lots for the Jews and the Gentiles were both fulfilled and are now quite appropriately commemorated in the feast of Purim, which is interpreted to mean 'lots.'

The book concludes with a postscript (11:1) designed to authenticate Mordecai's festal message (9:29), and by implication the entire Book of Esther, which was probably deposited in some Jewish archive in Egypt.

It is appropriate to inquire into the motives of the elaborator of the canonical Book of Esther. Why did he think it desirable to supplement this book, and what are the characteristics of his additions?

It is well known that the Book of Esther, unlike every other book in the Old Testament, makes not the slightest reference to the God of Israel. Furthermore, despite the danger and distress of the Jews, there is no mention of so fundamental a religious practice as prayer. Thus, when it is stated that the Jews 'wept and wailed,' and Mordecai 'cried with a loud and bitter cry,' the author refrains from saying that they cried to God. Even in a passing reference to fasting (4:16), no religious significance is given to what is essentially a religious practice.

Undoubtedly this avoidance of any explicit reference to religion was deliberate, and it has been explained in various ways. Some have thought that the author was a secular-minded Jew more interested in Judaism as a nationalism than as a religion. On the other hand, because the book as a whole illustrates the working of divine Providence by implying that Esther was an instrument of God's will in securing her people's deliverance, it may be that the author wrote at some period when it was extremely dangerous to make any open profession of the worship of Jehovah.

For whatever reason, several generations later the continuator of Esther decided to expand the book with six supplementary pieces, all but one of which contains the name of God. The fact that in Addition F the name of God is mentioned nine times in as many verses amply illustrates one purpose of the supplementation. The theology in these Additions is that of the so-called 'normative' type of Judaism. God is referred to as omniscient (13:12; 14:15–16; 15:5), omnipotent (13:9, 11; 14:12, 19; 16:16, 18), righteous (14:7), holy (14:6), the redeemer (13:16), the God of Abraham (13:15; 14:18) who chose Israel (13:16; 16:21)—in fact, the only true God (14:3).

The two prayers included in Addition C breathe a spirit of deep devotion to and dependence on God. Thus the Additions testify to the desire to introduce into the book certain religious elements which are conspicuously absent from the Hebrew narrative.

At the same time it must be recognized that the work of the Greek continuator, laudable as it may be in one respect, is far from being entirely commendable. The literary style of the Additions tends to be wordy, not to say bombastic. More serious are the discrepancies and contradictions which have been introduced. For example, according to the Hebrew text Mordecai discovered the plot against the king sometime after the seventh year of the reign of Ahasuerus (2:16–21), whereas the Greek Addition A suggests that this occurred in the second year of the king's reign. Other discrepancies relate to the nationality of Haman (in 16:10 he is called a Macedonian, but in Esther 3:1 his father's name is Persian and he is called the Agagite, that is, Amalekite); the date fixed for the massacre of the Jews (in 13:6, the fourteenth of Adar, but in Esther 3:13 it is the thirteenth of Adar); and the time when Haman's sons were put to death (compare 16:18 with Esther 9:13).

Most serious of all is the increase of anti-Semitism and the answering hostility against the Gentiles which are to be found in the Additions (for example, 10:10). Understandable as this note may be in the historical background of the origin of the Greek Additions, it is scarcely to be compensated for by the copious use of the name of the deity.

VI

The Wisdom of Solomon

TWO OF THE BOOKS OF THE APOCRYPHA — THE
WISDOM OF SOLOMON AND ECCLESIASTICUS —
BELONG TO THAT GENRE OF ANCIENT LITERATURE
known as sapiential or 'wisdom' literature. The authors of this
type of literature were called wise men or sages. Among the
Jews, as well as in other ancient cultures, the wise man occupied
a position in national life almost as distinct and prominent as the
prophet and the priest (the three are mentioned together in Jer.
18:18 as of equally recognized status). The wise man differed
from the priest in that he had no ceremonial duties in connection
with the Temple, and from the prophet in that he did not preface his remarks with 'Thus saith the Lord.' He might or might
not be a scribe, that is an expounder of the national scriptures.
The earliest sages in Israel elaborated occasional riddles (Judges
14:4), parables (II Sam. 12:1–6), and proverbs (Ezek. 18:2).
Later sages made the pursuit of wisdom the chief aim of life.
Sober reflection, from a religious point of view, upon all aspects
of existence, and the terse generalization of that reflection, resulted in the formation of collections of the sayings of the wise.

The most famous of these collections, going back to Solomon, Agur, Lemuel, and other sages, is known as the Book of Proverbs in the Old Testament.

It was after the Exile that Wisdom literature attained its highest development among the Jews. After the reorganization under Ezra (Ezra 7:6, 10), when the intellectual life of the people was gradually confined by the priests within the limits of a rigid legalism, the wise men found a new sphere for their activity. In addition to collecting detached aphorisms, such as the Book of Proverbs, they wrote on popular morals, handling ethical topics at length in a combination of narrative and rhythmical composition. Examples of this type of work contained in the Old Testament are the books of Job and Ecclesiastes, and perhaps Psalm 73.

The two books of Wisdom which are included in the Apocrypha are in many respects the heirs of the treasures garnered by earlier sages. Though agreeing in several of their general emphases, these two books differ widely in their special interests. Ecclesiasticus, whose roots go deep into Palestinian Judaism, is concerned with wisdom chiefly as it pertains to practical ethics and general human conduct regulated by divine statutes; the Wisdom of Solomon, on the other hand, is concerned to unite the conventional piety of orthodox Judaism with the Greek philosophical spirit current at that time in Alexandria. The former is largely a book of maxims; the latter aspires to be a theological treatise.

One of the most outstanding features of these two books is their development of the doctrine of Wisdom itself. Already in the Old Testament is to be found the beginning of the personification of Wisdom (Job 28 and Proverbs 8:22-31). Based squarely upon such a foundation, Ecclesiasticus reiterates that Wisdom is eternal (1:1), universal (24:6), unsearchable (1:6), the formative creative power in the world (24:3), yet created (1:4; 24:9) and established in the midst of the people of God in Jerusalem (24:10f.). In one passage (24:3ff., 'I . . . covered the earth as a mist'), Wisdom appears to be identified with the creative Word of God.

The Wisdom of Solomon carries the personification of Wisdom to its highest point in the Apocrypha. In a manner analogous to that of the Stoic teaching concerning the all-pervading Logos, the author identifies Wisdom with the spirit of the Lord (9:17), with the hand of God (14:6), with God's providence (14:3) and power (1:3). In an enumeration of the attributes of Wisdom (7:22-24), she is said to possess intelligence, holiness, beneficence, omnipotence, and omniscience (see also 9:11). These functions and attributes mark her as being very near to God himself. The writer regards her as far more than a literary personification; he accumulates such expressions as breath, effluence, mirror, and image of God (7:25-26) in order to assert her divineness. Yet the author stops short of attributing to Wisdom deity, separate from and outside of God himself.

After these preliminary remarks on the nature of Wisdom literature in general, more detailed consideration may now be given to the treatise on Wisdom which is ascribed to Solomon.

The Apocryphal book which is called the Wisdom of Solomon, or simply Wisdom, appears to have been composed in Greek sometime between about 100 B.C. and A.D. 40. In order to gain a wider audience for his literary work, the author writes in the name of Solomon, reputed to be the wisest king of Israel. Who the author was has been the subject of much learned debate, and many names have been proposed, ranging from Philo of Alexandria to Apollos before he became a Christian. The most that can be said with certainty is that he was an orthodox

Hellenistic Jew of Alexandria with a philosophical education.

The author appears to have written with several kinds of readers in mind. Some, perhaps many, of his fellow Jews in Alexandria had deserted the religion of their ancestors. He attempts to rekindle in them a genuine zeal for God and his Law (chapters 1 to 5). Other Jews, perplexed and disheartened by disappointments and persecutions, would find in his book an *apologia* that was calculated to encourage and fortify their faith and practice (chapters 10–12 and 16–19). Finally, with an eye upon possible Gentile readers of his book, he attempts to prove to thoughtful pagans the truth of Judaism (chapters 6-9) and the foolishness of idolatry (chapters 13-15).

In greater detail, the book discloses the following outline. Impersonating King Solomon, the writer addresses the rulers of the earth advising them to seek wisdom and follow righteousness (1:1-5). He declares that lawless deeds and impious words lead to spiritual death, but that 'righteousness is immortal' (1:6-15).

The apostate Jews, by their works and words, have made a covenant with death (1:16-2:1a). Like the author of the canonical Book of Ecclesiastes, they deny providence, immortality, and judgment, while greedily pursuing riotous pleasures and persecuting the righteous Jews (2:1b-12), whose life and faithfulness are a standing rebuke to them (2:13-40). The cause and consequence of these errors and crimes are succinctly stated: 'Through the devil's envy death entered the world, and those who belong to his party experience it' (2:24).

On the one hand, the sufferings of the righteous in this world are only a chastening which prepares them for a blessed eternity; at the judgment they will triumph over the ungodly, and thereafter will reign forever over the nations in the Kingdom of God (3:1-9). On the other hand, the wicked even in this life are miserable, their labors are unprofitable, and their children are cursed (3:10–16). In fact—and here the author digresses—true happiness does not consist, as many Jews supposed, in having many children and attaining a ripe old age, but in being humble amid prosperity and in giving assistance to the poor (3:17-4:10).

Resuming his general argument, the author reminds his readers that the premature death of the righteous is preferable to the longevity of the wicked, for, as in the case of Enoch of old, God thereby ushers them into eternal blessedness (4:10-19). There follows a description of the anguish and remorse of the ungodly in the Judgment, who, recognizing that the despised righteous are now numbered among the sons of God, will be forced to acknowledge the sinful folly of their course (4:20-5:23).

Pseudo-Solomon then calls upon the rulers of the earth to seek wisdom from the Lord, for without wisdom they cannot discharge their responsibilities (6:1-11). Wisdom responds to those who seek her (6:12-16), and leads those who desire her to true kingship and immortality (6:17-21). Next the author, still impersonating King Solomon, discloses how he attained wisdom; God bestowed it upon him, not because he was superior to other ordinary mortals, but because he had sought it through prayer (6:27–7:14). The diversified characteristics of wisdom are described with twenty-one, or 3 x 7, attributes (7:15-8:1; especially 7:22b–23).

The sage tells how he had begun to seek wisdom in his youth, and describes how she teaches men all the virtues (he enumerates the four cardinal virtues of Plato and the Stoics, 8:7) and instructs them in all knowledge (8:2-9). Through his possession of wisdom he will become a wise ruler, highly esteemed by his own subjects and by foreign peoples (8:10-16). He therefore prays that God may grant him this greatest of all boons

(8:17-21). The prayer (9:1-18), which is an expansion of the much briefer accounts in II Kings 3:7-9 and II Chron. 1:8-10, begins on a majestic note: 'O God of my fathers and Lord of mercy, who hast made all things by thy word, and by thy wisdom hast formed man, . . . give me the wisdom that sits by thy throne, and do not reject me from among thy servants' (9:1, 4).

This prayer is followed by a meditation upon the activity of wisdom in Israel's history. So marked are the change in style and the deterioration of form and content of the remaining part of the book that many scholars believe these chapters to be the work of a different author from the one who had attained the literary heights of the first part of the book. It may well be, however, that pseudo-Solomon discovered what many another author has discovered, namely, that the sublimest inspiration does not abide forever, and that in place of noble thoughts mere commonplaces and bathos can also come from one's pen. Whatever the explanation, it must be acknowledged that whoever was responsible for the last half of the book unfortunately kept on writing long after he had anything fresh or important to say. The rhetoric of this portion often degenerates into bombast, and there is a marked lack of spontaneity. Yet it is true to say that even in this part there are occasional passages which both in style and subject-matter are reminiscent of the author of the first half at his best.

The main theme of this section of the book (10:1-19:22) is the demonstration from history that wisdom, by God's providence, saved the Israelites and chastised her adversaries, the Egyptians and other heathen. The author develops in great detail the idea that God used the very things that benefited his people to punish their enemies (11:5). But he is so much enthralled by this notion, and manages to find it operative in so many unusual circumstances, that the modern reader's patience and interest are exhausted. Curiously enough, the concept of wisdom is found only in the brief opening chapter of this section (10:1-11:1), and the word 'wisdom' occurs but twice in the remainder of the book. It is also worthy of notice that in developing his religio-philosophical sketch of history, the author confines himself almost entirely to events mentioned in the Pentateuchal narratives of the Old Testament.

Wisdom, the author says, preserved and guided the patriarchs, from Adam to Joseph, and, through the instrumentality of Moses, led the Israelites victoriously from Egypt (10:1-21). Here, as also later, the author indulges in a literary conceit; he never once mentions by name the Old Testament worthy about whom he may be writing, but leaves it to the imagination of the reader to infer his identity from the context.

In a comparison between the Egyptians and the Israelites, the author points out that water, used by God in plaguing the former, became a source of blessing for the latter (11:1-14). Digressing from his subject, the author dwells on the principle that 'one is punished by the things through which he sins' (11: 16), and illustrates it by considering how God sent plagues of animals (frogs and lice) upon the Egyptians for their senseless worship of irrational animals (11:15-26). The Canaanites were also punished for their abominable sins (12:1-11); yet in their case, as also in the case of the Egyptians, God showed his mercy and desire that sinners should repent (12:12-27).

At this point the author digresses again in order to explain the nature and origin of idolatry (polytheism). With an extremely bitter tirade against the heathen, pseudo-Solomon dwells upon the demoralizing influence of idolatry upon all of life. The least blameworthy form of idolatry (though even this is inexcusable) is the worship of the natural elements and the heavenly bodies, by whose beauty men were naturally attracted

(13:1-9). He bluntly declares that the worship of beasts and stones and images made by human hands is ridiculous (13:10-19). After reiterating that idols and idolators are odious to God (14:1-11), the author adopts and somewhat modifies the theory of the origin of the gods which the Greek writer, Euhemerus, had popularized about 300 B.C., namely that they are nothing but deified human beings (14:12-21). From such image-worship come all the frightful vices of society, for which men will surely be punished (14:22-31).

Contrasted with this idolatry is Israel's faithfulness to God; as his chosen people they know him, his long-suffering and mercy, and therefore they are not led astray by 'the evil design of human art' (15:1-6). On the contrary, Israel's enemies fell into the childish absurdity of thinking that their idols, products of their own hands, were gods (15:7-19).

Returning now to the history of God's dealings with his ancient people, the author compares the punishments that God meted out to the Egyptians and to the erring Israelites. Unclean animals, worshiped by the Egyptians, were sent as plagues upon them, preventing them from eating, while clean animals (quails) were supplied as food for the Israelites in the desert (16:1-4). True enough, the Israelites were plagued by serpents in the desert, but this was for their admonition, and God healed those who by this chastisement were put in remembrance of the oracles of his Law (16:5-14).

Continuing the subject of the punishment of the Egyptians, the author elaborates with repeated exaggeration that the very elements were inimical to them, but showed themselves friendly to the Israelites (16:15-29). Drawing upon imaginary and often fantastic details, which are doubtless echoes of Jewish legend, pseudo-Solomon describes how the Egyptians in a horror of darkness were haunted by monstrous apparitions while the Is-

raelites had light and guidance and the comfort of a pillar of
fire and a friendly sun (17:1-18:4). The Egyptians were punished in yet another way, namely by the death of their first-
born children when God's almighty Word, a fierce warrior,
leaped down from heaven into the doomed land of Egypt, while
the plague which devastated the Israelites after the rebellion of
Dathan and Korah was subdued by the mediation of Aaron
(18:5-25). The author's imagination embroiders the account of
the crossing of the Red Sea, when 'land animals were trans-
formed into water creatures, and creatures that swim were
changed over to the land,' and there was a miraculous transmu-
tation of the elements (19:18-19). Here the book ends quite
abruptly; no culminating point has been reached nor does the
argument find a natural conclusion. It may be, as some have
suggested, that the author became so fatigued with his turgid
rhetoric, elaborated with tedious repetition, that he simply
dropped the whole subject.

The theological doctrines taught in the Wisdom of Solomon
are basically derived from the Old Testament, yet modified at
significant points by Greek philosophical ideas current in Alexandria at the time of its composition. For example, the author's
teaching of divine and human wisdom, or objective and sub-
jective wisdom as it may be termed, is an explication of the earlier ideas on this subject expressed in the Book of Proverbs, with
a metaphysical twist borrowed from the Stoic conception of the
universal Logos, that impersonal mediator between God and
creation. In other respects also pseudo-Solomon approaches the
language and doctrines of Hellenistic philosophy. Thus, in
speaking of the creative work of God, the writer describes him
as having 'created the world out of formless matter' (11:17),
adopting here the very phrase which Platonists used to describe

the pre-existent matter out of which the world was made, and implying that this unformed matter was itself uncreated.

As for man, his body is regarded as a mere weight and clog to the soul (9:15), a view which is foreign to both Old Testament and New alike. It was but a short step from this strain of thought to that gnostic heresy in the early Church which regarded all matter as inherently and irredeemably evil. Another Platonic doctrine which the author borrows is the pre-existence of souls ('. . . a good soul fell to my lot; or rather, being good, I entered an undefiled body,' 8:19-20). Sin, which is disobedience to God's moral law, and death are represented as having been introduced into the world by the devil (2:24). This appears to be the first time in Jewish literature that such a conception is expressed. The ideas that there is a world-soul (1:7; 7:24; 8:1) and that God has 'arranged all things by measure and number and weight' (11:20) are likewise derived from Greek and not from Hebrew sources.

It is particularly in the realm of eschatology that pseudo-Solomon more than once passes quite beyond the Old Testament. From Platonism he draws the doctrine that man is inherently immortal. Instead of an after-life in the shadow-land of Sheol, to which according to the Old Testament good and bad alike go at death, he teaches that one's moral character determines one's future destiny. The righteous will have peace and glory forever in 'a place of great delight in the temple of the Lord,' which is one of the first intimations of heaven as the abode of the godly (3:14; 5:15-16); whereas the wicked will be in torment (4:18-20; 17:21). The final judgment will follow death and precede entrance upon one's eternal abode (3:18; 4:20).

In a passage of great beauty and comfort, the author encourages the faithful to be undaunted by death.

The souls of the righteous are in the hand of God,
and no torment will ever touch them.
In the eyes of the foolish they seemed to have died,
and their departure was thought to be an affliction,
and their going from us to be their destruction;
but they are at peace.
For though in the sight of men they were punished,
their hope was full of immortality.
Having been disciplined a little, they will receive great good,
because God tested them and found them worthy of himself
(3:1-5).

It is obvious that here Platonic ideas of the inherent immortality of the soul have supplanted the Hebraic (and Christian) doctrine of the resurrection of the body, a doctrine found in Daniel 12:2 and throughout the New Testament.

The early Christians prized the Wisdom of Solomon for what were interpreted as several clear predictions of the passion of Christ. The text, 'Blessed is the wood through which righteousness comes' (14:7), when isolated from its context (the ark of Noah), was seized upon as a reference to the Cross on which Jesus died. Another passage (2:12-20) was taken by many Church Fathers (for example, Augustine in his *City of God*, XVII. 20) as prophesying most plainly the conspiracy of those responsible for the death of Christ. In this passage pseudo-Solomon pictures a righteous sufferer who protests against the apostasy, injustice, and persecuting policy of highly placed freethinkers. Several of the more striking sentences may be quoted:

Let us lie in wait for the righteous man,
because he is inconvenient to us
He professes to have knowledge of God,
and opposes our actions. . . .

> and calls himself a child of the Lord. . . .
> Let us test him with insult and torture,
> that we may find out how gentle he is,
> and make trial of his forbearance (2:12, 13, 19).

Whether the author here has in mind some contemporary Jewish martyrdom known to him, or whether he drew upon the stories in the Books of Maccabees for a generalized description of suffering for the Jewish faith, cannot be determined. He may also have been influenced by Glaucon's description in Plato's *Republic* of the binding, scourging, and crucifixion of the perfectly just man who is esteemed to be unjust.[1] In both cases the parallel to Christ's sufferings is more apparent than real.

Still another passage in this book has long been interpreted messianically. At an early date the imagination of Church Fathers was caught by pseudo-Solomon's dramatic and vivid reference to God's 'all-powerful word [the Logos] that leaped from heaven, from the royal throne, into the midst of the land' (18:15). Despite the context, which refers to the destruction of the first-born among the ancient Egyptians, these words came to be applied to the Incarnation. The influence of this Patristic interpretation can be seen even today in the Roman Missal, which incorporates these words in the Introit of the Mass for the Sunday within the Octave of Christmas as well as in the Introit of the Mass for the Vigil of Epiphany.

---

1. Glaucon's description of a hypothetical perfectly just man who is deemed to be unjust concludes with these words: '[He] will be scourged, racked, fettered, will have his eyes burnt out, and at last, after all manner of suffering, will be crucified' (*Rep.* 362A). It is not surprising that Clement of Alexandria, quoting this passage, describes Plato as 'all but foretelling the dispensation of salvation' (*Strom.* 5. 14).

VII

Ecclesiasticus, or the Wisdom of Jesus
the Son of Sirach

ECCLESIASTICUS IS NOT ONLY THE LONGEST BUT ALSO ONE OF THE MOST IMPORTANT AND MOST HIGHLY ESTEEMED OF THE APOCRYPHAL BOOKS. Its alternative title, 'The Wisdom of Jesus the Son of Sirach,' indicates that it belongs to the category of Wisdom literature.[1] The purpose of the book is to set forth the true nature of wisdom, and to indicate the religious and social duties which must be performed in all of the vicissitudes of life. Wisdom is conceived of in a very wide sense and includes such diverse activities and skills as aptitude in craftsmanship, business capacity, cleverness, cunning, caution in word and act, discernment, self-control, wise dealing, discretion, learning, right living—all culminating in the fear of the Lord. In fact, according to Ecclesiasticus, worldly wisdom is the same in kind as divine wisdom, and differs from it only in degree.

This is the only Apocryphal book the author of which is known. The writer tells us that his name is 'Jesus [Hebrew,

---

1. For an account of Wisdom literature in general, see above, pp. 65ff.

Joshua; Aramaic, Jeshua] the son of Sirach the son of Eleazer, of Jerusalem' (50:27, though the text of the latter part of this verse is uncertain). From various hints which he gives about his background we may infer that Ben Sira,[2] as he is frequently called, had mulled long over portions of the Old Testament, particularly the Book of Proverbs and the Pentateuch. His attitude toward the Law as well as his cordial way of referring to the Scribes, or students of the Bible (10:5; 38:24 f.; 44:4), make it probable that he himself belonged to this profession. From his invitation, 'Draw near to me, you who are untaught, and lodge in the house of instruction' (51:23), it is fair to conclude that he conducted an academy in Jerusalem where he would lecture to the youth on ethical and religious subjects. According to 34:11-12 he did not spend his entire life in Palestine, but traveled to some extent in foreign lands. In common with other 'wise men' he had no doubt served on diplomatic missions and was personally acquainted with life in the courts of kings (39:4).

In about 180 B.C. this seasoned scribe and sage began to commit to writing the distilled wisdom which he had been accustomed to impart orally. Though Aramaic was then the vernacular of the Jews in Jerusalem, Ben Sira chose to write in Hebrew, the classical language of the Old Testament. About half a century later a grandson of the author, whose name is not recorded, took a copy of his grandfather's *magnum opus* to Egypt. Believing that the large Jewish population of Alexandria would profit from his ancestor's wisdom, he made a translation of the book into Greek, the language widely used at that time in Egypt as well as elsewhere. In his preface the translator modestly begs the reader to be indulgent of any infelicities in his work; 'for,' he explains, 'what was originally expressed in Hebrew does not

---

2. Ben Sira is Hebrew for 'son of Sirach.'

have exactly the same sense when translated into another language.' This divergence, he goes on to say, exists in current translations of even the Law itself, the prophecies, and the rest of the books of the Old Testament.[3] Therefore, if divergence appears in his own work it will not be unique. And so he bids his readers to 'be indulgent in cases where, despite our diligent labor in translating, we may seem to have rendered some phrases imperfectly.' Such sentiments find a sympathetic echo in every translator's mind. They also suggest the great advantage which the expositor of the Bible has if he has studied the original languages of Scripture.

The problems of ascertaining the original text of the book of Ecclesiasticus are difficult and complicated. The extant Greek manuscripts of this book are disfigured by numerous interpolations, omissions, and transpositions. By studying these it is seen that the manuscripts fall into two groups, one of which is thought to represent a translation of the original Hebrew text and the other of which may be a rendering of a Hebrew text revised by a disciple of the original author. There are also two Syriac versions of the book, one of which was made from a Hebrew original, the other from a Greek version. Four fragmentary Hebrew manuscripts dating from the eleventh and twelfth centuries, discovered in Egypt just before the beginning of this century, preserve about two-thirds of the book. There is no unanimity of opinion as to the worth of these manuscripts. Some scholars maintain that they were translated from the Greek; others hold that they go back ultimately to Ben Sira's original text, though containing today certain modifications derived from the Greek and Syriac versions. In the autumn of

3. Here the translator, living about 130 B.C., bears witness to the threefold division of the books of the Hebrew Old Testament, namely the Torah, the Prophets, and the Writings.

1952 several other small fragments of the Hebrew text of a work similar to Ecclesiasticus were found in a cave near Qumran by the Dead Sea, but their relationship to the original work of Ben Sira has not yet been investigated.

Besides these there are still other translations which have been made, with more or less fidelity, from the Greek or the Syriac. The Old Latin rendering, which Jerome did not revise, is characterized by the presence of many doublets; in some cases a passage appears in three forms. It is noteworthy that the rather colorless name by which Ben Sira's literary work is commonly known today (Ecclesiasticus) comes from the title of the Latin version, and is generally explained to mean 'The Church Book,' that is, the most important, or at least the longest, of the books not recognized as fully canonical and yet read in Church. The popularity of Ecclesiasticus is witnessed by the existence of still other ancient daughter-versions, including the Coptic versions (Sahidic, Bohairic, and Achmimic), the Ethiopic, Armenian (in two forms), Georgian, Old Slavonic, and Arabic (in several forms).

The presence of variations among both the primary and the secondary versions is partly to be explained by the literary form in which Ben Sira couched his teaching. Like the Book of Proverbs in the Old Testament, Ecclesiasticus is cast in a rhythmical pattern involving couplets of parallel lines. This unit was easy to imitate and to supplement, as many variants in the manuscripts show, and it was also easy to omit. At times the translator-grandson of Ben Sira undoubtedly found parallelism where it did not exist, and at other times he may have missed it where it did. Furthermore, it must have happened more than once that the meaning and/or the legibility of the original was not clear. In such cases the translator had no alternative except to use conjecture for the text or the sense. Of course, when he came to the alphabetic acrostic at the end of the book, he was no more able to represent in Greek this artificiality in the Hebrew than most other translators, ancient and modern[4] alike, are able to do when rendering certain Psalms and portions of the Book of Lamentations, where the same artificial arrangement appears in the Hebrew.

The material of Ecclesiasticus is so loosely arranged that a detailed table of contents would require more space than can be given here. The book deals with all the ordinary social and religious duties. The author shows wide acquaintance with men and things, and his advice is usually full of good sense and as applicable today as it was two thousand years ago. Whether it is upon the subject of behavior at table, or a father's treatment of a headstrong daughter, or the need of keeping guard over one's tongue, or recommendations concerning the relationship between husband and wife, or the folly of a fool, or the delights of a banquet, or whether the author is dealing with self-control, borrowing, loose women, diet, slander, the miser, the spendthrift, the hypocrite, the parasite, keeping secrets, giving alms, standing surety, mourning for the dead—these and a host of other subjects give us a valuable picture of many aspects of the Judaism of Palestine during the second century B.C. In view of this large variety of topics in a book which has no apparent progression of thought or logical arrangement, what follows are selected passages which, in one way or another, illustrate some of the author's excellencies as well as some of his shortcomings.

Writing with naïve candor, Ben Sira reveals more of his own likes and dislikes than any other ancient Jewish author of wis-

---

4. Msgr. Ronald Knox is one of the few modern translators who has attempted to preserve in English the acrostics in Ecclesiasticus 51, Psalm 25, 34, 37, 111, 112, and 119, and Lamentations 1-4.

dom literature. It is clear from his book that he was a townsman, born and bred in the city, and with a love for the life of the town. He has his prejudices and makes no secret, for example, of his intense dislike of women.

As to literary form, it will be observed that Ecclesiasticus, though obviously influenced by the Book of Proverbs, is in one respect a development of Proverbs—it now and again expands pithy though isolated proverbs into more meditative passages, which are the beginning of an essay. Furthermore, Ben Sira can attain poetic heights, as when he writes of God's handiwork in nature:

> By his command he sends the driving snow
>   and speeds the lightnings of his judgment.
> Therefore the storehouses are opened,
>   and the clouds fly forth like birds. . . .
> He scatters the snow like birds flying down. . . .
> He pours hoarfrost upon the earth like salt,
>   and when it freezes, it becomes pointed thorns.
> The cold north wind blows,
>   and ice freezes over the water;
> it rests upon every pool of water,
>   and the water puts it on like a breastplate (43:13–14, 17, 19–20).

The longest sustained theme in the book is the celebrated section on the Praise of Famous Men, chapters 44 to 50. The introductory words to it are some of the best known in the Apocrypha:

> Let us now praise famous men,
>   and our fathers in their generations.
> The Lord appointed to them great glory,
>   his majesty from the beginning.
> There were those who ruled in their kingdoms,
>   and were men renowned for their power,

giving counsel by their understanding,
    and proclaiming prophecies;
leaders of the people in their deliberations . . .
those who composed musical tunes,
    and set forth verses in writing . . .
all these were honored in their generations,
    and were the glory of their times. . . .
Peoples will declare their wisdom,
    and the congregation proclaims their praise (44:1–4, 5, 7, 15).

Another remarkably fine section is devoted to the subject of physicians.[5] Ben Sira defends them against doubts and objections which some for religious scruples may have leveled against them.

Honor the physician with the honor due him, according
    to your need of him,
  for the Lord created him;
for healing comes from the Most High (38:1f.).
The Lord created medicines from the earth,
    and a sensible man will not despise them (38:4).
And give the physician his place, for the Lord created him;
    let him not leave you, for there is need of him.
There is a time when success lies in the hands of physicians,
    for they too will pray to the Lord
that he should grant them success in diagnosis
    and in healing, for the sake of preserving life (38:12–14).

At the same time, Ben Sira writes what seems on the surface to be a disparagement of the physician:

He who sins before his Maker,
    may he fall into the care of a physician (38:15).

5. In liturgical churches this section on 'The Praise of the Physician' (38:1–15) is quite appropriately designated to be read on the Feast of St. Luke, 'the beloved physician' (Col. 4:14).

His thought, however, is not that the physician is a bugbear; rather it is that the man who sins against God will be punished by sickness, and will thus require the healing ministrations of the physician.

As for matrimony, Sirach speaks in no uncertain terms. One wonders whether some of the following epigrams reflect conditions in his own household.

> I would rather dwell with a lion and a dragon
> than dwell with an evil wife.
> The wickedness of a wife changes her appearance,
> and darkens her face like that of a bear.
> Her husband takes his meals among the neighbors,
> and cannot help sighing bitterly.
> Any iniquity is insignificant compared to a wife's iniquity;
> may a sinner's lot befall her!
> A sandy ascent for the feet of the aged —
> such is a garrulous wife for a quiet husband
>
>   . . . .
>
> A dejected mind, a gloomy face,
> and a wounded heart are caused by an evil wife.
> Drooping hands and weak knees
> are caused by the wife who does not make her husband
> happy.
> From a woman sin had its beginning,
> and because of her we all die (25:16-20, 23-24).

At the same time Ben Sira is not entirely ignorant of the happiness which a good wife brings to her husband. It is noteworthy that this section is much shorter than the preceding one.

> Happy is the husband of a good wife;
> the number of his days will be doubled.
> A loyal wife rejoices her husband,
> and he will complete his years in peace.

A good wife is a great blessing;
> she will be granted among the blessings of the
> man who fears the Lord.
Whether rich or poor his heart is glad,
> and at all times his face is cheerful (26: 1–4).

In the training of children Ben Sira recommends sternness and severity.

He who loves his son will whip him often,
> in order that he may rejoice at the way he
> turns out (30: 1).
Bow down his neck in his youth,
> and beat his sides while he is young,
Lest he become stubborn and disobey you,
> and you have sorrow of soul from him (30: 12).

This is a far cry from what is associated with modern methods of progressive education and freedom of self-expression!

Turning to somewhat lighter subjects, Ben Sira includes instructions as to how one should conduct oneself at a stylish dinner party. His rules of etiquette include the following:

Are you seated at the table of a great man?
> Do not be greedy at it,
> and do not say, 'There is certainly much upon it!' . . .
Do not reach out your hand for everything you see,
> and do not crowd your neighbor at the dish.
Judge your neighbor's feelings by your own,
> and in every matter be thoughtful.
Eat like a human being what is set before you,
> and do not chew greedily, lest you be hated.
Be the first to stop eating, for the sake of good manners,
> and do not be insatiable, lest you give offense.
If you are seated among many persons,
> do not reach out your hand before they do (31: 12, 14–18).

On the subject of making after-dinner speeches, Ben Sira has some practical advice to give. If there is also to be an entertainment, 'do not pour out talk' (32:4); and at any dinner party his recommendation is:

> Speak concisely, say much in few words;
>   be as one who knows and yet holds his tongue (32:8).
> Leave in good season and do not be the last;
>   go home quickly and do not linger (32:11).

He has counsel for the toastmaster:

> If they make you master of the feast, do not exalt
>   yourself;
>   be among them as one of them (32:1).

Despite this sound advice directed to others, it must be observed that modesty was not one of Ben Sira's virtues. He has a most exalted opinion of his position and abilities as a teacher.

> I have yet more to say, which I have thought upon,
>   and I am filled, like the moon at the full.
> Listen to me, O you holy sons,
>   and bud like a rose growing by a stream of water (39:12-13).

It may even be that Ben Sira considered his book to be the equal of inspired Scripture; such, at any rate, can be the implication of the following:

> I was the last on watch;
>   I was like one who gleans after the grape-
>   gatherers;
>   by the blessing of the Lord I excelled,
>   and like a grape-gatherer I filled my wine press.
> Consider that I have not labored for myself alone,
>   but for all who seek instruction (33:16-17).

In Ecclesiasticus doctrinal truths are presupposed rather than expounded. Theologically, Ben Sira often leans toward the point of view which came to be identified with that of the Sadducees. Thus, he is reticent about expressing belief in a future life and has no doctrine of a resurrection (compare Matt. 22: 23). It is only here on earth that God rewards and punishes by awarding 'good things and bad, life and death, poverty and wealth' (11:14); the wicked man, he says in effect, may enjoy prosperity all his life, but God may cause his last hours of life to be so terrible that all his former enjoyment of life becomes obliterated (11:26-28).

Two other traits also indicate a Sadducean leaning. He is intensely interested in the sacred rites of the Temple worship, and holds the priests of the Lord in highest reverence (7:29-31). Furthermore, though in the eyes of most Jews in Ben Sira's day the great national hero, Ezra, was acclaimed second only to Moses himself, Ben Sira passes him over in silence when enumerating the Fathers of old. Since Ezra, the scribe *par excellence*, was the spiritual forebear of those of the Pharisaic school, our author's silence is explicable as reflecting allegiance to a somewhat different religious tradition.

This tradition, however, was in many other points similar to that of the Pharisees, and orthodox Judaism in general. God is 'mighty in power and sees everything ... he knows every deed of man' (15:18-19). He created heaven and earth (16:26-17:9), and made man in his own image (17:1-10; etc.). As almighty sovereign of mankind, God is holy (4:14), just (35:12), and merciful (2:11; 48:20). It is particularly upon Israel that God has been pleased to disclose his covenanted mercies (36:12-17; see chapters 44-49).

Wisdom, while dwelling in Israel as its proper home (24:12 f.), was yet, in a measure fixed by God, poured out from the beginning on all mankind (1:10; 24:9-11). In spite of this God-given endowment, Ben Sira observes that many people are far from living in accord with divine precepts. He explains this defectibility of the human soul by referring to an inherent propensity to moral evil. This 'inclination' or 'impulse' or 'purpose' (the technical Hebrew term is yetser ha-ra') in man habitually leads him to misuse his free will in choosing evil rather than the way of Wisdom. (Why such a yetser ha-ra' is found in *every* man, he leaves unexplained.) Yet out of evil God draws good in many ways. In the Law, God gives guidance as to how to avoid sin, and the practice of the Law gives moral stamina to keep the evil impulse in check (11:15, 17; 15:15f.; 21:12). Furthermore, God is compassionate toward man's shortcomings, and through prayer (22:33-23:6) man can 'flee from sin as from a snake' (21:2). Even when the sinful impulse proves too strong for a man, repentance draws one close to God again, and amendment cancels its effects (17:20-28; 34:30f.; 35:5).

The importance of the book of Ecclesiasticus as a whole is to be found in its function as an important link in the development of ancient Judaism. It is the last great example of the type of wisdom literature represented in the Old Testament; it is the first specimen of a form of Judaism part of which thereafter developed into the sect of the Sadducees and part into Talmudic rabbinism.

VIII

Baruch

THE BOOK OF BARUCH IS NOTEWORTHY AS BEING
THE ONLY BOOK OF THE APOCRYPHA WHICH IS
FORMED ON THE MODEL OF THE OLD TESTAMENT
prophets, and though it is lacking in originality, one can still detect, even at second-hand, something of the ancient prophetic
fire. It purports to have been written during the Babylonian
captivity by the hand of Baruch the son of Neriah (1:1), the
companion and secretary of the prophet Jeremiah (Jer. 32:12;
36:4; 51:59). Actually it appears to be a composite work of un-
even quality written by two or more authors, the latest of
whom may have lived during the first century before Christ or
even the first century of the Christian era. The clearest and
sharpest division in the book comes at about the middle (between 3:8 and 3:9). Not only does the style change at this point
from prose to poetic parallelism, but God is spoken of in quite
different ways in the two parts. In the former half (1:1–3:8)
the terms which the author employs to refer to the deity are:

Lord—used twenty-two times,

Lord our God—used fifteen times,

Lord Almighty, the God of Israel—used twice.

None of these occur in the second half (3:9–5:9), where another set of expressions appears, apparently characterized by an attempt to define the nature of the deity more exactly. 'Lord' (which represents the sacred name of Jehovah) does not appear at all, but is replaced by 'God.' In addition to this change in nomenclature, one observes that only in the second part does the author refer to God as 'the Everlasting,' 'everlasting Savior,' and 'the Holy One,' none of which occurs in the former section.

What parts of this work were written originally in Hebrew and what in Greek has been the subject of much debate among scholars. Today the book is extant in Greek, from which various ancient versions were made (two in Latin, two in Syriac, others in Coptic, Armenian, Ethiopic, and Arabic).

The composite character of the treatise will be still more evident from the following analysis of its contents.

The book opens with the statement that Baruch, having written this book in Babylon in the fifth year after the destruction of Jerusalem (presumably after 586 B.C.), read it in the hearing of the Jeconiah, the deposed king of Judah, and his fellow exiles by the river Sud. So profoundly were they moved by the reading that 'they wept, and fasted, and prayed before the Lord; and they collected money, each giving what he could; and they sent it to Jerusalem' (1:5-7). The message which accompanied the money explained that it was to be used for the purchase of offerings for the altar of the Lord. Surprisingly enough, the people of Jerusalem are urged to pray for the health of Nebuchadnezzar and his son Belshazzar, in order that the exiles may dwell in peace. The captives also requested prayer on their own behalf, 'for we have sinned against the Lord our God, and to this day the anger of the Lord and his wrath have not turned away from us' (1:13). At the same time the prescription is laid down that this book, as a confession of sin, should be read publicly in the Temple on the feast days and at appointed seasons.

There follows immediately the confession of sin, put into the mouth of Israel as a whole and accompanied by prayers that God will at length pardon his people whom he has so justly punished (1:15–3:8). It opens with words found also in Dan. 9:7f., 'Righteousness belongs to the Lord our God, but confusion of face to us . . . because we have sinned before the Lord. We have disobeyed him and have not heeded the voice of the Lord our God' (1:15-17). The past history of the nation is briefly reviewed to show that notwithstanding God's mercy Israel had been disobedient to him and had forsaken him. For this reason the calamities of which Moses had warned (see Deut. 28) have now come upon them in righteous retribution for their disobedience (1:15-2:10).

The prayer for divine mercy which follows (2:11-19) is marked by a poignant pathos which reminds one of the traditional laments and supplications associated with the Wailing Wall. Certain passages from the books of Daniel, Jeremiah, and Deuteronomy are recalled, and special stress is laid on Israel's sin in refusing to serve the king of Babylon despite the solemn injunctions by the prophets (2:20-26; compare Jer. 27:11–12; 29:5–6). Though Israel is a stubborn and stiff-necked people, they will repent in the land of their captivity; as a result God will bring them to their land once again, and will renew his covenant with them (2:27-35). This section is concluded with another prayer for mercy combined with an anguished confession of past iniquities (3:1-8).

Thus far the book is in prose; at this point a rhythmical, poetic style begins. Though made up largely of reminiscences of older works, the second half of the book is written with deep feeling and no little skill.

The first part (3:9-4:4) is in the style of Hebrew wisdom-literature. Here it is reiterated that Israel has been visited with calamities because she has forsaken God, the fountain of wisdom. The true wisdom is hidden from the world, and none of the Gentile sages have found her. Her ways cannot be searched out. Only God who knows all things, and whom the light and the stars obey, encompasses all wisdom, and he has given wisdom to Israel in the Law which endures forever.

> All who hold her fast will live,
>   and those who forsake her will die.
> Turn, O Jacob, and take her;
>   walk toward the shining of her light.
>
>   . . . . . .
>
> Happy are we, O Israel,
>   for we know what is pleasing to God (4:1-2, 4).

Quite different is the final section of this short book (4:5-5:9). Like the opening words of the second part of the Book of Isaiah, the author begins with a song of comfort and encouragement. Four times in twenty-five verses he reiterates the refrain, 'Be of good cheer,' or its equivalent (4:5, 21, 27, and 30). Speaking in the name of the Lord, the writer addresses Israel in a tone that is partly reproachful, partly reassuring. Jerusalem is represented as a sorrowing widow bereft of her children, uttering a pathetic lamentation over them (4:9-29). The lament, reminiscent of the dirges in the Book of Lamentations, ends with words of hope and comfort:

> For he who brought these calamities upon you
>   will bring you everlasting joy with your salvation (4:29).

From this point on to the end (4:30-5:9) the book contains spirited messages of hope and a promised restoration. Jerusalem is bidden to rejoice, for her children are to be led back to her from their captivity. The holy city is to be re-established for ever and ever, and the oppressors of Israel are to be humbled in the dust. Striking an exalted lyrical note, the final lines ring out with courageous optimism and splendid faith:

> Arise, O Jerusalem, stand upon the height
> and look toward the east,
> and see your children gathered from east and west,
> at the word of the Holy One,
> rejoicing that God has remembered them.
>
> . . . . . .
>
> For God has ordered that every high mountain and the
> everlasting hills be made low
> and the valleys filled up, to make level ground,
> so that Israel may walk safely in the glory of God.
> The woods and every fragrant tree
> have shaded Israel at God's command.
> For God will lead Israel with joy,
> in the light of his glory,
> with the mercy and righteousness that come from him
>
> (5:5, 7–9).

During subsequent centuries, so far as we know, the influence of the book of Baruch was much more pronounced in Christian circles than in Jewish circles. At the close of the fourth century Jerome stated that the Hebrews neither read nor even possess this book (Prologue to his translation of Jeremiah). It is probable that he referred to Palestinian practice only. How far it was used among the Diaspora Judaism is not clear, though there is a certain amount of evidence that it was adopted in the liturgy of lamentation observed on the 9th of Ab (approximately our July), the traditional date of the double burning of the Temple.

On the other hand, many early Fathers of the Church quoted the book as Scripture. Often they cited passages from it as the utterances of Jeremiah. It was evidently assumed that because Baruch was the amanuensis of the prophet, a book attributed to Baruch would contain the words of the prophet himself. Such an assumption was no doubt strengthened by the fact that in the Greek Bible the book appears as an appendix to the Book of Jeremiah. In fact, several important early manuscripts, including the famous Codex Vaticanus of the fourth century and the Codex Alexandrinus of the fifth century, place Baruch between the canonical books of Jeremiah and Lamentations.

The passage in Baruch which, above all others, attracted the attention of early Christian writers is 3:36-37:

> He [that is, God] found the whole way to knowledge,
>   and gave her to Jacob his servant
>   and to Israel whom he loved.
> Afterward she appeared on earth and lived among men.

(Another translation of the last line is 'and conversed with men.') In view of the notorious lack of exegetical discrimination displayed by many Fathers, it is not surprising that the natural meaning of these verses was abandoned for a mystical interpretation that saw here a witness to the doctrine of the Incarnation. Especially after the rise of Arianism in the fourth century this passage was frequently appealed to by the orthodox as a proof that Christ is God. It is quite understandable, therefore, that the Church was tempted to regard as canonical the book which contained a sentence that lent itself to so convenient a use in theological debate.[1]

---

1. Even though this passage in Baruch may be an early interpolation made by some Christian scribe (as several modern scholars think), it remains true that the Fathers who quoted it did so thinking it was Baruch's prophecy.

IX

The Letter of Jeremiah

THE SO-CALLED LETTER OF JEREMIAH STANDS
AT DIFFERENT PLACES IN DIFFERENT MANU-
SCRIPTS AND EDITIONS OF THE APOCRYPHA. IT IS
placed after Lamentations in two ancient Greek codices of the
Old Testament (the fourth-century Codex Vaticanus and the
fifth-century Codex Alexandrinus), in the Syriac Hexapla
manuscript in the Ambrosian Library at Milan, and in the Arabic
version. In other Greek and Syriac manuscripts, as well as the
Latin version, it is attached to the Apocryphal book of Baruch,
and consequently most English translations of the Apocrypha
print it as the final (sixth) chapter of that book. Since, however,
the Letter is a quite independent composition, and has nothing
to do with Baruch, the Revised Standard Version prints it as a
separate book.

Contrary to its title and opening sentence (1:1), this little
pamphlet is not a letter nor was it sent by Jeremiah to those who
were about to be led into Babylonian exile. It is an earnest,

though rambling appeal written by an unknown author who was concerned lest his fellow countrymen should exchange the religion of the prophets for any lower form of faith and life. One might perhaps characterize it as an impassioned sermon which is based on a verse from the canonical Book of Jeremiah. This verse, the only one in Jeremiah which happens to be written in Aramaic, probably reflects a situation in which Jews were invited by their heathen neighbors to participate in idol-worship, and it supplies the reply to be made in such circumstances: 'Thus shall you say to them: "The gods who did not make the heavens and the earth shall perish from the earth and from under the heavens"' (Jer. 11:10). Elaborating upon this text, the author of the Letter of Jeremiah ridicules the folly of idolatry, showing by a variety of arguments the utter impotence, whether for good or ill, of gods of wood and silver and gold.

A hint as to the date when it was written may be found in verse 3, where the author speaks of the captivity of the Jews as lasting for seven generations. This would suggest a date of composition some time about 300 B.C. or thereafter. Though extant today in Greek, certain characteristics of language and style have led most scholars to conclude that the 'letter' was originally composed in Hebrew (or Aramaic).

The style of the little tractate is florid and declamatory. There seems to be no logical connection in the order of the arguments. The author simply jumps from one idea to another, ringing the changes on the helplessness, lifelessness, uselessness, and destructibility of heathen idols. He mechanically divides his homily into sections by a refrain repeated eleven times, conveying with slight variations in expression the general sense, 'This shows that they are no gods' (verses 16, 23, 29, 30, 40, 44, 49, 52, 56, 64, 69).

Although the author speaks of 'gods' in general, only once

mentioning the name of a deity (the god Bel, verse 41), he seems to have particularly in mind the god Tammuz. This deity in the Babylonian pantheon, like its counterpart in other religions of the ancient Near East—such as Hadad in Syria, Attis in Asia Minor, Eshmun in Phoenicia, Mot at Ras Shamra, Osiris in Egypt, Adonis in Greece—was the god of vegetation, whose death was commemorated with mourning at midsummer in the month to which his name was given (the month Tammuz corresponds roughly with July). The licentious fertility rites which were associated with this deity, to which Herodotus, Strabo, and Lucian make reference, are alluded to in verse 43. The Tammuz ritual, in which women played a prominent part in lamenting the death of the god (as is indicated in Ezek. 8:14), was patterned upon a funeral ceremony, similar to a wake (see verses 30-32).

At the same time, what this author reiterates about the folly of idolatry was doubtless intended to be applicable to all pagan cults. The images of the gods require constant care and ritual supervision; they are provided with lighted lamps (verse 19), carried in procession (verse 26), decked in luxurious garments (verses 11-12), and supplied with scepters, daggers, and battle axes (verses 14-15). The author ridicules those who worship idols that are unable to keep bats, swallows, birds, and cats from perching on their bodies and heads (verse 22). So impotent are they that they cannot prevent thieves and robbers from despoiling them (verses 15 and 57f.). If a fire breaks out in the temple, the idols burn up like the timbers around them (verse 55).

The author's parting thrust is the declaration that these idols are 'like a scarecrow in a cucumber bed, that guards nothing . . . [or] like a thorn bush in a garden, on which every bird sits; or like a dead body cast out in the darkness. By the purple and linen that rot upon them you will know that they are not gods; and they will finally themselves be consumed, and be a reproach in the land' (verses 70-72).

Whether this fierce invective against the folly of idolatry was intended for the common benefit of 'the Dispersion among the Greeks' (John 7:35) or for some particular community of Jews, we do not know. In any case it took its place among the growing number of Jewish attacks on heathenism (compare the stories of Bel and the Dragon, the second part of the Wisdom of Solomon, and the implications of the Prayer of Manasseh).

Later this type of polemical literature was adopted and adapted for similar situations which confronted the Church in a pagan environment. Christian apologists drew freely upon arguments that had been hammered out on a Jewish anvil in order to meet new forms of a paganism that was always alluring and at times oppressive and persecuting. During the first half of the second century a Christian by the name of Aristides, a philosopher in the city of Athens, addressed a spirited defense of the Christian religion to the Emperor Hadrian, who reigned from 117 to 138. A comparison of his Apology with the Letter of Jeremiah reveals several striking similarities of technique and occasionally even of argument. At about the middle of the fourth century, the Sicilian rhetorician, Firmicus Maternus, composed a lengthy denunciation of dying paganism (De errore profanarum religionum), in which he quotes at length (xxviii.4-5) from this Jewish tractate against idolatry (verses 5-10, 21-24, 28-31, and 50-57).

X

The Prayer of Azariah and the Song of
the Three Young Men

THE ANCIENT GREEK AND LATIN VERSIONS OF
THE BOOK OF DANIEL CONTAIN A NUMBER OF AD-
DITIONS WHICH ARE NOT FOUND IN THE ORIGINAL
Hebrew and Aramaic text. Among many minor accretions to
the text, there are three principal Additions, included among
the Apocrypha as separate 'books' under the respective titles:
The Prayer of Azariah and the Song of the Three Young Men;
the History of Susanna; and Bel and the Dragon. Before they are
considered separately, a few preliminary remarks about them
as a group may be useful.

The ancient versions differ as to the arrangement of these
additional portions within the Book of Daniel. Their position
in the Latin Vulgate is as follows. The Prayer of Azariah and
the Song of the Three Young Men forms part of chapter 3 of
Daniel; the account of Susanna follows the last chapter of Daniel (which in Hebrew is chapter 12), and is numbered chapter
13; and the story of Bel and the Dragon forms chapter 14 of the
Vulgate. In many Greek copies, however, the sequence is different. The story of Susanna forms the introduction to the Book

of Daniel, being prefixed to chapter 1. Doubtless the reason for placing the tale here is that in it Daniel is represented as a mere youth. As is the case with the Latin Vulgate, the Prayer of Azariah and the Song of the Three Young Men stands in chapter 3. Furthermore, in some Greek manuscripts the chief parts of this composition are given a second time among the group of Odes or Hymns at the close of the Psalter. Here their titles are 'The Prayer of Azariah' and 'The Hymn of Our Fathers' (another form of the latter title in later manuscripts is 'The Hymn of the Three Men'). Bel and the Dragon is added at the close of chapter 12 of Daniel; in some manuscripts it is preceded by a title which plainly distinguishes it as the work of another author.

Since there is usually nothing in the manuscripts of the early versions of the Book of Daniel to indicate that these sections are interpolations, most of the Church Fathers quoted from them as parts of the canonical Daniel. Those few, however, who knew and adhered to the Hebrew canon rejected them. Jerome in particular called attention (in his Preface to Daniel) to their absence from the Hebrew Bible, and instead of making comments of his own added a brief résumé of Origen's remarks 'on the fables of Bel and Susanna.'

The date of the composition of these Additions may be placed sometime within the second or first century B.C. Whether they were written originally in Hebrew or Aramaic or Greek has been debated by scholars. Of the three Additions the Prayer of Azariah and the Song of the Three Young Men has the best claim to have been composed in Hebrew. The presence of two puns in the Greek version of Susanna has inclined most scholars to favor Greek as the original language of that Addition.

The only one of the Additions to Daniel that, strictly speaking, supplements the canonical Book of Daniel is the Prayer of

Azariah and the Song of the Three Young Men, which is introduced into the narrative of the third chapter of Daniel between
verses 23 and 24. It will be remembered that, according to Dan.
3, three Jews, Shadrach, Meshach, and Abednego, refused to
worship the golden image which Nebuchadnezzar had set up. By
way of punishment for their refusal they were bound and
thrown into the burning fiery furnace (Dan. 3:23). Then follows the interpolation. After an introductory sentence (verse
1), a prayer is ascribed to Azariah in the fiery furnace (Azariah
is his Hebrew name, Abednego, his pagan name; see Dan. 1:7).
The purpose of the prayer is not to secure deliverance from the
fire; on the contrary, Azariah makes no mention of the fiery
furnace. The author doubtless supposed that these confessors,
who readily submitted to be thrown into the fire in which they
remained for some time, would employ their leisure in prayer
to the God whom they so fearlessly confessed. Accordingly,
Azariah is represented as praising God, confessing his people's
sins, and imploring national deliverance (verses 2-22). In answer to this prayer, we are told, the Angel of the Lord came
down into the super-heated furnace, from which flames were
streaming out above the door forty-nine cubits, and made the
'midst of the furnace like a moist whistling wind' (verse 27).
At this all three martyrs, 'as with one mouth, praised and glori-
fied and blessed God in the furnace' (verse 28).

The lengthy hymn which follows has been traditionally entitled, 'The Song of the Three Holy Children,' where the word
'children' is used in a religious and not in a chronologic sense
(compare the phrase 'the children of Israel'). The three young
men call upon all God's creatures, animate and inanimate, to
join them in praising him. A certain solemnity is achieved by
the regularly recurring refrain, 'Sing praise to him and highly
exalt him for ever.' (This refrain occurs thirty-two times.) The

following verses will suggest something of the majestic rhythm
of the antiphonal arrangement.

> Bless the Lord, all works of the Lord,
>   sing praise to him and highly exalt him for ever.
> Bless the Lord, you heavens,
>   sing praise to him and highly exalt him for ever.
> Bless the Lord, you angels of the Lord,
>   sing praise to him and highly exalt him for ever.
> Bless the Lord, all waters above the heaven,
>   sing praise to him and highly exalt him for ever.

. . . .

> Bless the Lord, you whales and all creatures that
>   move in the waters,
>   sing praise to him and highly exalt him for ever.
> Bless the Lord, all birds of the air,
>   sing praise to him and highly exalt him for ever.
> Bless the Lord, all beasts and cattle,
>   sing praise to him and highly exalt him for ever.
> Bless the Lord, you sons of men,
>   sing praise to him and highly exalt him for ever.
> Bless the Lord, O Israel,
>   sing praise to him and highly exalt him for ever.

. . . .

> Bless the Lord, you who are holy and humble in heart,
>   sing praise to him and highly exalt him for ever.
> Bless the Lord, Hananiah, Azariah, and Mishael,
>   sing praise to him and highly exalt his name for ever;
> for he has rescued us from Hades and saved us from the
>   hand of death,
> and delivered us from the midst of the burning fiery
>   furnace;
>   from the midst of the fire he has delivered us
>   (verses 35–38, 57-61, 65–66).

The quarry from which this liturgy was derived is, of course, the Old Testament, and primarily the Psalter. It obviously owes much to Psalm 148:

> Praise the Lord from the heavens,
>   praise him in the heights!
> Praise him, all his angels,
>   praise him, all his host!
>
> . . . . . .
>
> Praise the Lord from the earth,
>   you sea monsters and all deeps,
> fire and hail, snow and frost,
>   stormy wind fulfilling his command!
> Mountains and all hills,
>   fruit trees and all cedars!
> Beasts and all cattle,
>   creeping things and flying birds!
> Kings of the earth and all peoples,
>   princes and all rulers of the earth!
> Young men and maidens together,
>   old men and children! (Psalm 148:1–2, 7–12).

As for the antiphonal form, the unknown author imitates Psalm 136, where the refrain, so familiar in the traditional phraseology, 'For his mercy endureth for ever,' appears twenty-two times.

The date of the composition of this Addition to Daniel was probably sometime during the strenuous persecution of the Jews by the Seleucid Emperor, Antiochus Epiphanes (about 167–163 B.C.). Then the fierce adversities that befell the nation must have seemed like a furnace of affliction. In verse 9 the lamentation, 'Thou hast given us into the hands of lawless enemies, most hateful apostates, and to an unjust king, the most wicked in all the world,' is doubtless an echo of the description of apostate Jews mentioned in I Macc. 1:11-15, and of the cruelties of King Antiochus (see I Macc. 1:20-24, 41-64). Some scholars have thought that the obvious difference in tone between the despondent strain of penitence that marks the Prayer of Azariah in the first half of the Addition, and the jubilant exultation throughout the Song of the Three Young Men, must imply a different time of composition of the two parts—one during the persecutions of Antiochus and the other just after they had ceased.

The theology of this Addition is what one would expect of the Judaism of that period. God is declared to be the only Lord of heaven and earth (verse 22). The calamities that have befallen the nation are condign punishment for the sins of the people (verses 5-8 and 14). The author rises from the priestly, or ritual, to the prophetic, or spiritual, view of sacrifice. Penitence takes the place of animal sacrifice:

> Yet with a contrite heart and a humble spirit may
>   we be accepted,
>   as though it were with burnt offerings of rams and
>   bulls,
>   and with tens of thousands of fat lambs;
>   such may our sacrifice be in thy sight this
>   day (verses 16-17).

The influence of this ancient Jewish Addition to the Book of Daniel has extended far and wide throughout the Christian Church. It was included as part of the Book of Daniel not only in the Greek and Latin versions, as was already mentioned, but also in other ancient Bible translations, such as the Syriac, Coptic, Ethiopic, Armenian, Georgian, and Arabic. The Song of the Three Young Men also came to be used in the litany of the early and medieval Church, from which it has passed into modern liturgies. In the Roman office it occurs in the private thanksgiving of the priest after the Mass, as well as at Lauds on Sundays and festivals. Because the passage opens with the words, 'Benedicite, omnia opera Domini,' the canticle is commonly called 'The Benedicite.' In the Morning Service in the Anglican or Episcopal Prayer Book, the Benedicite stands as an alternate to the Te Deum and begins with the familiar words, 'O all ye works of the Lord, bless ye the Lord.' One must acknowledge that this ancient song of praise is an altogether worthy link between Jewish and Christian forms of piety and worship.

XI

Susanna

OF THE CYCLE OF TRADITIONS ABOUT DANIEL
WHICH WERE ADDED TO THE BOOK OF DANIEL
WHEN IT WAS TRANSLATED INTO GREEK,[1] THE
story of Susanna is undoubtedly the gem. One of the best short
stories in the world's literature, it is based on the familiar motif
of the triumph of virtue over villainy, the narrow escape from
death of an innocent victim. Like its companion piece, Bel and
the Dragon, this Apocryphal Addition to Daniel is among the
earliest detective stories ever written.[2] While inculcating lessons of morality and trust in God, the story also grips the reader's
interest from the outset.

The time and place of composition of this story are quite unknown. If the original was in Hebrew or Aramaic, as some scholars believe to be true, it is probable that the author lived in Judea.

---

1. For general information about the several Additions to Daniel, see above,
pp. 99f.

2. These two stories stand at the beginning of Miss Dorothy Sayers's first
anthology of mystery stories entitled *Omnibus of Crime* (1929).

If it was composed in Greek, as the presence of two puns in the course of the Greek narrative may lead one to infer, Alexandria is as good a guess as any. No more exact date can be fixed than sometime during the two centuries preceding the Christian era.

Susanna was the beautiful wife of a prominent Jew of Babylon, named Joakim. Susanna's beauty was matched by her piety, for her parents had grounded her in the law of Moses. Joakim was held in honor by all, and to his large estate the Jewish elders and judges of Babylon used to come and hold court. Among them were two old judges, who, the author declares, were characterized by the passage in Scripture which says, 'Iniquity came forth from Babylon, from elders who were judges, who were supposed to govern the people' (Jer. 23:15, Septuagint; compare Jer. 29:21–23 in the English versions).

When those who had suits at law departed at noon, Susanna would go into her husband's spacious garden to walk, where the two elders used to see her every day. Unmindful of God and his judgments, they became inflamed with unlawful passion for her. Fully conscious of the impropriety of their desires, they tried to conceal them from one another. But one day, having ostensibly departed each to his home for the midday meal, they both slunk back again and met! This required a mutual explanation, and they were forced to admit their lust. Then they arranged for a time when they could find Susanna alone (verses 1–14).

One very hot day, while the elders were hidden in the garden, Susanna decided to bathe in the garden pool. So she sent her maids to shut the garden doors against intrusion, and to bring her what she needed for her bath. No sooner had the maids disappeared than the two elders ran to Susanna and said, 'Look, the garden doors are shut, no one sees us, and we are in love with you; so give your consent, and lie with us. If you refuse, we will testify against you that a young man was with you, and this was why you sent your maids away' (verses 20–21).

Susanna sighed deeply and said, 'I am hemmed in on every side. For if I do this thing, it is death for me; and if I do not, I shall not escape your hands. I choose not to do it and to fall into your hands, rather than to sin in the sight of the Lord' (verses 22–23). As she called for help, the two elders also set up a shout, and one of them ran and opened the garden doors. When the household servants came to investigate the commotion, the elders told their concocted story—that they had found Susanna committing adultery with a young man, who dashed away when they attempted to detain him. The servants were greatly shocked, for no word of scandal had ever before been breathed against their mistress's virtue (verses 24–27).

On the following day the two judges, while hearing law suits at Joakim's house, summoned Susanna before them. She well knew the reason of the summons, and came accompanied by her parents, her children, and all her kindred. As she was veiled, the wicked men ordered her to be unveiled, that they might feast upon her beauty. But her family and friends and all who saw her wept. Then the two judges repeated publicly their false indictment, laying their hands on the head of the accused in accordance with the Levitical code (Lev. 24:14). The accusation, being made by two such highly respected judges, was believed to be true, and she was convicted and sentenced to death.

Protesting her innocence, Susanna lifted her voice in prayer to God. Nor did she pray in vain, for just as she was being led away to execution, the proceedings were dramatically interrupted by a young man, Daniel, who demanded the right to interrogate the witnesses (verses 28–49).

Appeal from the verdict was granted, and as counsel for the defense, Daniel cross-examined Susanna's two accusers separately. Summoning one of them, he boldly addressed him, 'You old relic of wicked days, your sins have now come home, which you have committed in the past, pronouncing unjust judgments, condemning the innocent and letting the guilty go free, though the Lord said, "Do not put to death an innocent and righteous person." Now then, if you really saw her, tell me this: Under what tree did you see them being intimate with each other?' (verses 52–54). The elder replied that it was under a mastic tree.

Putting him aside, Daniel commanded that the other elder be brought. Confronted with the same question, this one replied that the sinful act had taken place under an evergreen oak.

Since it was evident now that their accusation had been false and malicious, Susanna was honorably acquitted and the guilty elders were promptly put to death (in accord with the statute in Deut. 19:18–21). The story closes with the statement that Susanna's parents and husband and all her kindred praised God who had saved an innocent woman from death, 'and from that day onward Daniel had a great reputation among the people' (verse 64).

From a literary point of view, this story is a model of artistic fiction. In a natural and very effective manner, Susanna's destiny is made to hang in the balance. Plot, surprise, struggle, unfolding of character, are present here in just the right proportions; and the whole is told succinctly and pungently. If it is a part of art to conceal art, this story qualifies as great literature.

In Hebrew the name Susanna means 'a lily,' and the name Daniel means 'God has judged.' Besides the obviously appropriate symbolism of these two names for the hero and the heroine, the Greek text of the narrative contains two puns which are lost in any literal translation. When the first elder declared that he saw Susanna and her lover under a mastic tree (Greek, *schinos*), Daniel replied, 'Very well! You have lied against your own

head, for the angel of God has received the sentence from God
and will immediately cut (*schisei*) you in two' (verse 55). After
the second elder said that the two were under an evergreen oak
(*prinos*), Daniel retorted, 'Very well! You also have lied against
your own head, for the angel of God is waiting with his sword
to saw (*prisai*) you in two, that he may destroy you both' (verse
59). To represent in English these instances of ironic word-play
one would perhaps paraphrase in some such fashion as, 'Under
a *clove* tree . . . the Lord will *cleave* you,' and 'Under a *yew*
tree . . . the Lord will *hew* you.'

The moral of the story has been variously explained. Besides
inculcating obvious lessons of purity, trust in God, and the
efficacy of prayer, which lie on the surface of the narrative, the
author's purpose may also have been to show how, when the elders or aged men of Israel had corrupted their ways, God would
raise up champions of his truth and righteousness from among
the young men. Indeed, some scholars regard this story as a tract
of the times, satirizing the current administration of justice. Believing that the unknown author was concerned about a certain
laxity, or even abuses, in the method of conducting legal proc-
esses, they interpret Daniel's role as that of reformer of judicial
procedures. Thus, the author advocates a more rigid examination of the witnesses where collusion might be suspected (verse
48), and as a deterrent to perjury demands the infliction of the
same punishment on the perjurer as his victim would have suffered had not the deceit been detected (verse 62). Whatever
may be thought about the legitimacy of such an interpretation
of the author's purpose, the ordinary reader will continue to enjoy the story on the basis of its own obvious merits.

Of some importance for the history of the interpretation of
this book is the significance which certain Church Fathers at-

tached to the several characters in the story. Early in the third
century Hippolytus, bishop of Rome, wrote, 'Susanna is a type
prefiguring the Church; Joakim her husband prefigures the
Messiah. The garden is the election of the saints, who, like trees
that bear fruit, are planted in the Church. Babylon is the world;
and the two elders are set forth as a figure of the two peoples
that plot against the Church—the one, namely, of the circumcision, and the other of the Gentiles.' This allegorical interpretation no doubt accounts for the frequent occurrence of pictorial
representations of Susanna in early Christian art. Frescoes in
Roman catacombs and sculpture on sarcophagi from southern
Gaul and Italy depict Susanna veiled and standing in the attitude
of prayer between the two elders. Sometimes Daniel appears in
the scene as judge and deliverer. In the cemetery of Praetextatus
there is a painting which represents a lamb standing between
two wolves, with a Latin inscription identifying them as Susanna
and the elders. In connection with such an artistic representa-
tion it is interesting to read St. Chrysostom's sermon on Susanna
in which the celebrated preacher of Constantinople elaborates
upon her steadfast chastity. 'Susanna stood as a lamb between
two wolves. She was left alone between these two beasts, with
no one to help her but God alone. He looked down from heaven,
and suffered the dispute to make clear both the chastity of Susanna and the wickedness of the elders; so that she might become
a glorious example to women of all times. Susanna endured a
severe fight, more severe than that of Joseph. He, a man, con-
tended with one woman; but Susanna, a woman, had to contend
with two men, and was a spectacle to men and to angels. The
slander against her fidelity to her marriage-vow, the fear of
death, her condemnation by all the people, the abhorrence of
her husband and relations, the tears of her servants, the grief of
all her household—she foresaw all this, and yet nothing could
shake her fortitude.'

During the Middle Ages the story attained great popularity
in various literary forms among the nations of Europe. About
the beginning of the twelfth century Hildebert, Archbishop of
Tours, paraphrased the story in a lengthy Latin poem. During
the fourteenth and fifteenth centuries at least five versions in
alliterative and riming stanzas circulated in Scotland. In these
versions the original story is much adorned with imaginative
details.[1] In the sixteenth century a translation from German into
Ladino, the dialect used in the Upper Engadine Valley in Switzerland, was adapted for presentation as a drama. The elders are
called Achab and Sedechias; the maids are Spondea and Promp-
tula; and other characters are individualized.

In more modern times, an edifying exposition in English verse
circulated in the seventeenth century; it was prepared by Robert Aylett, D.C.L., for the benefit of 'our Judges in Westminster
Hall.' In 1682 an ornate paraphrase in Greek elegiac verse was
published at Venice. As will be pointed out later (pp. 227ff.),
the plight of Susanna has inspired old masters and modern painters alike.

---

1. For a quotation of part of a typical stanza of this poem, see below, p. 208.

XII

Bel and the Dragon

ONE OF THE OLDEST DETECTIVE STORIES IN THE
WORLD IS EMBODIED IN THE APOCRYPHAL ADDI-
TION TO THE BOOK OF DANIEL ENTITLED BEL AND
the Dragon.[1] This brief treatise is obviously intended to pour
ridicule upon the folly of idolatry and to discredit heathen
priestcraft. At the same time the polemic against idol worship is
cast in a most vivid and dramatic form.

Bel, whose proper name was Marduk, was perhaps the most
popular god in the Babylonian pantheon, and in about 2250 B.C.
became the patron deity of Babylon. One of the seven wonders
of the ancient world was the temple of Bel, a colossal structure
of magnificent proportions. Cuneiform tablets have been discovered telling how Nebuchadnezzar lavished upon it elaborate decorations of gold, silver, costly woods, and lapis lazuli.
Several sources of evidence testify to the quantities of various
animals, fish, and fowl, as well as honey, milk, fine oil, and vari-

---

1. For general information about the several Additions to Daniel, see above,
pp. 99f.

ous kinds of wine which were presented as offerings to Marduk as part of the daily ritual. After generations of worshipers had come to this magnificent temple, in 479 B.C., so Herodotus tells us, it was plundered and destroyed by Xerxes I on his return from Greece.

Daniel is introduced as a companion of Cyrus the king of the Persians, and the most honored of that select group known as the king's Friends. One day the king inquired of Daniel why he did not join him in worshiping the idol called Bel. The Jewish exile answered, 'Because I do not revere man-made idols, but the living God, who created heaven and earth and has dominion over all flesh' (verse 5).

The king was convinced that Daniel was mistaken, and as proof that Bel was a living god he pointed to the immense quantity of food and drink consumed by Bel every day—twelve bushels of fine flour and forty sheep and fifty gallons of wine. Then Daniel laughed and said, 'Do not be deceived, O king; for this is but clay inside and brass outside, and it never ate or drank anything' (verse 7).

Nettled by this reply the king called his priests and said to them, 'If you do not tell me who is eating these provisions, you shall die. But if you prove that Bel is eating them, Daniel shall die, because he blasphemed against Bel' (verse 9). The priests of Bel, seventy in number, agreed to let the king set forth Bel's food and seal the temple door overnight. The reader is informed that they were unconcerned, for beneath the god's table they had made a hidden trap door, through which they used to enter and consume the provisions (verses 11-13).

When the priests had gone out and the king had set forth the food for Bel, Daniel ordered his servants to sift fine ashes over the floor of the whole temple. In the night the priests came with their wives and children, as they were accustomed to do, and ate and drank everything (verses 14f.).

Early the next morning the king and Daniel came to the temple, and Daniel certified that the seals were unbroken. As soon as the doors were opened, the king looked at the table and shouted in a loud voice, 'You are great, O Bel; and with you there is no deceit, none at all' (verse 17).

Then Daniel laughed, and restraining the king from going in he said, 'Look at the floor, and notice whose footsteps these are.' Recognizing the footprints of men and women and children, the king was enraged at the undeniable chicanery of the priests, and seizing them he forced them to disclose the secret entry to the temple. Thereupon the king ordered them to be executed, with their families, and permitted Daniel to destroy the image of Bel and the temple (verses 18–22).

As a sequel to this tale, the unknown author recounts another episode in which Daniel's prowess is involved. The Babylonians also venerated a monstrous dragon, or serpent, as a god. The king urged that, as this was obviously alive, there was no reason why Daniel should not worship it. Daniel, however, refused, saying, 'I will worship the Lord my God, for he is the living God. But if you, O king, will give me permission, I will slay the dragon without sword or club.' Believing in the immortality of the dragon, the king granted permission to Daniel to try to kill it. Then Daniel prepared a concoction of pitch, fat, and hair, which he boiled and made into cakes. He fed these to the dragon, which immediately burst open (verses 23–27).

The Babylonians, enraged by this treatment of their god, accused the king of having become a Jew. They demanded that he hand Daniel over to them, or else they would kill him and his royal household in retaliation for the destruction of the image of Bel, the slaying of the dragon, and the execution of the priests.

So, under compulsion, King Cyrus handed Daniel over to them.
Then they threw Daniel into the lions' den,[2] where he remained
for six days. There were seven lions in the den, and every day
they had been given two human bodies and two sheep; but these
were not given to them now, so that they might become even
more rapacious and devour Daniel (verses 28–32).

The scene shifts abruptly, and we are told that in Judea the
prophet Habakkuk was on the point of bringing pottage and
bread to the reapers, when the angel of the Lord commanded
him to take the food to Babylon, to Daniel, in the lions' den.
When Habakkuk remonstrated that he had never seen Babylon
and knew nothing about the den of lions, 'the angel of the Lord
took him by the crown of his head, and lifted him by his hair and
set him down in Babylon, right over the den, with the rushing
sound of the wind itself' (verse 36). After Daniel praised God
for remembering him in this way, he ate the dinner, and in a
twinkling of an eye the angel of the Lord returned Habakkuk
to his home in Palestine (verses 33–39).

On the seventh day, when the people's indignation had begun
to cool down, the king came to mourn for Daniel, but found him
sitting unharmed in the lions' den. The king then shouted with a
loud voice, 'Thou art great, O Lord God of Daniel, and there is
no other besides thee.' He pulled Daniel out and threw into the
den the men who had attempted Daniel's destruction, and they
were devoured immediately before his eyes (verses 40–42).

The motifs of these yarns, grotesque and preposterous as they
appear to us today, were doubtless highly appreciated by the

---

2. It scarcely needs to be pointed out that this is a quite different incident
from the occasion when, according to the canonical text of Daniel (chap. 6),
King Darius had Daniel cast into the lions' den because he had refused to pray
to any except God.

original readers of this supplement to Daniel. Like the raconteur of the Arabian Nights, the author of the Addition knows how to rouse and keep the attention of his audience. With a minimum of verbiage, he goes straight to the point, emphasizing the moral that those who worship the true and living God will be sustained in every kind of trial. So concise is he that at several points one could wish to ask him for further explanation. Thus, does he intend us to understand that it was by a secret formula that Daniel concocted some poisonous food for the dragon, or that with merely a ridiculous mixture of harmless ingredients he was able to overcome the frightful beast? Again, did the reapers, whose dinner was taken to Daniel, receive any compensation? But such queries as these, raised by prosaic Westerners, would probably have seemed irrelevant, if not even irreverent, to the pious Jewish storyteller. He had dedicated his vivid imagination to the defense of monotheism, and to this end he ingeniously elaborated and embellished a nucleus of Biblical references to Daniel (Dan. 6) and Ezekiel (Ezek. 8:3).

When and where the unknown author lived cannot be determined with certainty. If he wrote originally in Hebrew or Aramaic, as a number of present-day scholars believe, he probably resided in Palestine. If he wrote in Greek, he may have lived almost anywhere in the eastern Mediterranean world. In either case it is likely that the stories were composed sometime during the second or first century B.C.

In international folklore, the dragon or serpentine monster has had a long history. In the ancient Near East the serpent was frequently regarded as a religious symbol, and the Bible contains traces of serpent worship among the ancient Hebrews (Num. 21:8f. and II Kings 18:4). On Babylonian seals and cylinders men are depicted worshiping gods apparently serpentine in

form. It must be admitted, however, that though the Addition
to Daniel gives the impression that the dragon was a live snake
(as distinct from an image) worshiped as a god, there is no
evidence outside this narrative that such was the custom in
Babylon.

In the alchemy of Semitic mythology certain attributes of
a serpentine dragon were attributed to the huge sea monster,
Leviathan. Isaiah promised that in the future 'the Lord with his
hard and great and strong sword will punish Leviathan the fleeing serpent, Leviathan the twisting serpent, and he will slay the
dragon that is in the sea' (Isa. 27:1). During subsequent centuries the tradition developed among the Jews that at the Messianic banquet to be held in the coming age, the flesh of this
monster would be roasted and served to the righteous remnant.
The growth of the belief may be seen in the following representative quotations. An early stage is found in the Psalter:
'Thou didst crush the heads of Leviathan, thou didst give him
as food for the people' (Psalm 74:14, margin). A later speculation associates with Leviathan another huge monster, a land
animal called Behemoth. In the Apocryphal book of II Esdras,
the author speaks of God, 'Thou didst keep in existence two living creatures; the name of one thou didst call Behemoth and the
name of the other Leviathan . . . and thou hast kept them to be
devoured by whom thou wilt, and when thou wilt' (II Esdras
6:49,52). According to the Babylonian Talmud (*Baba Bathra*,
74b), on the fifth day of creation God made two pairs of these
creatures, male and female, but lest they should destroy the
earth they were rendered incapable of having progeny. The female Leviathan was killed and salted for the future enjoyment
of the righteous, and the two Behemoths were reserved for the
same purpose. In modern times the American writer, Louis Untermeyer, amplified this ancient speculation in his rousing poem,

'Roast Leviathan.' The huge monster is described in the most extravagant language:

> The smallest scale upon his tail
> Could hide six dolphins and a whale.
> His nostrils breathe—and on the spot
> The churning waves turn seething hot. . . .
> And when he drinks what he may need,
> The rivers of the earth recede.

After Leviathan has been slain,

> Then come the angels!
> With hoists and levers, joists and poles,
> With knives and cleavers, ropes and saws,
> Down the long slopes the gaping maws,
> The angels hasten; hacking and carving,
> So nought will be lacking for the starving
> Chosen of God, who in frozen wonderment
> Realize now what the terrible thunder meant.
> How their mouths water while they are looking
> At miles of slaughter and sniffing the cooking! [3]

The Christian adaptation of the ancient dragon-motif is hardly less spectacular than the Jewish. In the New Testament the author of the Book of Revelation has obviously felt the impact of the earlier traditions, for he adopts the figure of the dragon to represent the epitome of evil ('the great dragon was thrown down, that ancient serpent, who is called the Devil and Satan, the deceiver of the whole world,' Rev. 12:9). In later Christian folklore, Daniel destroying the dragon without a sword or club was metamorphosed into St. George slaying the dragon with his lance. According to tradition a certain Georg-

---

3. Louis Untermeyer, *Roast Leviathan* (New York, 1923). By permission of Harcourt, Brace and Company, publishers.

ius was a military tribune and martyr under Diocletian at Nicomedia in A.D. 303. Medieval legends elaborated his prowess by telling of his bravery in slaying a dragon that had been menacing the populace of Silene in Lybia. During the Crusades and later, St. George became the patron saint of English soldiery, of chivalry, and of the Order of the Garter. In 1415, by the Constitutions of Henry Chichele, Archbishop of Canterbury, St. George's Day was made a major double feast, and ordered to be observed the same as Christmas Day, all labor ceasing. Such is the long journey from the ancient story of Daniel and the Dragon to him of whom Edmund Spenser wrote,

> For thou, emongst those Saints whom thou doest see,
> Shalt be a Saint, and thine owne nations frend
> And patrone: thou *Saint George* shalt called bee,
> *Saint George* of mery *England*, the signe of victoree
>
> (*The Faerie Queene*, I. x. 61, 8–9).

XIII

The Prayer of Manasseh

ONE OF THE FINEST PIECES IN THE APOCRYPHA
IS THE LITTLE CLASSIC OF PENITENTIAL DEVO-
TION KNOWN AS THE PRAYER OF MANASSEH. CON-
structed in accord with the best liturgical patterns, and full
without being drawn out, this beautiful prayer breathes
throughout a deep and genuine religious feeling.

Its literary origin is obscure. The author, of whose identity
there is no evidence, seems to have had as his chief aim to set
forth the mercies of God, from which even the worst offenders
against his law were not excluded, provided they sought divine
pardon through true repentance. A signal illustration of the
Lord's compassion was to be found in the account of one of the
wickedest of the kings of Judah, Manasseh the son of good
king Hezekiah.

According to the Old Testament records (II Kings 21:1-18
and II Chron. 33:1-20), during his long reign of fifty-five years
Manasseh 'did what was evil in the sight of the Lord, according
to the abominable practices of the nations whom the Lord drove

out before the people of Israel,' for he erected altars to Baal, worshiped all the host of heaven, burned his son as an offering, practiced soothsaying and sorcery, and dealt with mediums and necromancers. He even placed a carved image of Asherah in the house of God. Prophets sent by the Lord declared that because of these abominations Jerusalem and the Temple were to be destroyed and Judah was to suffer banishment in the Babylonian captivity (II Kings 23:36f.; 24:3f.; Jer. 15:4). As a prelude to the future national punishment, the writer of Chronicles records that Manasseh himself tasted of the bitter waters of exile. His account is as follows:

> The Lord spoke to Manasseh and to his people, but they gave no heed. Therefore the Lord brought upon them the commanders of the army of the king of Assyria, who took Manasseh with hooks and bound him with fetters of bronze and brought him to Babylon. And when he was in distress he entreated the favor of the Lord his God and humbled himself greatly before the God of his fathers. He prayed to him, and God received his entreaty and heard his supplication and brought him again to Jerusalem into his kingdom. Then Manasseh knew that the Lord was God. . . . Now the rest of the acts of Manasseh, and his prayer to his God, and the words of the seers who spoke to him in the name of the Lord the God of Israel, behold, they are in the Chronicles of the Kings of Israel. And his prayer, and how God received his entreaty, and all his sin and his faithlessness, and the sites on which he built high places and set up the Asherim and the images, before he humbled himself, behold, they are written in the Chronicles of the Seers
>
> (II Chron. 33:10–13, 18–19).

As can be learned from this account, when the canonical Book of II Chronicles was compiled, two other works were reputed to contain Manasseh's prayer. These records having been lost, it is not surprising that some devout Jew endeavored to supply the lack by drawing up such a prayer as might have been used by the repentant king. It may be that the unknown author had in mind the practical use of this prayer by way of providing a suitable penitential devotion for those of his countrymen who, having fallen into idolatry, could be reclaimed from the error of their way.

The question of the date of the composition of the Prayer is difficult to decide. Though there is no positive evidence, many scholars place it sometime during the last two centuries B.C. Whether it was composed in Hebrew or Aramaic or Greek is disputed. Though lacking in any clear reference to the place of composition, the ideas embodied in the Prayer are far more in accord with the teachings of Palestinian Judaism than with those of the Hellenistic Judaism of, for example, Alexandria.

The outline of the Prayer is typical of the Jewish liturgical forms current after about 400 B.C. It opens with an introductory ascription of praise to the Lord Almighty, whose majesty is displayed in creation (verses 1–4), as well as his mercy in granting repentance to sinners (verses 5-8). Then follows a personal confession:

> For the sins I have committed are more in number than the sand
>> the sea;
>> My transgressions are multiplied, O Lord, they are multiplied!
> I am unworthy to look up and see the height of heaven
>> because of the multitude of my iniquities.
> I am weighted down with many an iron fetter,
>> so that I am rejected because of my sins,
>> and I have no relief;
> for I have provoked thy wrath
>> and have done what is evil in thy sight,
>> setting up abominations and multiplying offenses
>>>>> (verses 9–10).

The acknowledgment of sin is followed by supplication to God for pardon:

> And now I bend the knee of my heart,
>   beseeching thee for thy kindness.
> I have sinned, O Lord, I have sinned,
>   and I know my transgressions.
> I earnestly beseech thee,
>   forgive me, O Lord, forgive me!
>   Do not destroy me with my transgressions!
> Do not be angry with me for ever or lay up evil for me;
>   do not condemn me to the depths of the earth (verses 11–13).

The prayer concludes with a petition for grace (verse 14), and a doxology:

> For all the host of heaven sings thy praise,
>   and thine is the glory for ever. Amen (verse 15).

The phraseology employed by the author discloses a theology which resembles that of later Judaism. For example, God is called the 'God of the righteous' (verse 8) and the 'God of those who repent' (verse 13), and supernatural power is ascribed to the sacred Name (verse 3). The two main religious ideas which permeate the Prayer are God's infinite mercy and the efficacy of true repentance.

The repentance and restoration of King Manasseh furnished the subject of many legendary stories, of which this Prayer was one among several elements. For example, the Targum of Chronicles adds, after II Chron. 33:11, the story of how 'the Chaldeans made a copper mule, and pierced it all over with little holes, and shut him [Manasseh] up therein, and kindled fire all around him. And when he was in straits, he besought help of all the idols which he had made, and was not helped, because they were worthless. And he turned, and prayed before the Lord his God, and humbled himself exceedingly before Jehovah, the God of his fathers...' etc., etc.[1] The first Christian book to refer to the story is the *Didascalia*, a third-century manual of ecclesiastical procedures and of rules governing Christian behavior, later incorporated into the *Apostolic Constitutions*. In the section of the latter which deals with the duties of the Bishop in admonishing sinners (Book ii, chap. xxii), the example of Manasseh is told in language drawn mostly from II Kings 21 and II Chron. 33, though with various supplementary details. For example, after giving the full text of Manasseh's prayer of penitence, the reader is informed of the outcome: 'The Lord heard his voice and had compassion on him. And there appeared a flame of fire about him, and all the iron shackles and chains which were about him fell off; and the Lord healed Manasseh of his affliction, and brought him back to Jerusalem unto his kingdom,' etc. Other early Christian writers made occasional use of the Prayer, either by way of exhortation in sermons or as a model of true penitential discipline. In more modern times the saintly Bishop Lancelot Andrewes, one of the translators of the King James Version of the Bible in 1611, incorporated the greater part of the Prayer in his book of *Devotions*, and thus made it familiar to many.

Despite the inherent worth of this ancient Prayer, it has had a curiously difficult time to establish itself in a fixed position textually. In fact, the position of the Prayer in Biblical manuscripts and in printed Bibles varies considerably. Contrary to what one might have expected, it appears that no Greek manuscript of the Old Testament contains this section in connection

1. Quoted by C. J. Ball in Henry Wace's edition of the *Apocrypha*, Vol. II (London, 1888), p. 371.

with II Chronicles.[2] In several copies, including the famous Codex Alexandrinus of the fifth century, it stands among the fourteen Canticles or Odes which are appended to the Psalter. Beginning with the Middle Ages, manuscripts of the Latin Vulgate attach the Prayer to the end of II Chronicles. A few Syriac, Armenian, Old Slavonic, and Ethiopic witnesses likewise have the Prayer, some at the end of II Chronicles, some at the close of the Psalter. Its position in printed Bibles varies. Luther, who had translated the Prayer during an early part of his career and had published it prior to the publication of the Old Testament, finally placed the Prayer at the close of the Apocrypha. Among English versions it usually stands among the Apocrypha before I Maccabees, although the Roman Catholic Douay Bible of 1609–10 places it, along with III and IV (i.e. I and II) Esdras, in an appendix after II Maccabees. In editions of the Latin Vulgate printed before the Council of Trent, the Prayer is placed after II Chronicles; in all official printings of the Vulgate since the Council, it is placed in an appendix after the New Testament. In the Geneva Bible of 1560, used widely by the Puritans, it follows II Chronicles,[3] as it does also in the Modern Greek Bible published in St. Petersburg in 1876.

---

2. Sir Henry H. Howorth revived the view argued long ago by St. Thomas Aquinas (*Summa Theol.*, III. 984, 10) that the prayer was once an integral part of II Chronicles (*Proceedings of the Society of Biblical Archaeology*, Vol. XXXI [1909], pp. 89–99).

3. See below, pp. 187f.

XIV

The First Book of the Maccabees

THE BOOKS DESIGNATED I MACCABEES AND II
MACCABEES DERIVE THEIR NAMES FROM THEIR
RECITAL OF THE HEROIC EXPLOITS OF THAT
doughty defender of Jewish independence and religious freedom, Judas Maccabeus. Though the derivation and significance
of the word 'Maccabeus' are disputed, a widely held view is that
it comes from a Hebrew word meaning 'the Hammerer' and
was given to Judas as an honorific commemorating his victories.
It was afterward applied also to other Jewish patriots of this
period.

The two books of the Maccabees give an account of the struggle of the Jews for religious and political liberty in the second
century B.C. The narratives, though independent of each other,
cover much of the same material, but are written by two authors
of quite different interests and capabilities. I Maccabees begins
with the accession of Antiochus Epiphanes, 175 B.C., and ends
about forty years later (in 134 B.C.) with the death of Simon,

the last of Judas's brothers. The narrative is told in a simple and unadorned style, obviously the work of a plain and honest chronicler who set down the facts in their historical sequence, with scarcely any attempt to theorize upon them or to emphasize their significance. The historical framework of II Maccabees, on the other hand, extends from the last year of the reign of Seleucus IV (175 B.C.) to the defeat of Nicanor fifteen years later (13 Adar, 160). The interest of the author is concentrated upon religion, and his purpose is primarily to furnish instruction and admonition to the scattered and oppressed Jewish people. By way of briefly characterizing the two authors of I and II Maccabees (though with the attendant danger of oversimplification), it may be said that the former was a sober historian who wished to glorify Israel and its heroic Maccabean leaders, and that the latter was a moralizing theologian who wished to emphasize the immeasurable superiority of Judaism over heathenism.

The First Book of the Maccabees was undoubtedly written in Hebrew, and copies of this continued to have a limited circulation until the time of Origen and Jerome. It was, however, in a literalistic Greek translation that the book was most widely read; the Jewish historian of the first Christian century, Flavius Josephus, obviously depended on this version and knew nothing of the Hebrew original. Several 'daughter-versions' were made from the Greek, including two translations into Latin and two into Syriac.

The unknown author of I Maccabees wrote probably about 100 B.C. or soon after. The intimate knowledge of the Palestinian countryside which he displays in tracing the military campaigns shows that he was a Palestinian himself. His knowledge of the world outside Palestine is slight and vague. That the author had a deep regard for the Mosaic Law, the Temple, and the Temple worship is evident throughout his work. At the same time he is careful not to obtrude the religious element into his narrative—being quite different in this respect from the author of II Maccabees. He is reticent about using the holy names of 'God' and 'Lord,' always employing in their stead a surrogate like 'Heaven,' or using simply the second or third person pronoun in referring to the Deity (for example, 'They [i.e. Judas and his men] sang hymns and praises to Heaven, for his mercy is good and ever-lasting,' 4:24). Since the Pharisees were likewise scrupulous in thus avoiding the possibility of profaning the name of God, it has sometimes been thought that our author was a member of this party. On the other hand, not a few traits appear in his book which point to affinities with the Sadducean party. For example, there is no reference to angels or spirits, and no hint of belief in the resurrection of the dead, even where it might naturally be expected to appear (e.g. 2:51; 3:59; 9:9f.). Furthermore, there is observable a certain relaxation of the strictest rules of Sabbath observance (2:40f.). For these reasons, some scholars have classified I Maccabees as a product of the Sadducean school of thought.

It may well be, however, that the author of I Maccabees was neither a Pharisee nor a Sadducee; what is certain is that his book is permeated with an authentic and unmistakable piety. Divine Providence is throughout acknowledged as overruling all the machinations of the enemy, and, after full preparation has been made for battle, prayer is offered up to Heaven for good success (3:18f., 44, 48, 53, 60; 4:10; 5:34, 54; 7:36–38, 41f; 9:45, etc., etc.). In a word, the author unites an ardent trust in God with a practical-minded conviction that victory in battle will depend also upon good generalship and military strategy.

The narrative of I Maccabees, which is cast in a strictly

chronological order, is concerned almost wholly with military events. It may be summarized as follows. After the briefest possible introduction, beginning with the conquests of Alexander the Great (336–323 B.C.), the division of his empire, and the origin of the Seleucid empire (1:1–9), the first main division of the book describes the desperate condition of the Jews under the Seleucid emperor, Antiochus Epiphanes (1:10–64). The name 'Epiphanes' means 'manifest' and was chosen by Antiochus because he regarded himself as a god manifest in human flesh. His enemies, however, dubbed him Antiochus Epimanes, meaning Antiochus the madman. In order to unify his empire Antiochus sought to impose a veneer of Greek culture on the diverse peoples over whom he ruled. Throughout Judea, as elsewhere, he erected heathen altars; he introduced pagan customs even within the holy city of Jerusalem itself. On a fateful day toward the close of the year 167 (the 25th of Chislev, approximately our December), Antiochus's henchmen desecrated the altar in the Temple by offering on it swine's flesh to the Olympian Zeus. Furthermore the emperor sought to abolish the Jewish religion by a series of edicts forbidding, on pain of death, the observance of the Sabbath, the circumcision of male children, and even the possession of a copy of the Old Testament Law.

The heroes of the book are introduced in chapter 2, with an account of the strong resistance shown by Mattathias and his five sons at Modein when a Syrian officer came to enforce the decree of Antiochus that all Jews should offer heathen sacrifices. They not only steadfastly refused to comply with the decree, but slew both a Jew who had come forward to sacrifice and the royal officer; then they fled to the mountains. With a group of like-minded Jews, called Hasidim, that is, 'the Pious,' Mattathias conducted a guerrilla-type of warfare, slaying not only Antiochus's soldiers but apostate Jews as well.

The main part of the book relates in detail the exploits of three of Mattathias's sons: Judas Maccabeus (3:1–9:22), Jonathan (9:23–12:53), and Simon (13:1–16:24). Temporary victories gained by the Jews under the leadership of Judas, subsequent to the death of his father, resulted in the rededication of the Temple (4:36–61). They cleaned out the debris, erected another altar and provided new vessels, and offered a sacrifice to purify the Temple and to dedicate the new altar. This ceremony took place on the 25th of Chislev, exactly three years after the Temple had been profaned.

But peace did not last long, for the Jews in Gilead, east of the Jordan, as well as in Galilee sent an appeal to Judas for aid against the Gentiles, who were threatening to destroy them (5:1–16). Dispatching his brother Simon to Galilee, Judas and his brother Jonathan went to defend their brethren in Gilead; both campaigns were successful (5:17–68).

After the death of Antiochus Epiphanes in 163 B.C., the war was carried on between Judas and Lysias, the general of the Syrian forces (6:1–17). Besides infantry and cavalry, the Syrian army also boasted of thirty-two military elephants. (This is the first time in the annals of warfare that elephants appear to have been utilized.) A brother of Judas, Eleazar, seeing that one of the beasts, larger than the others, was equipped with royal armor, courageously ran into the midst of the phalanx to reach it. Getting under the elephant, 'he stabbed it from beneath and killed it; it fell to the ground upon him and there he died' (6:46). Despite such heroic self-sacrifice, the Jewish forces were demoralized in the face of the overpowering might of the Syrians. Owing to the Levitical restrictions imposed during a sabbatical year, the Jews at Beth-zur and Jerusalem were compelled to surrender (6:47–54). Lysias, however, upon hearing of the threatening attitude of Philip (see 6:14), persuaded the young king,

Antiochus Eupator, to sign a peace treaty with the Jews, grant-
ing them religious freedom once again (6:55-63).

The detailed account of subsequent intrigues and counter-
intrigues (7:1-8:32), the death of Judas in 160 B.C. (9:1-22),
the succession of Jonathan as military leader of the Jews, and
later as high priest (10:15-21), his battles and relations with the
Syrian kings, his embassies to Rome and to Sparta (12:1-53),
and his death when treacherously taken prisoner by his temporary ally, Trypho (12:39-53)—all these carry the narrative
on to about 143-142 B.C.

The last of the five sons of Mattathias, Simon, was then chosen
by the Jews to be their leader (13:1-9). Under him the Jews
at length secured their political independence (142 B.C.) and began to date their documents and contracts 'In the first year of
Simon the great high priest and commander and leader of the
Jews' (13:42). A later generation looked back on Simon as the
ideal Jewish ruler, and in I Macc. 14:4-15 there is a Greek translation of a Hebrew panegyric in his honor. The poet first lists
his conquests, including Joppa, Gazara, Beth-zur, and the citadel
of Jerusalem itself, whose garrison was finally starved out; but
more important were the peacefulness and security of his government, and the spirit of justice which marked his rule.

In order to recognize publicly the services of Simon, a formal
decree was passed, engraved on tablets of bronze, and set up
conspicuously in the Temple, declaring that Simon and his line
should fill the offices of high priest, civil ruler, and military commander in perpetuity (14:25-49).

All was not yet quiet politically. Although Antiochus VII
had confirmed Simon's autonomy, allowing him to coin money
(15:1-9; some of these coins have been found by archaeolo-
gists), later he revoked all these concessions (138 B.C.) and issued an ultimatum that Simon should hand over to him certain

conquered cities as well as the tribute from them, or pay an indemnity of 1000 talents of silver (15:10–31). When Simon offered a mere 100 talents, Antiochus ordered his general, Cendebeus, to enforce the entire ultimatum. Simon sent his two older sons, Judas and John, to resist the Syrians, saying, 'Take the place of me and my brother, and go out and fight for our nation, and may the help which comes from Heaven be with you' (16:3). Under their leadership the Jews were successful in routing Cendebeus and a very large force (16:4–10).

In 134 B.C. Simon and his two sons Mattathias and Judas were treacherously murdered by Simon's own son-in-law (16:11–16). Simon's son, John, at once seized his father's authority as ruler and high priest. This stirring book then closes (16:23f.) with a reference to a chronicle (now lost) relating the achievements and brave deeds of John, known to historians as John Hyrcanus, who ruled from 134–104 B.C.

As will have been gathered from what has been said above, I Maccabees is eminently worth reading for its own sake as an inspiring record of a dauntless little group fighting for and achieving independence. Many artists and poets have chosen themes from its pages. It is no less prized by the historian as one of the few surviving records of the important, but relatively obscure, period of Jewish history just prior to the beginning of the Christian era. More than one group whose presence is taken for granted in the pages of the New Testament had its roots in this tumultuous age. From the Maccabees came the Zealots of later times. The rank and file of the Hasidim are the spiritual forebears of the Pharisees as a sect and the devout and humble folk of Jesus' time. From the Hellenized, pro-Syrian party came eventually the calculating, worldly Sadducees and the Temple aristocracy.

It must be admitted that, from one point of view, it is some-what strange that so Jewish a book as I Maccabees was not accepted by the Rabbis as part of the Scriptures, and that the Hebrew original was allowed to disappear. Perhaps the fact that the later Maccabees became completely secularized in their outlook and were therefore disapproved of by the Pharisees (whose views ultimately prevailed in 'normative' Judaism) explains the relatively limited influence of the book in subsequent ages. On the other hand, the obvious value of the narrative in itself and in revealing the times which it records has been appreciated by many among both Jews and Christians. For example, Martin Luther acknowledged, 'This is another of those books not included in the Hebrew Scriptures, although in its style, in language and words, it closely resembles the rest of the books of Holy Scripture, and would not have been unworthy to be reckoned among them, because it is a very necessary and useful book for the understanding of the eleventh chapter of the prophet Daniel' ('Preface to the First Book of the Maccabees,' Luther's translation of the Bible, ed. 1534), and Samuel Taylor Coleridge once declared that the story of the Maccabees was inspiring enough to be inspired.

During the centuries the heroic exploits of the Maccabees have been recalled in the annual Jewish winter festival of Hanukkah (also spelled Chanukah). This celebration, commemorating the rededication of the Temple on the 25th of Chislev, is referred to in the Gospel of John as 'the feast of Dedication' (John 10:22). Because of the prominence of lamps in its observance, Josephus calls it 'the feast of lights.' Like the celebration of Passover, Hanukkah is still observed in Jewish households today with a simple but appropriate ritual, calculated to impress the story of the Maccabees upon the children of the family. Often the family will have a special Hanukkah candlestick, with eight receptacles arranged about a central shaft. Accompanied with songs and stories, at sundown on each day of the eight-day festal period a candle is lighted. Some groups of Jews, however, light all eight the first evening and remove one candle each day afterward. Special foods are prepared during this week, varying with the locale, and children receive gifts from parents and relatives. Games and riddles have been a characteristic feature of the domestic celebration of Hanukkah. The most popular of the children's games is played with a square top (called the *drehdel*), on each side of which is inscribed one of the four Hebrew letters, *nun*, *gimmel*, *he*, and *shin*. These are regarded as the initial letters of the sentence, *Nes gadol hayah sham* ('A great miracle happened here'). The allusion is to a legend, mentioned in the Babylonian Talmud (*Shabbat* 23b), to the effect that when the Temple was rededicated it was discovered that all the oil for the lamp in the Sanctuary had been desecrated by the invaders. After a diligent search, however, a single cruse of undefiled oil sealed by the High Priest was found. In it was oil enough for the lamp to burn but a single day. Then a miracle was wrought for the Maccabees; the oil was multiplied so that it proved to be sufficient to burn for eight days. While playing with the *drehdel*, therefore, as well as in the lighting of the candles, it is possible to recount to the children the main elements of the history and legends associated with the pious and intrepid Maccabees.[1]

1. One of the best popular volumes dealing with the observance of this feast is *Hanukkah, the Feast of Lights,* compiled by Emily Solis-Cohen, Jr. (Philadelphia, 1937). Besides essays on the history of Hanukkah, the book contains music and songs, games, dramas, candle drills, and poems appropriate for the celebration of this joyous Jewish feast.

XV

The Second Book of the Maccabees

THE BOOK KNOWN AS II MACCABEES IS A NARRA-
TIVE OF THE RESISTANCE OFFERED BY THE HASI-
DIM, OR PIOUS JEWS, AGAINST THE PROGRAM OF
paganization which the Seleucid dynasty attempted to promote
in Judea. As was remarked in the comments on I Maccabees,
the two books differ from each other not only in scope but
even more markedly in manner of treatment of material. The
events narrated by II Maccabees fall within a period of about
fifteen years, from a time shortly before the accession of Antiochus Epiphanes (175 B.C.) down to the year 160. Thus the
book is in the main parallel to the first seven chapters of I Maccabees, though independent of this work. The author declares
(2:23ff.) that he has epitomized a larger work, consisting of
'five books,' composed by a certain Jason of Cyrene. Some scholars think that they can detect in II Maccabees the junctures
which correspond to the endings of each of the five books of
Jason's work, namely 3:40, 7:42, 10:9, 13:26, and 15:27.

Unlike the sober and often unadorned style of I Maccabees,
the author of this book regards his task as that of rewriting in
more rhetorical form (2:29-31) the narrative which has come

to his hands. In fact, his work of popularization has produced a romanticized melodrama in the artificial and florid style so popular in Alexandria at that period. A special aim of the author seems to have been the honoring of the Temple at Jerusalem. Not only does he frequently refer to it with obvious affection and reverence (as in 2:19, 22; 3:12; 5:15-21; 14:31; 15:18; etc.), but he is concerned to relate fully the circumstances connected with the institution of a great national festival—the purification and dedication of the Temple after its desecration by Antiochus Epiphanes.

An unmistakable characteristic of the author is the amplifying of religious and miraculous elements in his narrative; flashing apparitions of heavenly horsemen fight in behalf of the Jewish patriots, and both victory and defeat suggest to the author appropriate moral lessons. Despite the air of unreality produced by these stories of celestial helpers, undoubtedly a genuine piety prompted their composer, whether Jason of Cyrene or the Epitomist. In nearly every case the apparition is the result of prayer, thus testifying to a trust in divine protection.

As for the date of the composition of II Maccabees, two stages must be distinguished. As was mentioned above, the book is confessedly an abridgment of a history in five volumes written by Jason of Cyrene (2:19-23). Who Jason was and when he wrote are not known. Some scholars have suggested that he is to be identified with the Jason of I Macc. 8:17 (possibly a nephew of Judas), who was sent on an embassy to Rome; others think that he was a contemporary of Philo of Alexandria (about 20 B.C. to about A.D. 54). In any case he was a strict Jew who composed his work in Greek for the instruction and edification of his people. The unknown Epitomist was no doubt an Alexandrian Jew in full agreement with the aims and spirit of Jason. When it was that he made his digest of Jason's five-volume work is uncertain. Scholars have conjectured dates ranging from about 120 B.C. to the first half of the first Christian century.

The reason for preparing this abridgment, the Epitomist explains, was to provide a simplified account for the general reader, who would be bewildered at 'the flood of numbers . . . [and] the mass of material' (2:24) in the original work of Jason. The Epitomist candidly acknowledges that 'the toil of abbreviating . . . is no light matter but calls for sweat and loss of sleep. . . . However, to secure the gratitude of many we will gladly endure the uncomfortable toil, leaving the responsibility for exact details to the compiler, while devoting our effort to arriving at the outlines of the condensation' (2:26-28).

The popularity of the Epitomist's work is attested by the loss to posterity of Jason's original five-volume history and the continued circulation of the digest. The Greek text of the latter was subsequently translated into Latin, Syriac, Coptic, and Armenian.

Prefixed to the Maccabean record proper are two introductory letters purporting to have been sent by the Jews of Palestine to the Jews of Egypt (1:1-2:18). The central theme of these letters pertains to the purification and dedication of the Temple; the author thereupon proceeds (2:19ff.) to show how this had been the life work of Judas.

The first part of the book sets forth the pre-Maccabean history and the causes that provoked the Jewish rebellion (3:1-7:42). The author begins with the unsuccessful attempt made by Heliodorus, envoy of the Syrian king Seleucus IV, to plunder the Temple at Jerusalem—an attempt that was miraculously frustrated by angelic beings (3:1-40). Next follows a melancholy recital of how by intrigues and bribery the high-priesthood changed hands several times, and of how the renegade high-priests, Jason and Menelaus, as well as Simon, overseer of the Temple, collaborated with the Seleucids in an attempt to Hellenize the Jews in Jerusalem (4:1-50). As a result of many sacrilegious acts committed with the connivance of a secularized priesthood, terrible calamities befell Jerusalem. The appearance of battling horsemen in the sky for almost forty days (5:1-4) was a warning of the pogrom soon to be unleashed by Antiochus against the Jews. The occasion of it was the sudden attack on Jerusalem made by Jason in the hope of regaining the high-priesthood. But through his reckless butchery Jason aroused such hostility against himself that he was forced to flee again to the Ammonites (5:5-10). Antiochus Epiphanes, interpreting Jason's attack as a revolt of Judea against himself, came with fury against Jerusalem and wreaked frightful vengeance. He massacred forty thousand Jews and sold the same number into slavery. Accompanied by the traitorous high-priest, Menelaus, Antiochus desecrated the Holy of Holies and carried off eighteen hundred talents of plunder from the Temple, leaving behind governors to afflict the people. But Judas Maccabeus, with a few others, escaped to the mountains and lived in temporary hiding (5:11-27). The author explains that God did not intervene to save his people on this occasion, as he had done when Heliodorus attacked them (see 3:22-30), because of his holy anger against the Jews for their sins (5:17-20).

Then began a series of anti-Semitic persecutions. Antiochus commanded that the Temple at Jerusalem be dedicated to the Olympian Zeus; he permitted the Gentiles to fill the Temple precincts with revelings and debauchery; and, worst of all, he compelled the Jews to participate in monthly festivals in honor of the god Dionysus (6:1-9). Two women were tortured and then killed for having circumcised their infants, and pious Jews were burned to death in a cave, where they were observing the

Sabbath (6:10-11). Once again the author moralizes and urges 'those who read this book not to be depressed by such calamities, but to recognize that these punishments were designed not to destroy but to discipline our people' (6:12).

Noteworthy among the examples of immovable faithfulness to the traditions of the fathers was the aged scribe Eleazar, who chose to endure tortures rather than to eat swine's flesh (6:18-31). This account is followed by the famous chapter which relates in piteous detail the inhumane atrocities by which seven brothers were, one by one, put to death in the presence of their mother, who, after urging each son to remain steadfast, was herself a martyr for her faith (7:1-42).

The remainder of the book (chapters 8-15) corresponds broadly to I Macc. 3-7, and describes the rise and progress of the Maccabean insurrection until the crushing defeat of the Syrian general Nicanor at the hands of Judas. The early victories of the Maccabees over Nicanor (8:8-29) and over Timothy and Bacchides, with the obviously exaggerated reports of the number of Syrians killed and the amount of booty seized (8:20 and 30), are followed by a highly embroidered account of the death of Antiochus Epiphanes (chap. 9; this account differs irreconcilably from the account of Antiochus's death reported in I Macc. 6:1-16). After retreating in disorder from Persepolis, where he had attempted to rob the temples and control the city, Antiochus determined to take vengeance by making 'Jerusalem a cemetery of Jews' (9:4). But he was suddenly stricken by the Lord with wracking pains (9:5-6), and was run over by his chariot (9:7-8). The fall was so hard as to injure every part of his body. As if this were not enough, the narrator relates with obvious relish that 'the ungodly man's body swarmed with worms, and while he was still living in anguish and pain, his flesh rotted away, and because of his stench the whole army felt revulsion at his decay' (9:9). Broken in spirit, he vowed to make full restitution to the Jews, and even to become a Jew himself (9:11-17). His deathbed repentance led him to write a friendly letter to the Jews, informing them of his afflictions and urging them to be loyal to his successor, Antiochus V, Eupator (9:18-27).

The author now follows with an account of the purifying of the Temple under the guidance of Judas, and the inauguration of the Feast of Dedication (10:1-9). By an error of chronology, this is said (10:3) to have taken place two years (instead of three years, see I Macc. 4:52, compared with I Macc. 1:54-59) after the altar had been desecrated.

Troubles for the Jews, however, were not over. The enemy, led by Timothy, invaded Judea with a very large force of mercenaries. After earnest supplications for divine assistance, Judas met him near Jerusalem and was able to rout the opposing army owing to the miraculous appearance of five celestial horsemen (10:24-38).

Committing another anachronism, the author goes on to relate the first expedition of Lysias, which, according to I Macc. 4:26-35, took place before the death of Antiochus Epiphanes. Lysias was defeated by Judas after the appearance of a horseman, clothed in white and brandishing weapons of gold, who rode at the head of the Jewish forces (chap. 11).

A patched-up peace was short-lived, and new troubles broke out at Joppa (12:2-5), at Jamnia (12:6-12), and at several other places (12:13-45). A second victory over Lysias in 163 B.C. (chap. 13; compare a less distorted account I Macc. 6:28-63) resulted in three years of peace (14:1). This was broken by an attack on the part of Nicanor whom Demetrius I had sent as the Syrian governor of Judea. After an initial clash of forces, Nicanor unexpectedly dispatched an embassy to give and receive pledges of friendship (14:18-20). Later, however, at the insistence of Demetrius, Nicanor reopened the conflict. Several hair-raising stories which are not in I Maccabees (see particularly the ghastly account of the suicide of a certain Razis, a highly esteemed elder in Jerusalem, 14:37-46) come to a climax in the rousing account of an all-out battle between the two forces. Judas encouraged his men by relating a dream in which he saw the deceased high-priest Onias praying for his countrymen, and the prophet Jeremiah presenting Judas a golden sword (15:11-19). In the battle the Jews laid low no fewer than thirty-five thousand of the enemy and, discovering the corpse of Nicanor, took his head and right arm to Jerusalem, where they were exhibited publicly (15:27-35). The victory was celebrated annually on the 13th of Adar, the day before the Feast of Purim instituted to celebrate Esther and Mordecai's triumph over their enemies (13:36).

So the Epitomist closes his book, having blended historical fact and colorful style, for (he says) just as 'wine mixed with water is sweet and delicious and enhances one's enjoyment, so also the style of the story delights the ears of those who read the work' (15:39).[1]

---

1. Although it is commonly unnoticed, the author's allusion here ('the style of the story delights the ears of those who read the work') is a clear testimony to the prevalence in antiquity of reading aloud, even to oneself. Similarly, it was because the Ethiopian treasurer was reading aloud to himself (Acts 8:30) that Philip was able to know that the passage was from the prophet Isaiah. For other ancient testimonies to the practice of reading aloud in antiquity, see Josef Balogh, 'Voces paginarum,' *Philologus*, Vol. LXXXII (1926-27), pp. 84-109, 202-231; G. L. Hendrickson, 'Ancient Reading,' *Classical Journal*, Vol. XXV (1929), pp. 182-196; and E. S. McCartney, 'Notes on Reading and Praying Audibly,' *Classical Philology*, Vol. LXIII (1948), pp. 184-187. Furthermore, the fact that ancient scribes wrote without leaving spaces between words and sentences (*scriptio continua*) would obviously necessitate reading aloud, syllable by syllable; see A. Brinkmann, 'Scriptio continua und Anderes,' *Rheinisches Museum*, Vol. LXVII (1912), pp. 609-630.

To the secular historian II Maccabees, with its palpable exaggerations and its frequent moralizings, is less valuable than the sober and straightforward account in I Maccabees. But to the student of religions II Maccabees is of paramount importance, for it throws welcome light on the development of Judaism before the beginning of the Christian era. It is just because the avowed aim of the author was not to recount a series of dry facts in chronological order, but rather to select certain events from the period which he treats, and to arrange, embellish, and comment upon them, that we can determine what were the beliefs and practices which he and like-minded Jews of the period defended. His pronounced Pharisaic standpoint is reflected in the confidence that God has ordained even the most minute affairs of his people and marvelously protected the sanctity of his Temple in Jerusalem. The calamities which befell the Jews are regarded as a temporary visitation for their sins (4:16f.; 5:17-20; 6:12, 17; 7:32f; 12:40). The book, moreover, speaks of the interposition of angels for the welfare of the people (10:29, 13:2; etc.) and other supernatural manifestations (3:25; 5:2; 13:2; etc.) as of common occurrence. Allied to the author's belief in the active energy of beings of the unseen world is the importance he assigns to dreams (15:11).

Furthermore, the doctrine of Providence is worked out in a most minute parallelism of the retributive punishment of the wicked in a manner exactly appropriate to the crime. Thus, Andronicus was put to death on the very spot where he had murdered Onias (4:38), and Jason, 'who had cast out many to lie unburied . . . had no funeral of any sort and had no place in the tomb of his fathers' (5:10). The torments suffered by Antiochus are likened to those which he had inflicted on others (9:5–6). The fate that befell Menelaus 'was eminently just; because he had committed many sins against the altar whose fire and ashes were holy, he met his death in ashes' (in an incinerator, 13:4-8). The hand and tongue of Nicanor, with which he had blasphemed, were hung up as 'a clear and conspicuous sign to every one of the help of the Lord' (15:32-35). On a larger scale the same idea is developed in the contrasted relations of Israel and the heathen to the divine Power. The former is 'God's people,' 'God's portion' (1:26; 14:15), who are chastised in love; the latter are left unpunished until the full measure of their sins precipitates their destruction (6:12-17).

Even more striking in the author's theology is the definiteness and fullness with which the doctrine of the resurrection of the body is expressed. He not only believed in survival after death, but in eternal life for the righteous (7:36), in contradistinction to the punishment which awaits the wicked. Moreover, the resurrection will include the restoration of the body (7:11, 23; 14:26), and will involve reunion with the members of one's family (7:6, 9, 14, and 29).

Still other doctrines and practices are enunciated clearly for the first time in this book. The unambiguous statement of the doctrine of *creatio ex nihilo* appears in 7:28, 'Look up at the heaven and the earth and see everything that is in them, and recognize that God did not make them out of things that existed.' Likewise, the reference to the offering of prayers and sacrifices in behalf of the dead, 'that they might be delivered from their sin' (12:43-46), involves a practice which is nowhere mentioned in the canonical Scriptures.

Thus, both by what it provides in the way of transition from the Old to the New Testament, as well as in the respects in which it stands alone, the Second Book of the Maccabees is of no little importance to the Christian theologian.

Likewise, the historian must recognize the profound influence which chapters 6 and 7 of this book have had on both Jews and Christians during succeeding centuries down to the present. In fact, it is probably true to say that in importance for the Christian Church no part of the Apocrypha has been so widely and deeply felt as the narrative of the sufferings of the martyrs recounted in this book. The steadfast faith of the Jewish mother and her seven sons, subjected to frightful persecution (chap. 7), became for Jewish and Christian readers alike an object lesson worthy of devout imitation. Sometime during the first century before or after the birth of Christ, a Hellenistic Jewish author composed a quasi-philosophical treatise entitled 'The Triumph of Reason,' which several of the Church Fathers attributed to Flavius Josephus. It is so unlike that writer's style and outlook, however, as to make this ascription of authorship altogether unlikely. Furthermore, this book stands in three of the great uncial manuscripts of the Septuagint (namely, the Codices Sinaiticus, Alexandrinus, and Venetus) under the title, 'The Fourth Book of the Maccabees.' The document contains an enlargement, not to say exaggeration, of the gruesome tortures endured by the Maccabean mother and her sons. Besides honoring the memory of the martyrs, the author's object is to illustrate the philosophical maxim that religious convictions are stronger than bodily passions, or the apprehensions of pleasure and pain.

During the early centuries of the Christian Church in times of Roman persecution, more than one Christian writer exhorted the faithful to imitate the Jewish martyrs, and to suffer the most excruciating tortures rather than renounce their faith (for example, Cyprian's *Exhortation to Martyrdom*, chap. 11; and Origen's *Exhortation to Martyrdom*, chap. 23). Later Christian authors went still further in heaping encomiums upon these eight staunch Jewish confessors. Panegyrics are found in the works of Ambrose, Chrysostom, Augustine, Gaudentius, Euse-

bius of Emesa, Leo, and others. In his 'Oration on the Maccabees' Gregory Nazianzen quotes at length from the treatise mentioned above, 'The Triumph of Reason.' As early as the third
century an annual service of commemoration of these martyrs
was instituted, a service which came to be observed throughout
the Eastern and Western Churches on the first day of August.

At the same time there were those who objected that it was
improper for the Church to enroll Jewish confessors in her catalogue of martyrs, on the ground that they died not for Christ
but for the Law of Moses. In reply Gregory Nazianzen urged
that 'if they suffered so bravely before Christ's coming, what
would they not have done, had they lived after him, and had
the death of Christ for their example!" Augustine defended the
practice of the Church thus: 'They could not confess Christ
openly, for the name of Christ was not yet revealed; yet they
died for the name of Christ veiled in the Law: for what is the
Old Testament but the New Testament veiled; what is the New
Testament but the Old Testament revealed?'

High as is their praise of the seven sons, the chief admiration
of Patristic authors was reserved for the mother, who (they
reasoned) made a sevenfold sacrifice and endured seven martyr-
doms, thus exhibiting a faith which far surpassed that even of
Abraham, who faced the sacrifice of one son. In his paean of
praise for the Jewish mother, Gregory Nazianzen recognizes in
her a foretype of the Mother of Sorrows at the crucifixion of
Christ.

A rash of popular legends and fancies regarding these Jewish
martyrs, now canonized by the Church, sprang up. Neither II
Maccabees nor IV Maccabees records the names of the sons and
their mother. Pious invention soon made up for this lack. In the
Calendar of Martyrs current in the Syrian Church, preserved
in a manuscript dating from A.D. 411, we find the name of the

mother given as Shamuni. In the following centuries the Greek
Menæa, or ritual books of the Eastern Orthodox Church, duly
record on August 1st the names of all the sons and that of the
mother, namely, Abion, Antonius, Gourias, Eleazar, Eusebonas,
Alim, Marcellus; their mother is here called Solomonis. Furthermore, the scene of their martyrdom was transferred from Jerusalem to Antioch, where a basilica, or large church, was erected
in their honor. In one of his sermons on the festival of the Maccabean martyrs, Augustine comments on the irony that the
church should have been erected in the city which bore the
name of the persecutor (Antiochus). It goes without saying that
interest came to be shown in their remains. At first it was supposed that their bones were preserved in the basilica at Antioch.
According to one legend these sacred relics were removed in the
sixth century from Antioch to Constantinople, and from there
to Rome in the Church of St. Peter ad Vincula, with whose festival their commemoration coincides. Later in the Middle Ages a
rivalry over the relics developed between Rome and Cologne,
for in the latter city a convent, dedicated to the holy Maccabees,
boasted that it possessed their heads, preserved in golden vases.

XVI

The Apocrypha and the New Testament

IT MUST BE SAID AT THE OUTSET THAT THE INDISPENSABLE AID FOR A CORRECT UNDER- STANDING OF THE NEW TESTAMENT IS THE OLD Testament. All of the authors of the books of the New Covenant presuppose the moral and religious foundations which lie deep in Hebrew history and are to be traced through all parts of the Old Covenant. Explicitly and implicitly the early Church regarded itself as the heir of the promises made by God to Abraham, Isaac, and Jacob, and therefore called itself the Israel of of God (Gal. 6:16).

At the same time, and without minimizing the role of the Old Testament, it should also be recognized that the social, political, and religious climate which pervades the New Testament differs in certain important aspects from that represented even in the latest strata of the Old Testament. It is here that the books of the Apocrypha play their part in disclosing the stages of development during the generations just prior to the coming of Christ. Though it would be altogether extravagant to call the

Apocrypha the keystone of the two Testaments, it is not too much to regard these intertestamental books as an historical hyphen that serves a useful function in bridging what to most readers of the Bible is a blank of several hundred years. To neglect what the Apocrypha have to tell us about the development of Jewish life and thought during those critical times is as foolish as to imagine that one can understand the civilization and culture of America today by passing from colonial days to the twentieth century without taking into account the industrial and social revolution of the intervening centuries.

Furthermore, it is altogether likely, as will be shown later, that several of the New Testament authors were acquainted with one or more books of the Apocrypha. The serious student of Shakespeare's plays seeks to determine what books were in the bard of Avon's library, so as to be able to assess and appreciate the poet's native genius the better. In a similar way our understanding of certain expressions and arguments in the New Testament will be enhanced if we take into account not only the Old Testament, which was the primary source-book of the New Testament authors, but the books of the Apocrypha as well.

A. *Literary Form and Doctrinal Development*

One may consider first of all the literary form of most of the documents in the New Testament. Of the twenty-seven books of the New Testament, twenty-one of them, or seven-ninths of the total number, are in the form of letters or epistles. In addition there are seven short letters to the Seven Churches, incorporated in chapters 2 and 3 of the Book of Revelation. The Old

Testament, on the other hand, contains only an occasional reference to letters. There is, for example, the letter which Hezekiah laid before the Lord (II Kings 19:14), and the letter of Jeremiah to the captives in Babylon (Jer. 29:1ff.); but none of the thirty-nine books of the Old Testament is in the form of a letter. What is the explanation of this curious and striking change in the form of Judeo-Christian religious literature? When and under what circumstances did the change come about? The books of the Apocrypha help to provide an answer to these questions. There we see certain literary forms coming to be utilized for religious purposes which are well-recognized and commonplace in the New Testament.

The writing of epistles, as distinct from letters, seems to have originated in Alexandria several centuries before the beginning of the Christian era. Letters, as Adolf Deissmann was fond of emphasizing, are generally private documents and deal with circumstances of the passing moment. Epistles, on the other hand, are on a higher level of literary effort, and are written with the intention of being both public and permanent. The examples in the New Testament combine features of both the letter and the epistle. When the Apostle Paul, for example, wrote to the Church at Colossae, he wrote in a most intimate and personal manner, from his heart to the hearts of the readers. His letter grew out of the specific situation that called it forth. At the same time his style is somewhat more formal than the off-the-cuff and haphazard style so characteristic of an ephemeral letter. Moreover, he himself envisages that his message to the Colossians will be read also by the congregation at Laodicea (4:16). Thus, in this literary form Paul manages to establish a warm and personal contact with the human heart, as well as to convey weighty religious instruction applicable to many besides the immediate recipients of the document. In the hands of the leaders in the early Church, communication by letters became one of the most important, if not the most important, means of consolidating and maintaining a sense of the common life and unity among the scattered members of the one universal Church. In fact, this literary form combined the advantages of a conversation and a treatise; it was possible to communicate truth, not abstractly, but in close relation to the condition of mind of the recipients.

The historical precedent for such a use of letters arose among the Jews during the Babylonian exile. By the division of the nation into two halves, one in Judea and one in Babylon, as well as by the founding of another large settlement of Jews at Alexandria in Egypt, a situation emerged in which, by means of letters, the separated parts of the nation sought to strengthen and encourage each other in mutual resistance to paganism and in loyalty to the faith of their fathers. It was in such circumstances that the Apocryphal Letter of Jeremiah, large sections of the book of Baruch, and the two letters at the beginning of II Maccabees find their origin and setting. Although these models were probably not consciously in the mind of Paul or Peter or James or other Christian authors of the first century, it is instructive to find similar circumstances calling forth similar types of literature.

It is, however, not merely as to literary forms that the Apocrypha throw light upon the New Testament; it is chiefly in broadly cultural, sociological, and theological respects that they assist us in understanding the thought and life of first-century Jews in Palestine, from whom the earliest Church was recruited. For example, nowhere in the Old Testament is there to be found a reference to the Pharisees or the Sadducees, both of which parties are referred to frequently in the New Testament. As was pointed out earlier, the historical origins of the Pharisees must be sought in the tumultuous times of the Maccabean uprisings and in the subsequent fortunes of the pious and sternly patriotic Jews who resisted the encroachments made by the Hellenizing policy of the Seleucid Empire. On the other hand, the small but powerful group of secularist priest-kings in Jerusalem, who not only accepted but welcomed collaboration with the outsiders, were the forebears of the Sadducees of Jesus' day.

Of especial importance were the deep-seated changes in Jewish theology and piety which took place during the intertestamental period and which are partially reflected in the Apocryphal and pseudepigraphic literature of the time. Thus, the doctrines of the Messianic hope, of personal immortality, and of the activity of angels and demons are three areas in which notable developments occurred subsequent to the close of the Old Testament period and prior to the opening of the New Testament age. Though aspects of some of these changes have been alluded to in previous chapters, it is appropriate here to discuss each one somewhat more fully.

Great strides were made in Jewish thinking concerning the person and work of the Messiah. In the Old Testament what may be called Israel's Messianic hope is without any precise or uniform formulation; in fact, the term 'Messiah' is scarcely ever employed by an Old Testament author with the specialized meaning that only afterward came to be attached to it. Building upon the foundation of an unshakable conviction that God would send Israel a king and deliverer to save the nation from her oppressors, the wonderful vitality of the Messianic hope progressively grew more explicit and more pervasive throughout Judaism. Such pseudepigraphic literature as the book of Enoch and the Psalms of Solomon contain many references to a personal Messiah, such as 'the Anointed One,' 'the Son of

Man,' 'the Elect One,'—all of which occur in the New Testament. Not only in certain books of the Apocrypha (notably II
Esdras), but also in literature discovered recently at Qumran
near the Dead Sea, one sees the increasing interest among certain groups of Jews in the fulfillment of Messianic expectations.
Under the tyranny of the Seleucid dynasty and the later Hero-
dian suzerainty under Rome, popular longing for a Jewish king
took on at times an almost feverish intensity. The hold that it
had obtained on the imagination of a large section of the people
is evidenced in the thrill of excitement which ran through many
of those who heard and responded to the proclamation made by
John the Baptist, 'The kingdom of heaven is at hand!' (Matt.
3:2ff.).

The doctrine which underwent perhaps the greatest development during the intertestamental period was that which pertains to the after-life. Speaking generally, the Old Testament is
a book about a people whose hopes and aspirations were directed
toward a goal lying within the horizon of this world. Whatever
intimations it contains of the next world, they are few in number and usually refer to a colorless life amid the grim shadows
and terrors of Sheol—an undefined state of bodiless existence
which is common to the good and bad alike. In the New Testament, on the other hand, both Jesus and his followers take for
granted the certainty of a future resurrection and the reality of
eternal bliss for the righteous and of eternal retribution for the
wicked. The intervening stages of the growth of these beliefs
are reflected particularly in the Wisdom of Solomon and II
Maccabees among the Apocrypha, and the Psalms of Solomon
and I Enoch among the pseudepigrapha. At first the idea of the
resurrection seems to have been restricted to the lot of the
godly, and it was usually contemplated as involved in the establishment of the Messiah's kingdom. Because that kingdom

had been delayed, those who had been overtaken by death before its realization—so it came to be believed—would be raised
to life again at the advent of the Messiah and his rule over the
nations. There also entered the vocabulary of certain Jews, particularly those in Alexandria who had been influenced by Greek
philosophical thought, such words as 'immortal' and 'immortality.' The first time that the word 'heaven' seems to have been
used to refer to the abode of the righteous subsequent to the day
of judgment is in the first century B.C.

Finally, among other noteworthy changes in the thinking of
the Jews, the growing appreciation of the reality and activity of
both angels and demons characterizes a certain amount of the
intertestamental literature. Such Apocryphal books at Tobit, II
Maccabees, and II Esdras, as well as I Enoch among the pseudepigrapha, reflect a rather highly developed angelology. In these
books angelic help is taken for granted as one of the regular re-
sources of the godly person. The book of Tobit shares certain
prevalent beliefs in magic as a means of controlling malevolent
spirits. Other apocryphal writings, however, resemble the Old
Testament in its reticence in these matters. The fact that in
Jesus' day the Sadducees are said to have rejected all belief in
angels, spirits, and the future resurrection (Acts 23:8), whereas
other Jewish sects held to them, shows the persistence of the
two types of theology which are reflected in the intertestamental literature.

B. *New Testament Parallels and Allusions to the Apocrypha*

Besides the help which the Apocryphal books provide by way of general orientation for the reader of the New Testament, the New Testament itself contains numerous instances of parallels to words, phrases, or whole sections in the Apocryphal literature. How to interpret these parallels—whether they are mere coincidences or are literary reminiscenses—is not always clear. In some cases, however, both the thought and the phrasing are so close between the two that it must be concluded that the Christian writers had been influenced directly or indirectly by the intertestamental books. Among the several New Testament authors, Paul, James, and the anonymous writer of the Epistle to the Hebrews display the greatest number of coincidences with the Apocrypha.

There is reason to think that both the Apostle Paul and the author of Hebrews had at some time read and were impressed by the Wisdom of Solomon. In the case of Paul, several verses in the first chapter of his Epistle to the Romans contain striking parallels to the thirteenth and fourteenth chapters of Wisdom. Some of them are the following:

ROMANS

WISDOM

(1:20) 'Ever since the creation of the world his [God's] invisible nature, namely, his eternal power and deity, has been clearly perceived in the things that have been made. So they are without excuse;

(21) for although they knew God they did not honor him as God or give thanks to him, but they became futile in their thinking and their senseless minds were darkened.

(22) Claiming to be wise they became fools, (23) and exchanged the glory of the immortal God for images resembling mortal man or birds or animals or reptiles.'

(26) 'For this reason God gave them up to dishonorable passions. . . .'

(29) 'They were filled with all manner of wickedness, evil, coveteousness, malice. Full of envy, murder, strife, deceit, malignity, they are gossips, (30) slanderers, haters of God, insolent, haughty, boastful, inventors of evil, disobedient to parents, (31) foolish, faithless, heartless, ruthless.'

(13:5) 'From the greatness and beauty of created things comes a corresponding perception of their Creator.'

(13:8) 'Yet again, even they cannot be excused; for if they had the power to know so much that they could investigate the world, how did they fail to find sooner the Lord of these things,'

(13:1) 'For all men who were ignorant of God were foolish by nature; and they were unable from the good things that are seen to know him who exists, nor did they recognize the craftsman while paying heed to his works.'

(12:24) 'For they went very far astray on the paths of error, accepting as gods those animals which even their enemies despised; they are deceived like foolish babes.'

(14:24) 'They no longer keep either their lives or their marriages pure, but they either treacherously kill one another, or grieve one another by adultery, (25) and all is a raging riot of blood and murder, theft and deceit, corruption, faithlessness, tumult, perjury, (26) confusion over what is good, forgetfulness of favors, pollution of souls, sex perversion, disorder in marriage, adultery, and debauchery.

(27) For the worship of unspeakable idols is the beginning and cause and end of every evil.'

A careful examination of these two columns will disclose that both authors emphasize three similar arguments: (a) mankind knows something of the greatness of God from observing his handiwork in nature; (b) rejecting these tokens of God's majesty, mankind turned to the worship of senseless idols made in the form of animals; and (c) as a result men have plumbed the depths of manifold crimes and immoralities.

Again, in Paul's discussion in chapter 9 of the same Epistle to the Romans there are several examples of marked similarities with statements in the latter part of the Wisdom of Solomon. These include the following:

ROMANS

(9:20) 'Who are you, a man, to answer back to God? Will what is molded say to its molder, "Why have you made me thus?"'

(21) Has the potter no right over the clay, to make out of the same lump one vessel for beauty and another for menial use?

(22) What if God, desiring to show his wrath and to make known his power, has endured with much patience the vessels of wrath made for destruction (23) in order to make known the riches of his glory for the vessels of mercy, which he has prepared beforehand for glory . . . ?'

WISDOM

(12:12) 'For who will say [to God], "What hast thou done?" Or who will resist thy judgment? Who will accuse thee for the destruction of nations which thou didst make?'

(15:7) 'For when a potter kneads the soft earth and laboriously molds each vessel for our service, he fashions out of the same clay both the vessels that serve clean uses and those for contrary uses, making all in like manner; but which shall be the use of each of these the worker in clay decides.'

(12:20) 'For if thou didst punish with such great care and indulgence the enemies of thy servants and those deserving of death, granting them time and opportunity to give up their wickedness, with what strictness thou hast judged thy sons . . . !'

Here one finds clear resemblances in the arguments which Paul and pseudo-Solomon employ. Each dwells on the impossibility of resisting the might and majesty of God. Each uses the illustration of the potter, and that not only in the sense in which several Old Testament writers do so (namely, God molds us as a potter does the clay), but both agree in giving a new twist to the old illustration—God fashions the good and the bad out of the *same* clay. Finally, each writer lays great stress on the patience and indulgence of God prior to his judgment upon the wicked. Not only is a similarity of argument discernible, but the student who consults the original Greek of both documents will discover verbal parallels which cannot easily be represented in translation. For example, a literalistic translation of Wis. 12:12 is, 'For who will say, "What [or, Why] hast thou made?" Or who will answer back to thy judgment?' With this compare the rendering of Rom. 9:20 given above.

Passages in several other New Testament letters likewise reveal parallels with expressions in the Wisdom of Solomon. Noteworthy in this respect are Eph. 6:11 and II Cor. 5:1-9. In the former passage the Apostle speaks of the whole armor of God—which is not, as is so often misrepresented, merely the armor which God supplies, but is the armor which God himself wears ('God's panoply'). Doubtless the germ of the idea is to be found in Isa. 59:17, 'He [the Lord] put on righteousness as a breastplate, and a helmet of salvation on his head'; but the Greek word *panoply* which the author of Ephesians uses, as well as the fuller details in his elaboration of the imagery, probably came to the Apostle from the book of Wisdom.

EPHESIANS

WISDOM

(6:13) 'Therefore take the whole armor [panoply] of God . . . (14) Stand therefore, having girded your loins with truth, and having put on the breastplate of righteousness, (15) and having shod your feet with the equipment of the gospel of peace; (16) above all taking the shield of faith, with which you can quench all the flaming darts of the evil one. (17) And take the helmet of salvation, and the sword of the Spirit, which is the word of God.'

(5:17) 'The Lord will take his zeal as his whole armor [panoply] and will arm all creation to repel his enemies; (18) he will put on righteousness as a breastplate, and wear impartial justice as a helmet; he will take holiness as an invincible shield, (20) and sharpen stern wrath for a sword, and the world will fight with him against the mad men.'

The passage in II Cor. 5: 1–9, which is too long to be quoted here in full, seems to have been influenced by what is said in Wis. 9: 10–19. Particularly noteworthy is the following comparison:

II CORINTHIANS

WISDOM

(5:1) 'For we know that if the earthly tent we live in is destroyed, we have a building from God, a house not made with hands, eternal in the heavens. . . . (4) For while we are still in this tent, we sigh with anxiety.'

(9:15) 'For a perishable body weighs down the soul, and this earthly tent burdens the thoughtful mind.'

In both sets of verses one finds the metaphor of the earthly tent and the idea of the body's weighing down the soul. Now, doubtless both these features were common enough in the teachings of contemporary Platonists and Stoics, and were there no other indications of parallelism it would not be necessary to infer from these any more than that Paul had a general acquaintance with Hellenistic philosophy. But the presence of certain verbal coincidences in the Greek of both passages points to a literary connection. For example, it is significant that the word *skēnos*, translated 'tent' or 'tabernacle,' appears *only* in these two passages in *all* of Biblical Greek—the entire Septuagint and the New Testament.

From a consideration of these several parallels one must doubtless conclude that both the language and the form in which Paul expressed some of his views on idolatry, on God's might and sovereignty, and on man's 'long home,' had been influenced by certain expressions in the Apocryphal book of the Wisdom of Solomon. At the same time it must be recognized that he obtained nothing further from it. The manifest dissimilarities not only as regards broad content, but the different uses made of certain terms common to both authors, are deep-seated and may not be underestimated. In view of these divergencies, the suggestion which Msgr. Ronald Knox once threw out, that perhaps Paul wrote the book of Wisdom before he became a Christian, is more facile than convincing. What one can legitimately deduce from the parallels observable between the two is that there can be little doubt that the Apostle had at one time made a close study of this Apocryphal book.

The anonymous author of the Epistle to the Hebrews seems to have been acquainted with several books of the Apocrypha. His roster of eminent Old Testament worthies in chapter 11 reminds one of the famous chapter in Ecclesiasticus which begins, 'Let us now praise famous men ...' (44:1). Near the close of this list of heroes of faith in the Epistle to the Hebrews reference is made to those who 'were tortured, refusing to accept release, that they might rise again to a better life' (11:35). As the Church Father Theodoret already saw in the fifth century, this is undoubtedly an allusion to the heroism of the Maccabean martyrs who steadfastly refused to save their lives by eating swine's flesh. In fact, the Greek word for 'tortured' used here is related linguistically to that which appears in the description of Eleazar's death in II Macc. 6:19. Furthermore, again and again in the gruesome account of the persecution of the Jewish mother and her seven sons (II Macc. 7), emphasis is laid upon the hope of the resurrection as sustaining them in their tortures —just as is mentioned also in the verse quoted above from Hebrews (11:35).

In the opening paragraph of this same Epistle there are two rare Greek words which seem to be reminiscent of the eloquent passage in pseudo-Solomon describing divine Wisdom as 'manifold' and as a 'reflection' of eternal light (Wis. 7:22–26). By choosing these two words the writer to the Hebrews shows that he understands Jesus to embody fully and to reflect perfectly the Wisdom of God himself.

The short Epistle of James, a characteristic bit of 'wisdom literature' in the New Testament, contains numerous allusions not only to the Book of Proverbs in the Old Testament but also to the proverbs in the work composed by the Palestinian author, Jesus the son of Sirach. What appear to be reminiscences include the following:

'Let every man be quick to hear, slow to speak,' advises James (1:19), imitating Sirach's pithy proverb, 'Be swift in listening, but slow in answering' (5:11). Furthermore, James's essay on the use of the tongue, in chapter 3, has numerous points of contact with similar advice in Sirach 19:6–12; 20:5–7, 17–19; 25:5–10; and 28:13–26. The thought in Jas. 1:13, 'Let no one say when he is tempted, "I am tempted by God"; for God cannot be tempted with evil and he himself tempts no one,' may be compared with Sirach 15:11f., 'Do not say, "Because of the Lord I committed apostasy"; for he will not do what he hates. Do not say, "It was he who led me astray"; for he has no need of a sinful man.'

In another instance an expression in Sirach throws welcome light on the meaning of a passage in James. Probably many readers of the familiar promise in Jas. 1:5, 'If any of you lacks wisdom, let him ask God who gives to all men generously and without reproaching, and it will be given him,' would be at a loss to explain the significance of the words 'and without reproaching' (King James Version 'and upbraideth not'). But a comparison with the exhortation in Ecclus. 18:15, 'My son, do not mix reproach with your good deeds, or cause grief by your words when you present a gift,' suggests at once that according to James God's gifts are made in such a manner as never to embarrass the recipient for his asking.

Finally, among many other parallels in thought and language between the two books, the following indubitably points to James's familiarity with the work of Jesus the son of Sirach. The New Testament author addresses the wicked rich, 'Your gold and silver have rusted, and their rust will be evidence against you and will eat your flesh like fire' (Jas. 5:3). The Greek verb translated here 'will be rusted' occurs only twice in the entire Greek Bible, in this verse and in Ecclus. 12:11, where it refers to a metal mirror tarnishing. Moreover, the Greek noun which is translated 'rust' in James occurs nowhere else in the New Testament with this meaning, but it appears in a verbal form in a passage where Sirach addresses the rich of his day, 'Help a poor man for the commandment's sake . . . Lose your silver for the sake of a brother or a friend, and do not let it rust under a stone and be ruined' (29:9–10). Furthermore only in these passages throughout the entire Bible and the Apocrypha does the figure occur of rust affecting unused silver and gold. In view of all this it is hard to doubt that both the simile and the verbal expression of it in the Epistle of James were derived from Ecclesiasticus.

When all these examples are taken together, one must conclude that James was undoubtedly familiar with the book of Ecclesiasticus, and had at some time mulled over its precepts. At the same time it is also fair to add that a comparison of the two books discloses to most readers the immense spiritual difference between the two authors.

The last book of the New Testament contains, in addition to much imagery derived from the Old Testament, a striking parallel to a passage in Tobit. Tobit's 'prayer of rejoicing' (13:1ff.) contains a remarkable poetic passage which looks forward to the time when

> Jerusalem will be built with sapphires and emeralds,
> and her walls with precious stones,
> and her towers and battlements with pure gold.
> The streets of Jerusalem will be paved with beryl and
>   ruby and stone of Ophir (13:16–17).

It may well be that these words were in the mind of John when in the Book of Revelation he describes the New Jerusalem as a city of pure gold, with walls of jasper, sapphire, emerald, beryl, and all kinds of precious stones (21:18–21).

If first-century Christians, including Paul, the author of the Epistle to the Hebrews, James, and John reveal a certain amount of evidence that they were acquainted with several books of the Apocrypha, can the same be said of the Founder of Christianity, Jesus himself? In evaluating the evidence in the Gospels one must always bear in mind that, because Jesus left nothing in writing himself, it is possible to explain certain parallels between his teaching and statements in the Apocrypha as originating with those who were responsible for the oral and written transmission of his words. To the extent, however, that one finds reason to believe that Jesus' teachings have been transmitted with a minimum of extraneous coloration, to that extent the following evidence will probably suggest that he too was acquainted with a certain amount of the intertestamental literature.

On several occasions the book of Ecclesiasticus seems to be recalled in the form of Jesus' sayings. In this book wisdom is made to say of herself, 'Those that eat me will be hungry for more, and those that drink me will be thirsty for more' (Ecclus. 24:21). In John 6:35 Jesus is reported as saying, 'He who comes to me shall not hunger, and he who believes in me shall never thirst.' Here one observes points of contrast as well as of comparison. The wisdom known to the son of Sirach was so good that men would long to eat and drink of her again; but John means that Jesus Christ, the bread of life and the water of life, is all-satisfying and will leave no longing in the souls of those whom he feeds. Whether the choice of the language to express this idea consciously reflects Ben Sira's phrases is a question that can be answered with more assurance after several other similar examples in the Gospels have been examined.

The familiar and comforting invitation of Jesus, 'Come to me, all who labor and are heavy-laden, and I will give you rest. Take my yoke upon you, and learn from me; for I am gentle and lowly in heart, and you will find rest for your souls. For my yoke is easy, and my burden is light' (Matt. 11:28–30), contains what may be several echoes of similar language in Ecclesiasticus.

> Draw near to me, you who are untaught,
>> and lodge in the house of instruction. . . .
> Put your neck under the yoke,
>> and let your souls receive instruction . . . .
> See with your eyes that I have labored little
>> and found for myself much rest (Ecclus. 51:23, 26, 27;
>>>> compare also Ecclus. 6:24-25 and 24:19-22).

Jesus' parable of the Rich Fool reminds one of Ben Sira's description of a secular-minded rich man. In each we find a prosperous and self-centered man, whose self-satisfied soliloquy anticipates a life of ease; in both cases death comes unexpectedly, and his goods are dispersed to others. The following are the two passages.

> There is a man who is rich through his diligence and self-denial,
>> And this is the reward allotted to him:
> When he says, 'I have found rest,
>> And now I shall enjoy my goods!'
> He does not know when his time will come;
>> He will leave them to others and die (Ecclus. 11:18-19).

Jesus told them a parable, saying, 'The land of a rich man brought forth plentifully; and he thought to himself, "What shall I do, for I have nowhere to store my crops?" And he said, "I will do this: I will pull down my barns, and build larger ones; and there I will store all my grain and my goods. And I will say to my soul, Soul, you have ample goods laid up for many years; take your ease, eat, drink, be merry." But God said to him, "Fool! This night your soul is required of you; and the things you have prepared, whose will they be?" So is he who lays up treasure for himself, and is not rich toward God' (Luke 12:16-21).

Other parallels between Jesus' teachings and the book of Ecclesiasticus involve certain similar precepts. Thus, Jesus' warning, 'In praying do not heap up empty phrases as the Gentiles do; for they think that they will be heard for their many words' (Matt. 6:7), may be compared with Ben Sira's counsel, 'Do not prattle in the assembly of the elders, nor repeat yourself in your prayer' (7:14). Again, Ben Sira says, 'Forgive your neighbor the wrong he has done, and then your sins will be pardoned when you pray' (28:2), while Jesus affirms at the close of the Matthean form of the Lord's Prayer, 'If you forgive men their trespasses, your heavenly Father also will forgive you; but if you do not forgive men their trespasses, neither will your Father forgive your trespasses' (Matt. 6:14–15). With this may be compared also Jesus' word in Mark (11:25), 'Whenever you stand praying, forgive, if you have anything against anyone; so that your Father also who is in heaven may forgive you your trespasses.'

Finally, both Jesus and Ben Sira make a comparison based on the difference between old and new wine. 'Forsake not an old friend,' counsels the latter, 'for the new one does not compare with him; a new friend is like new wine: when it is aged, you will drink it with pleasure' (9:10). After speaking of putting new wine into old wineskins, Jesus declares, 'And no one after drinking old wine desires new; for he says, "The old is good"' (margin, 'is better,' Luke 5:39).

In assessing the significance of these parallels between sayings of Jesus reported in the Gospels and passages in Ecclesiasticus, it is obvious that taken singly each involves no more than an everyday expression which was either commonplace or proverbial among Palestinian peasantry. On the other hand, the similarities do exist, and there is nothing antecedently improbable in the supposition that Jesus of Nazareth may have read and recollected phrases in the Wisdom of Jesus the son of Sirach. In any case, however, it is obvious that the dominant influence in our Lord's teaching as a whole came from the Old Testament, particularly from Deuteronomy, Isaiah, and the Psalms, and that the influence from Ecclesiasticus was, so to speak, marginal, affecting an occasional form rather than the content of his teaching.

It is just possible that another Apocryphal book—the book of Tobit—may also have been known to Jesus. He may have expanded the concise statement of the angel Raphael to Tobit and Tobias, 'Prayer is good when accompanied by fasting, almsgiving, and righteousness' (12:8). Part of the Sermon on the Mount, as reported by Matthew, contains three consecutive sections referring to right attitudes in almsgiving, praying, and fasting (Matt. 6:2, 5, and 16), and the whole is introduced by Jesus' warning against practicing one's piety before men in order to be seen by them (Matt. 6:1), where the Greek word translated 'piety' is the same as that rendered 'righteousness' in the verse quoted from Tobit.

Another parallel between the two is to be found in the presence in Tobit of the negative form of the Golden Rule, 'What you hate, do not do to anyone' (4:15), with which the positive form in Jesus' teaching has often been compared, 'As you wish that men would do to you, do so to them' (Luke 6:31; see also Matt. 7:12).

Finally, Jesus' exhortation, 'When you give a feast, invite the poor, the maimed, the lame, the blind, and you will be blessed, because they cannot repay you' (Luke 14:13–14), reminds one of the example set by Tobit, who at the feast of Pentecost, seeing the abundance of food on the dinner table, said to his son, 'Go and bring whatever poor man of our brethren you may find who remembers the Lord, and I will wait for you' (Tobit 2:2).

C. *The Significance of Parallels and Allusions*

In discussing the subject of parallels and allusions to the Apocrypha found in the New Testament, it is sometimes urged that no passage from the Apocrypha is ever expressly quoted by a New Testament author as proceeding from a sacred authority. This is doubtless true. On the other hand, however, it is also true that nowhere in the New Testament is there a direct quotation from the canonical books of Joshua, Judges, Chronicles, Ezra, Nehemiah, Esther, Ecclesiastes, the Song of Solomon, Obadiah, Zephaniah, and Nahum; and New Testament allusions to them are few in number.

Perhaps the emphasis in such enumerations has been wrongly placed. The absence in the New Testament of a direct quotation from, for example, the prophet Nahum does not remove his work from the list of canonical books. Nor, on the other hand, should the presence of allusions, more or less clear, to passages in the Apocrypha be construed as conferring upon these books any authority which they do not otherwise possess. The reason is obvious. When Paul quotes a line from the play *Thaïs* by the Greek comic poet, Menander, in I Cor. 15:33; or when Luke reports Paul's address in Athens as containing a snatch from the pantheistic 'Hymn to Zeus' composed by the Stoic philosopher, Cleanthes (Acts 17:28); or when the author of Titus 1:12 repeats the popular squib of the semi-legendary Epimenides about the Cretans—in none of these cases does the quotation by a New Testament writer impart a special sanctity to the words that are quoted.

More controversial, however, is the fact that Jude makes an express quotation (in verses 14 and 15) of a passage found in the pseudepigraphic book, I Enoch (1:9). Three different opinions were held in the early Church regarding the significance of this quotation. Tertullian, on the one hand, argued that Jude's testimony authenticates the entire book of Enoch as inspired Scripture (Tert. *de Cultu Fem.* i.3) and referred to Enoch as the most ancient prophet through whom the Holy Spirit spoke (Tert. *de Idol.* xv). On the other hand, according to Jerome many rejected the canonicity of Jude because he had dared to quote a pseudepigraphic book (Jer. *de Vir. Illust.* iv). Fortunately a mediating position represented by Augustine prevailed, one which permitted Jude to refer to a single sentence of Enoch without imagining that by so doing he conferred canonical status on the entire book (Aug. *Civ. Dei* XV, xxiii.4).

When one compares the books of the Apocrypha with the books of the Old Testament, the impartial reader must conclude that, as a whole, the true greatness of the canonical books is clearly apparent. Though the several books within the Old Testament are manifestly quite disparate and occupy varying levels, and though some readers would perhaps be willing to exchange passages in several Apocryphal books for others in the canonical books, yet it is probable that the judgment of most readers today would be in accord with that of Judaism and the earliest Church, both of which saw a profound difference between the two groups of books.

This chapter may be concluded with the quotation of a paragraph from a newly discovered essay left by John Henry Newman on 'The Connection in Doctrine and Statement of the Books of the Apocrypha with the New Testament.' This essay, of uncertain date but obviously from Newman's Anglican period (that is, prior to 1845), was found in manuscript form and was published for the first time in 1953. Though the editor regards the text as a more or less fair copy, the document as a whole undoubtedly lacks the finishing touch which Newman would have given it prior to passing it for publication.

After having examined a great number of parallels between the books of the Apocrypha and the New Testament, and after showing the influence of several Apocryphal books on the writers of the New Testament, Newman concludes:

'Providence never acts with harsh transitions, one thing melts into another. Day melts into night, summer into winter. So it is with His inspired Word. What is *divine*, gradually resolves into what is human. Yet, as nevertheless summer and winter have for practical purposes a line of division, as St. Paul dissuaded the shipmen from sailing because the fast was already past and sailing dangerous, so we too for practical purposes are obliged to draw a line and say what is safe and sure to take as a canon for our faith, and what we cannot be sure will not mislead us. Without therefore, far from it, denying that God's supernatural hand is in the Apocrypha, yet, knowing that it was not included in that Canon which Christ sanctions, and that His Church has not spoken so clearly on the subject as to overcome the positive face of the argument deducible from this silence, therefore we do not see our way clear to receive it as canonical.' [1]

---

1. Jaak Seynaeve, *Cardinal Newman's Doctrine on Holy Scripture* (Louvain, 1953), pp. 50*–51*.

XVII

A Brief History of the Apocrypha in the Christian Church

A. *The Apocrypha in the Early Church, down to the Reformation*

THE EARLY CHRISTIAN CHURCH, WHICH BEGAN WITHIN THE BOSOM OF PALESTINIAN JUDAISM, RECEIVED HER FIRST SCRIPTURES (THE BOOKS of the Old Testament) from the Jewish synagogue. Since, however, the Gentile converts to Christianity could not read Hebrew, the Greek translation of the Old Testament (called the Septuagint), which many Jews had also come to use, was widely employed by the Church. Because of the antagonism which developed between the Synagogue and the Church, the Jews abandoned the use of the Greek Septuagint, and this circulated henceforth solely among the Christians. Almost the only manuscript copies of the Septuagint which have come down to us today were written by Christian scribes. What is important to notice here is that these Greek Bibles have an arrangement

of the books of the Old Testament very different from that
which prevailed in Judaism. The threefold division into Law,
Prophets, and the Writings is replaced by a sequence in which
the Law and the historical books stand first, the poetic and
didactic books follow, and the prophets come at the end, as in
our English Bibles. There is also another difference. The copies
of the Septuagint contain a dozen or more other books interspersed among the books of the Hebrew canon. Most of these
are identical with the traditional Apocrypha, but with certain
differences. The apocalyptic book of II Esdras is not found in
any Greek codex of the Old Testament. The Prayer of Manasseh is not in all copies of the Septuagint, and when it is present
it is found among the odes or hymns which in some manuscripts
are appended to the Psalms. On the other hand, some Septuagint manuscripts include III and IV Maccabees and Psalm 151,
which are not generally reckoned among the traditional books
or parts of the Apocrypha.

It should be understood that these various books stand in the
copies of the Septuagint with no indication that they are not
included in the Hebrew canon. From this fact some have
leaped to the conclusion that the Jews of Alexandria, who used
Greek, regarded these books as being inspired in the same sense
as the Law, the Prophets, and the Writings. For several reasons,
however, such a conclusion appears to be unfounded. In the first
place, the number of Apocryphal books is not identical in all
copies of the Septuagint. This circumstance suggests that there
was no fixed canon at Alexandria which included all these
peripheral books. In the second place, the manuscripts of the
Septuagint which contain these disputed books were all copied
by Christian scribes, and therefore cannot be used as indisputa-
ble proof that the *Jewish* canon included all the books in question. In the third place, though Philo, the greatest of the Jewish

Hellenists in Alexandria, knew the existence of the Apocrypha, he never once quoted from them, much less used them for the proof of doctrine, as he habitually uses most of the books of the Hebrew canon. It is extremely difficult, therefore, to believe that the Alexandrian Jews received these books as authoritative in the same sense as they received the Law and the Prophets.

The question remains, however, how such books came to stand so closely associated with the canonical books as they do in the manuscripts of the Septuagint. In attempting to find at least a partial answer to this problem, it should not be overlooked that the change in the production of manuscripts from the scroll-form to the codex or leaf-form must have had an important part to play in the ascription of authority to certain books on the periphery of the canon. The fact that there was a controversy in Talmudic times whether it was legitimate to include the Law, the Prophets, and the Writings all in a single scroll, indicates that the prevailing custom among the Jews was the production of separate volumes for each part of the Hebrew Bible. Some Rabbis went so far as to insist that each book of Scripture must form a separate volume.[1] The recent discovery of several scrolls in caves by the Dead Sea, each containing a copy of a single Biblical book, attests to the prevalence of this feeling among the Jews.

When the codex or leaf-form of book production was adopted, however, it became possible for the first time to include a great number of separate books within the same two covers. From all of the recently accumulating evidence from the papyri, it appears that it was the early Christians who changed from scrolls to codices as the format for their sacred books, perhaps in direct opposition to the usage of scrolls in the Synagogue. For

---

1. For an account of the rabbinical discussions, see Joel Müller's edition of *Masechet Soferim. Der talmudische Tractat der Schreiber* ... (Leipzig, 1878), pp. 41–43.

whatever reason the change was instituted, it now became possible for canonical and Apocryphal books to be brought into close physical juxtaposition. Books which heretofore had never been regarded by the Jews as having any more than a certain edifying significance were now placed by Christian scribes in one codex side by side with the acknowledged books of the Hebrew canon. Thus it would happen that what was first a matter of convenience in making such books of secondary status available among Christians became a factor in giving the impression that all of the books within such a codex were to be regarded as authoritative. Furthermore, as the number of Gentile Christians grew, almost none of whom had exact knowledge of the extent of the original Hebrew canon, it became more and more natural for quotations to be made indiscriminately from all the books included within the one Greek codex.

From the Greek Septuagint translation of the Old Testament an Old Latin Version was made, which of course also contained the Apocryphal books among the canonical books. It is not strange, therefore, that Greek and Latin Church Fathers of the second and third centuries, such as Irenaeus, Tertullian, Clement of Alexandria, and Cyprian (none of whom knew any Hebrew), quote the Apocrypha with the same formulas of citation as they use when referring to the books of the Old Testament. The small number of Fathers, however, who either had some personal knowledge of Hebrew (e.g. Origen and Jerome) or had made an effort to learn what the limits of the Jewish canon were (e.g. Melito of Sardis) were usually careful not to attribute canonicity to the Apocryphal books, though recognizing that they contain edifying material suitable for Christians to read.

Whether it was owing to the influence of Origen or for some other reason, from the fourth century onward the Greek Fathers made fewer and fewer references to the Apocrypha as inspired.

Theologians of the Eastern Church, such as Cyril of Jerusalem, Gregory of Nazianzus, and Amphilochius, drew up formal lists of the Old Testament Scriptures in which the Apocrypha do not appear.

In the Latin Church, on the other hand, a much higher estimate was generally accorded the books of the Apocrypha. Following the example of Tertullian and Cyprian, Augustine frequently quoted them as though they were not different from the canonical books of the Hebrew Old Testament. Furthermore, more than one Synodical Council justified and emphasized their use. Jerome, standing in this respect almost alone in the West, spoke out decidedly for the Hebrew canon, declaring unreservedly that books which were outside that canon should be ranked as Apocryphal. When he prepared his famous Latin translation of the Bible, the Vulgate, he scrupulously separated the Apocryphal Additions to Daniel and Esther, marking them with marginal notes as absent from the original Hebrew. Nevertheless, against his more considered judgment, he allowed himself to be persuaded by the importunity of two bishops, his friends, to make a hurried rendering of the books of Tobit and Judith. His translation of the former was dashed off at one sitting. In subsequent years, as Latin-speaking Christians came more and more widely to adopt Jerome's rendering of the canonical books, they added to his hasty translations of a few of the Apocryphal books the translations of the others which had been current in Latin before Jerome's time. Thus, during the Middle Ages there circulated throughout Europe manuscripts of the Latin Bible which contained the Apocryphal books mingled with the canonical books of the Old Testament. Many of these manuscripts also preserve Jerome's comments which he had prefixed to many of the books. In more than one of these prefaces he insists upon the fundamental distinction between the

canonical Scriptures and the books which, though of an edifying nature, were not to be used to establish doctrine.

Subsequent to Jerome's time and down to the period of the
Reformation a continuous succession of the more learned Fathers and theologians in the West maintained the distinctive and
unique authority of the books of the Hebrew canon.[2] Such a
judgment, for example, was reiterated on the very eve of the
Reformation by Cardinal Ximenes in the preface of the magnificent Complutensian Polyglot edition of the Bible which he
edited (1514-17). Moreover, the earliest Latin version of the
Bible in modern times, made from the original languages by the
scholarly Dominican, Sanctes Pagnini, and published at Lyons in
1528, with commendatory letters from Pope Adrian VI and
Pope Clement VII, sharply separates the text of the canonical
books from the text of the Apocryphal books. Still another Latin
Bible, this one an edition of Jerome's Vulgate published at Nur-
emberg by Johannes Petreius in 1527, presents the order of the
books as in the Vulgate but specifies at the beginning of each
Apocryphal book that it is not canonical. Furthermore, in his
address to the Christian reader the editor lists the disputed books
as 'Libri Apocryphi, sive non Canonici, qui nusquam apud He-
braeos extant.' Even Cardinal Cajetan, Luther's opponent at
Augsburg in 1518, gave an unhesitating approval to the Hebrew
canon in his *Commentary on All the Authentic Historical Books
of the Old Testament*, which he dedicated in 1532 to Pope
Clement VII. He expressly called attention to Jerome's separation of the canonical from the uncanonical books, and maintained that the latter must not be relied upon to establish points
of faith, but used only for the edification of the faithful.

2. For a list of some of these see P. F. Keerl, *Die Apokryphen des alten
Testaments. Ein Zeugniss wider dieselben auf Grund des Wortes Gottes*
(Leipzig, 1852), pp. 138-144.

B. *The Apocrypha and the Protestant Reformation*

The central aim of the Protestant Reformers was the examination and correction of current ecclesiastical practices and doctrines in the light of the Bible. In the controversies which
emerged they soon perceived the need to be certain which books
were authoritative for the establishment of doctrine and which
were not. It appears that Luther was first led to disparage the
books of the Apocrypha when his opponents appealed to passages in them as proof for the doctrines of Purgatory and of the
efficacy of prayers and Masses for the dead (II Macc. 12:43-
45). Likewise the emphasis that certain Apocryphal books lay
upon merit acquired through good works (Tobit 12:9; Ecclus.
3:30; II Esdras 8:33; 13:46, etc.) was naturally distasteful to
him.

The first discussion of the canon from a Protestant point of
view was a history-making book published at Wittenberg in
1520 by Andreas Bodenstein of Karlstadt, who is commonly
known by the name of his native town. Written in Latin and
entitled *De Canonicis Scripturis Libellus*—a small epitome of the
book was also issued at the same time in the vernacular German
—the treatise distinguishes the canonical books of the Old Testament (i.e. the Hebrew Old Testament) from the Apocrypha.
The books of the Apocrypha are further classified in two divisions. Of one group, containing Wisdom, Ecclesiasticus, Judith,
Tobit, and I and II Maccabees, Karlstadt says, 'These are Apocrypha, that is outside the Hebrew canon, yet are holy writings'
(section 114). In explaining his view of the status of these books,
he writes: 'If I were asked for my opinion as to reading such
books [he is thinking especially of Tobit, Wisdom, and Ecclesi-

asticus], I should answer thus: what they contain is not to be despised at once; still it is not right that a Christian should relieve, much less slake, his thirst with them . . . Before all things the best books must be read, that is those which are canonical beyond all controversy; afterwards if one has the time, it is allowed to peruse the controverted books, provided that you have the set purpose of comparing and collating the non-canonical books with those which are truly canonical' (section 118). The second group of Apocrypha, namely I and II Esdras, Baruch, the Prayer of Manasseh, and the Additions to Daniel, Karlstadt declares to be filled with ridiculous puerilities and therefore to be contemptuously discarded; 'These books,' he writes, 'are obviously Apocryphal, worthy of the censor's ban' (section 114).

Some of the principles embodied in Karlstadt's treatise on the canon were reflected in many editions of the Bible translated by Protestant scholars of various countries, as well as in personal statements and creedal documents which they issued.

The first Bible in a modern vernacular to separate the canonical Scriptures from the Apocryphal books was the Dutch Bible published by J. van Liesvelt in 1526 at Antwerp. Prepared by a group of scholars whose names have escaped record, the section from Genesis to the Song of Solomon and the whole of the New Testament are based on Luther's German version; the remaining books seem to follow the text, though not the arrangement, of the Cologne Low German Bible of about 1480 (a western dialect of Low German resembling Dutch). After Malachi there stands the section devoted to the Apocrypha, which is entitled, 'The Books which are not in the canon, that is to say, which one does not find among the Jews in the Hebrew.'

The first edition of the Zürich or Swiss-German Bible (1527-29), prepared by ministers of the Protestant Church in that city, presents in six volumes all of the portions hitherto published by

Luther (namely Genesis to the Song of Solomon and all of the New Testament) slightly revised and adapted throughout to the Swiss dialect. The Apocryphal books, translated by Leo Juda (or Jud), comprise the fifth volume, and are prefaced by the statement, 'These are the Books which are not reckoned as Biblical by the ancients, nor are found among the Hebrews.' A one-volume edition of the Zürich Bible, which appeared in 1530, contains the Apocrypha grouped together, in this case, after the New Testament. In commenting on the attitude of Protestants respecting the disputed books, Œcolampadius, perhaps on the whole the best representative of the Swiss Reformers, declared in a formal statement issued in 1530: 'We do not despise Judith, Tobit, Ecclesiasticus, Baruch, the last two books of Esdras, the three books of Maccabees, the Additions to Daniel; but we do not allow them divine authority with the others.'[3]

Luther's German translation of the entire Bible, completed in 1534, contained the books of the Apocrypha (except I and II Esdras) in an appendix at the close of the Old Testament. The reason he omitted the books of Esdras, he declares, is that 'they contain absolutely nothing which one could not much more easily find in Aesop or in even more trivial books' ('Preface to the Book of Baruch'; later editions of Luther's Bible contain the rendering of these two books made by Daniel Cramer, 1568-1637). Luther prefaced the section of his Bible in which the books of the Apocrypha were collected together with the statement: 'APOCRYPHA—that is, books which are not held equal to the Holy Scriptures, and yet are profitable and good to read.' This general view was further expanded in the special prefaces to the separate Apocryphal books, in which Luther freely ex-

---

3. Abraham Scultetus, *Annales Evangelii*, Vol. II (Heidelberg, 1618), pp. 313f.

pressed with characteristic vigor his judgment regarding each book. (For his opinion of the worth of Tobit, Judith, and I Maccabees, see the chapters above on these books.)

Luther's translation was the basis of several other early Bibles prepared by Protestants in countries that had felt the influence of the German Reformer. Thus, the first Bible to be published in Swedish (1541), in Danish (1550; this was used also in Norway), in Icelandic (1584), and in Slovenian (1584) imitate Luther's 1534 Bible in each of the following particulars. The books of the Apocrypha are gathered together and printed with a half title page after Malachi and before the New Testament. On this page stands Luther's prefatory statement defining the subordinate status of the Apocrypha, yet declaring them useful for reading. On the same page is a list of abbreviated titles of the Apocrypha as follows: Judith, Wisdom, Tobit, Sirach, Baruch, Maccabees, Parts of Esther, and Parts of Daniel. Though the Prayer of Manasseh is not mentioned in this table of contents, its text is printed at the close of the Apocrypha. Luther's prefaces to the individual books of the Apocrypha are given before the text of each book (except in the Danish Version). Curiously enough, in all these Bibles, including that of Luther himself, a colophon at the conclusion of the Apocrypha states that this is the end of the Old Testament.

The first Protestant version in French was prepared at the expense of the Waldensians by Pierre Robert Olivétan and printed in 1535 near Neuchâtel, Switzerland. In this edition the books of the Apocrypha are placed at the conclusion of the Old Testament with the preface, 'The Volume of all the Apocryphal Books contained in the Vulgate translation which we have not found in Hebrew or Chaldee.' This translation was reprinted several times, in one case (in 1545) with emendations made by John Calvin, who was Olivétan's cousin. The Bible was reissued at Geneva in 1551 with a new translation of the Apocrypha made by the Reformer Théodore de Bèze (Beza).

Though it is often asserted, there seems to be no evidence that Calvin collaborated with his kinsman in the original work of translation; he contributed, however, a Latin preface and an introduction to the New Testament. With respect to the separation of the Apocrypha from the canonical books, Calvin's influence may perhaps be detected indirectly. In his celebrated treatise of theology, the *Institutes of the Christian Religion*, Calvin makes more than four thousand references to the canonical Scriptures in support of his system of doctrine. It is instructive to note that he refers only ten times to books of the Apocrypha (they are Tobit, Wisdom of Solomon, Ecclesiasticus, Baruch, and I and II Maccabees), and in these cases he never uses the Apocrypha to substantiate any doctrine.[4]

As for English Bibles, the first complete translation to come from the press was that of Miles Coverdale in 1535. Following Luther's example, he gathered the Apocryphal books together (including in this case I and II Esdras, but not the Prayer of Manasseh or Baruch; the latter is printed after the Book of Jeremiah), and explained in a preface the subordinate place which they occupy at the end of the Old Testament. This preface is a curious example of the hesitating and ambivalent position which Coverdale took. On the one hand, he declares that he has placed them apart because they are 'not iudged amonge the doctours to be of like reputacion with the other scripture,' but this is only because they contain 'darck sentences' which seem

---

4. For Calvin's position regarding the Apocrypha, see his *Institutes*, IV, 9, §14, and particularly his Tract, 'Antidote to the Council of Trent,' especially his discussion of the Fourth Session of the Council. Besides stressing the lack of uniformity of tradition regarding the worth of the Apocryphal books, he points out that they display a marked inferiority to the canonical writings.

to differ from the 'open and manyfest trueth in the other bokes of the byble.' On the other hand, he has no wish that they should be 'despysed, or litle sett by,' for he is convinced that if they were compared with 'the other open scripture (tyme, place, and circumstaunce in all thinges considered) they shulde nether seme contrary, ner be vntruly and peruersly aledged.'

In 1537 an English Bible appeared which for the first time gathered in a separate group all the Apocryphal books which henceforth it became traditional to call the Apocrypha. This was the so-called Thomas Matthew Bible, which used as a preface to the Apocrypha a translation of the French preface in Olivétan's version.

Special notice should be taken of the Geneva Bible of 1560. This was one of the most popular and widely circulated of English versions of the Scriptures, until eventually it came to be superseded by the King James or so-called Authorized Version. About two hundred editions, either of the whole Bible or of the New Testament alone, were printed between 1560 and 1630. Its importance in the history of Bible translations may be appreciated from the fact that it is the first English Bible to adopt the practice of dividing the text into verses, the first to use italics for those words which the translators added because of English idiom, but which are not in the original, and the first to use the more easily read Roman type rather than the time-honored but clumsy black-letter type. The translators of the Geneva Bible were a group of scholarly Reformers who had fled from the impending persecution under Queen Mary, among whom were William Whittingham (who had married a sister of John Calvin's wife), Anthony Gilby, Thomas Sampson, and others of a strict Calvinistic persuasion. For many years this version was the household Bible of a large section of English-speaking Protestantism. It was the Bible used by Shakespeare, by John Bunyan, by the men of Cromwell's army, and was brought to America by the Pilgrims and other early settlers, many of whom would have nothing to do with the more recently translated (1611) King James Version. In view of this conservative background and wide appreciation of the Geneva Bible, it is instructive to consider the preface which introduces the section containing the Apocrypha. It is as follows (with modernized spelling):

'These books that follow in order after the Prophets unto the New Testament, are called Apocrypha; that is books, which were not received by a common consent to be read and expounded publically in the Church, neither yet served to prove any point of Christian religion, save inasmuch as they had the consent of the other Scriptures called canonical to confirm the same, or rather whereon they were grounded: but as books proceeding from godly men, were received to be read for the advancement and furtherance of the knowledge of the history, and for the instruction of godly manners: which books declare that at all times God had an especial care of his Church and left them not utterly destitute of teachers and means to confirm them in the hope of the promised Messiah, and also witness that those calamaties that God sent to his Church, were according to his providence, who had both so threatened by his Prophets, and so brought it to pass for the destruction of their enemies, and for the trial of his children.'

One curious feature of the Geneva Bible may be mentioned; alone of English Bibles it has the Prayer of Manasseh among the canonical books, between II Chronicles and Ezra. Its title is entered in the table of contents after II Chronicles thus: 'The prayer of Manasseh, apocryphe.' A note in the margin opposite the text of the Prayer itself informs the reader, 'This prayer is not in the Ebrewe, but is translated out of the Greke.' Why this special favor was shown to this Apocryphal prayer is not known. (See also below, p. 197, footnote 14.)

In the King James Version of 1611, which came to be called popularly the Authorized Version,[5] the disputed books stand between the Old and New Testaments, under the title 'Apocrypha' but without any preface or note. At the close of II Maccabees is the colophon, 'The End of Apocrypha.' A fact not generally known today is that in the original 1611 Bible an appreciable proportion of the relatively few references placed here and there in the margins of the canonical books directed the reader's attention to passages in the Apocrypha.[6] In the following century, when the margins came to be crowded with references, all references to the Apocrypha were omitted.

5. There is no evidence that the 'authorization' of the King James Version was anything more than permissive. The circumstances under which both the Geneva and the Bishops' Bibles continued to be used are decisive against an exclusive authorization. To call it, therefore, *the* Authorized Version is to confer on it a status which it never received officially.

6. The total number of references to the Apocrypha in the margins of the Old and New Testaments of the King James Version as printed in 1611 is 113. Of this number, 102 are in the Old Testament, and 11 in the New. The New Testament passages with the references to the Apocrypha are as follows:

IN THE MARGIN OF	IS A REFERENCE TO
Matt. 6:7	Ecclus. 7:14
Matt. 23:37	II Esdras 1:30
Matt. 27:43	Wisdom 2:15, 16
Luke 6:31	Tobit 4:15
Luke 14:13	Tobit 4:7
John 10:22	I Macc. 4:59
Rom. 9:21	Wisdom 15:7
Rom. 11:34	Wisdom 9:13
II Cor. 9:7	Ecclus. 35:9
Heb. 1:3	Wisdom 7:26
Heb. 11:35	II Macc. 7:7

Beginning about the middle of the sixteenth century various Churches issued formal creedal statements regarding the status and usefulness of the Apocrypha. The first general council of the Church ever to give a decision on the question of the limits of the canon was that held at Tridentum (Trent) in Italy (1545-63). In reaction to Protestant criticisms of the disputed books, on April 8, 1546, fifty-three Roman Catholic prelates at this Council pronounced an anathema upon any who would not receive the old Latin Vulgate Bible, with all of its books and parts, as sacred and canonical. Oddly enough, however, there were three books which, though included in many Latin manuscripts of the Vulgate, were denied canonical status by the Council; they are the Prayer of Manasseh and I and II Esdras. In the official edition of the Vulgate, published in 1592, these three are printed as an appendix after the New Testament, 'lest they should perish' from neglect. The other disputed books continued to be scattered throughout the Old Testament, in the positions to which Latin scribes had been accustomed to assign them. In the authorized English translation for Roman Catholics, called the Rheims-Douay Version (finished in 1609-10), these three books are printed as an appendix to the Old Testament. At the head of this section the following caption appears: 'The Prayer of Manasses, with the second [sic] & third [sic] Bookes of Esdras, extant in most Latin and vulgare Bibles, are here placed after al the Canonical bookes, of the old Testament: because they are not receiued into the Canon of Diuine Scriptures by the Catholique Church' (p. [1001]). Here II and III Esdras refer to what are called I and II Esdras in Protestant editions of the Apocrypha and to what Roman Catholics usually call III and IV Esdras. In fact, the actual titles and the running titles for the two books in this edition are 'Third Booke of Esdras' and 'Fovrth Booke of Esdras.' As most modern printings of the King James Version omit the books of the Apocrypha, so modern printings of the Rheims-Douay Version commonly omit these three books.

It was not easy for all Roman Catholic scholars to acquiesce to the unequivocal pronouncement of full canonicity which the Council of Trent made regarding books which, for so long a time and by such high authorities even in the Roman Church (see above, p. 180), had been pronounced inferior. Yet, despite more than one attempt by noted Catholic scholars to reopen the question, this expanded form of the Bible has remained the Scriptural authority of the Roman Church.

After the declaration made by the Council of Trent, various Protestant Churches[7] embodied in creedal statements the views on the status of the Apocrypha which had been enunciated by individual Reformers and had been embodied, explicitly or implicitly, in many vernacular translations of the Bible.

In the Belgic Confession, prepared in 1561 for the Protestant Churches of Flanders and the Netherlands, and used subsequently by Reformed Churches in other countries, the canonical books of the Old and New Testaments are distinguished from the Apocryphal, 'which the Church may read and take instruction from, so far as they agree with the canonical books; but they are far from having such power and efficacy as that we may from their testimony confirm any point of faith or of the Christian religion; much less to detract from the authority of the other sacred books' (Article VI).

The official position of the Church of England regarding the books of the Apocrypha, like its position in certain other doc-

---

7. The Lutheran Church, however, issued no formal, creedal statement on the canon. Evidently the principles embodied in Karlstadt's treatise on the canon, and applied in Luther's prefaces to the Apocryphal books in his German translation of the Bible, were deemed to be sufficient.

trinal disputes, was ambivalent. The Thirty-nine Articles of Religion, issued in 1562, contain statements that support two different positions respecting the status and function of the Apocrypha. On the one hand, after enumerating the books of the Old Testament, Article VI continues, 'And the other books (as Hierome [Jerome] saith) the Church doth read for example of life and instruction of manners: but yet doth it not apply them to establish any doctrine'; then there follows a list of the books of the Apocrypha. On the other hand, in Article XXXV, reference is made to the two Books of Homilies,[8] which are described as containing 'a godly and wholesome Doctrine.' It is not generally realized how much of the Apocrypha is used to enforce the 'godly and wholesome Doctrine' in these Homilies. Nineteen of the Homilies contain about eighty quotations from and references to all the books of the Apocrypha except the two books of Esdras and II Maccabees. These passages are often quoted in the same manner as passages from the canonical books. For example, in the Homily against Excess of Apparel, the book

8. The First Book of Homilies was issued in 1547 and is entitled, *Certayne Sermons or Homilies, appoynted by the kynges Maiestie, to bee declared and redde, by all persones* [i.e. persons], *Vicares, or Curates, euery Sondaye in their churches, where thei haue cure.* In 1563 *The Seconde Tome of Homelyes* was issued, being 'set out by the aucthoritie of the Quenes Maiestie; and to be read in euery paryshe churche agreablye.' In all there were thirty-three of these Homilies, each of which was divided into two or more parts—one or more to be used at the morning service and the remainder in the afternoon. According to Canon 49, issued in 1604, clergy not licensed to preach, that is, those who were 'lay readers,' were commanded to read the Homilies to their congregations and not to put forth sermons of their own.

In the following century, Joseph Addison, speaking through his literary creation, Sir Roger de Coverley, commended the practice of preaching others' sermons with studied dignity. 'A sermon repeated after this manner, is like the composition of a poet in the mouth of a graceful actor. I could heartily wish that more of our country-clergy would follow this example, instead of wasting their spirits in laborious compositions of their own . . . . This would not only be more easy to themselves, but more edifying to the people' (*The Spectator*, No. 106, July 2, 1711).

of Judith and the Additions to Esther are cited as 'Scripture.' In the Homily against Swearing, a quotation from Ecclesiasticus is introduced by the words, 'Almighty God by the wise man saith . . .' In a similar fashion, in the Homily on Alms-doing, a verse from Tobit is prefaced by the statement, 'The Holy Ghost doth also teach in . . . Scripture, saying.' Perhaps the strongest declaration of all is in the Tenth Homily of the Second Book, where the hearers are exhorted to learn from the book of Wisdom, as being the 'infallible and undeceivable word of God.'

Much more explicit and unequivocal was the position taken in 1647 by the Westminster Assembly of Divines and embodied in the Westminster Confession of Faith, which came to be accepted as the doctrinal standard of various Presbyterian and other Reformed Churches. Although it is sometimes supposed that the Westminster Assembly pronounced against the reading of Apocryphal books, actually the concern of the Divines was to differentiate between proper and improper uses of the Apocrypha. After an enumeration of the names of all the books of the Old and New Testaments and the statement that they alone are Holy Scripture, the following paragraph appears: 'The books commonly called Apocryphal, not being of divine inspiration, are of no part of the Canon of the Scripture; and therefore are of no authority in the Church of God, nor to be otherwise approved, or made use of, than other writings' (Chapter I, section iii).

The position of Eastern Orthodox Churches regarding the canon of the Old Testament is not at all clear. On the one hand, since the Septuagint version of the Old Testament was used throughout the Byzantine period, it is natural that Greek theologians, such as Andrew of Crete, Germanus, Theodore the Studite, and Theophylact of Bulgaria, should refer indiscriminately to Apocryphal and canonical books alike. Furthermore, certain Apocrypha are quoted as authoritative at the Seventh Ecumenical Council held at Nicaea in 787 and at the Council convened by Basil at Constantinople in 869. On the other hand, writers who raise the issue regarding the limits of the canon, such as John of Damascus and Nicephorus, express views which coincide with those of the great Athanasius, who adhered to the Hebrew canon. During the centuries following the definitive break between East and West in 1054, when Pope Leo IX excommunicated Patriarch Cerularius, the subject of the canon lay dormant; for while the theologians waxed furious over such controversies as the lawfulness of eating cheese in Lent, there is no sign of a dispute as to the canon of Scripture.

At the time of the Reformation much more definite positions were taken, *pro* and *contra*. Certain more enlightened priests, who had fallen under suspicion of heretical leanings toward Protestantism because of other teachings, saw fit to emphasize the distinction between canonical and Apocryphal. For example, in 1622 a Greek prelate, Z. Gerganos, who had studied at Wittenberg, published a Catechism in Greek which clearly reflects the position of the Synod of Dort in 1618, when the position represented in the Belgic Confession was reaffirmed. In 1625 another Greek theologian, named Critopoulos, who had studied at Oxford, drew up a Confession of Faith which is in close agreement with Anglican views on the canon.

By way of reaction, other leaders of Eastern Orthodoxy found it expedient, in confessions of faith and in decrees of synods, explicitly to place the Apocryphal books on a level with the canonical books. The Synod of Jassy (1642) condemned the illustrious Cyril Lucar of Constantinople, who had published a confession of faith which adhered to the ancient Hebrew canon, and in the following year the Catechism of Peter Moghila took a position opposed to that of Cyril. What was per-

haps the most important synod in the history of the Eastern
Church was convened at Jerusalem in 1672. Chiefly directed toward the continuing influence of Cyril and 'the party of the
Calvinists,' the Synod expressly designated the books of Wisdom, Judith, Tobit, Bel and the Dragon, Maccabees (four
books), and Ecclesiasticus as canonical.

The position of the Russian Orthodox Church as regards the
Apocrypha appears to have changed during the centuries. During the Middle Ages Apocryphal books of both the Old and the
New Testament exerted a widespread influence in Slavic
lands.[9] In the first Slavonic Bible to be published (at Ostrog in
1581), the Apocryphal books are distributed among the canonical books of the Old Testament. In subsequent centuries Constantinople's leadership gave way to the Holy Synod ruling
from St. Petersburg, whose members were in sympathy with
the position of the Reformers. Through a similar influence em-
anating from the great Universities at Kiev, Moscow, Petersburg, and Kazan, the Russian Church became united in its rejection of the Apocrypha. For example, the Longer Catechism
drawn up by the Metropolitan Philaret of Moscow and approved by the Most Holy Governing Synod (Moscow, 1839)
expressly omits the Apocrypha from the enumeration of the
books of the Old Testament on the ground that 'they do not
exist in Hebrew.'[10]

This Catechism was translated into Greek and had a wide

9. See Moses Gaster, *Greeko-Slavonic Literature and Its Relation to the Folk-lore of Europe during the Middle Ages* (London, 1887), pp. 25ff. and 191f.; Milivoy S. Stanoyevich, *Early Jugoslav Literature* (1000–1800), (New York, 1922), pp. 22f.; and Linda Sadnik, 'Das Schicksal der Apokryphen im Slaventum,' *Universitas*, Vol. II (1947), pp. 1051–4.

10. Philip Schaff, *The Creeds of Christendom*, Vol. II (New York, 1889), p. 451; cf. Martin Jugie, *Histoire du canon de l'ancien testament dans l'église grecque et l'église russe* (Paris, 1909).

circulation throughout Greece and in other localities where the position represented by Peter Moghila's Catechism had previously held sway. As a result, there appears to be no unanimity on the subject of the canon in the Greek Orthodox Church today. Catechisms directly at variance with each other on this subject have received the *Imprimatur* of Greek Ecclesiastical authorities, and the Greek clergy may hold and teach what they please about it.

C. *Controversies Over the Use of the Apocrypha*

After the Roman Catholic Church decided at the Council of Trent to regard most of the Apocryphal books as indisputably sacred and canonical, it was natural that certain theologians in other Churches should react against the Apocrypha. For, as Richard Cecil (1748–1810), one of the fathers of the evangelical school, sagely observed, 'Man is a creature of extremes. The middle path is generally the wise path; but there are few wise enough to find it. Because Papists have made too much of some things, Protestants have made too little of them . . . The Papist put the Apocrypha into his Canon—the Protestant will scarcely regard it as an ancient record.'[11]

In England the question was debated at various times, usually with more heat than light. The Puritans felt uneasy that there should be any books included within the covers of the Bible besides those which the Protestant Churches regarded as absolutely inspired.[12] One of their champions for a Bible con-

11. *The Remains of Richard Cecil, with Numerous Selections from his Works,* with an Introduction by his Daughter and Preface by R. Bickersteth, new edition (London, 1876), p. 364.

12. In general, members of the Society of Friends, as would be expected,

taining only the sacred and unimpeachable books acknowledged
as canonical was the Welshman, John Penry, better known under the nom de plume, Martin Marprelate. In one of his vigorous
tracts published in 1589 Penry attacked Archbishop John Whitgift for insisting that the Apocrypha be printed in the same volume with the inspired books. In his equally vigorous reply, as
reported by his biographer, John Strype, Whitgift asks, 'Who
ever separated the Apocrypha from the rest of the Bible from
the beginning of Christianity to that day? ... And shall we suffer this singularity in the Church of England, to the advantage
of the adversary, offense of the godly, and contrary to all the
world besides?' He said 'that he knew there was a great difference between the one and the other; yet that all learned men
had from the beginning given to the Apocrypha authority, next
to the Canonical Scriptures. And therefore that such giddy
heads as thought to deface them were to be bridled, and that it
was a foul shame, and not to be suffered, that such speeches
should be uttered against those books, as by some had been:
enough to cause ignorant people to discredit the whole Bible.' [13]

In course of time the Puritan aversion to the Apocrypha was
expressed by editions in which these books were omitted. The
earliest copies of the English Bible which exclude the Apocrypha were certain Geneva Bibles printed in 1599 mainly in the
Low Countries. This was apparently the work of the binders,
for the titles of the Apocryphal books occur in the list at the beginning of the Bible. Though the printed sheets containing the

sympathized with the position of the Puritans in rejecting the use of the Apocrypha, although in this case the Friends were inclined to bring the canonical
books down to the level of the Apocryphal writings; see Henry J. Cadbury,
'Early Quakerism and Uncanonical Lore,' *Harvard Theological Review*, Vol.
XL (1947), pp. 177-205.

13. John Strype, *The Life and Acts of John Whitgift*, Vol. 1 (Oxford,
1722), p. 590.

Apocrypha were omitted,[14] the Metrical Psalms are almost invariably found in these Bibles. It would seem that the practice of issuing copies of the Bible without the Apocrypha continued, for in 1615 George Abbot, Archbishop of Canterbury, who had been one of the strongly Calvinistic members of the committee that prepared the King James Version, 'directed public notice to be given that no Bibles were to be bound up and sold without the Apocrypha on pain of a whole year's imprisonment.'[15]

Despite the threat of this penalty, however, various printings of the King James Version appeared in London and Cambridge without the Apocrypha (copies lacking the Apocrypha are dated 1626, 1629, 1630, 1633). Like the Geneva Bibles of 1599, these also seem to have been the work of printers who perhaps wished to satisfy an increasing demand for less bulky and less expensive Bibles. The first English Bibles in which the deliberate omission of the Apocryphal books is discussed 'editorially' are those of the edition of the Geneva Version published at Amsterdam in 1640. In this edition a statement regarding the omission of the Apocrypha is inserted between Malachi and the books of the New Testament. The statement is said to be taken 'from the Dutch Bible recently published'; this Dutch Bible is doubtless the famous edition prepared under the order of the Synod of Dort and published in 1637 (see below, p. 200).

Among the voices that were raised against the presence of the Apocrypha in the same volume with the canonical Scriptures was that of the renowned Hebraist, John Lightfoot. In a sermon

14. The Prayer of Manasseh, however, continued to follow II Chronicles; see above, pp. 187f.

15. Edward Arber, *A Transcript of the Registers of the Company of Stationers of London*, Vol. v (Birmingham, 1894), p. xlix.

preached before the House of Commons in 1643 this scholar, who from his Talmudic and Midrashic studies had gained a rather low opinion of Jewish popular literature, bitterly denounced the custom of putting the Apocrypha between the books of the Old and New Testament. He expostulated: 'Thus sweetly and nearly should the two Testaments join together, and thus divinely would they kiss each other, but that the wretched Apocrypha doth thrust in between.' Making use of an irrelevant simile, he declared that, 'Like the two cherubims in the Temple-oracle,' the end of the Law and the beginning of the Gospel would touch each another 'did not this patchery of human invention divorce them asunder.' It is inconsistent, he urged, that the Reformed Churches should 'have refused these books out of the canon, but have reserved them still in the Bible: as if God should have cast Adam out of the state of happiness, and yet have continued him in the place of happiness.' The sentiment of the majority in the Church of England, however, was otherwise, and for several generations most printings of the King James Version continued to include the Apocrypha.

The Lectionary attached to the Anglican Prayer Book, from 1549 onward, has always contained prescribed Lessons from the Apocrypha. At different times the number and choice of these Lessons have varied, frequently in accordance with the amount and intensity of polemic against their use in Church services. (For present-day practice see below, p. 203.) In reply to those who urged the discontinuance of reading Lessons from the Apocrypha, as being inconsistent with the sufficiency of Scripture, the bishops at the Savoy Conference, held in 1661, replied that the same objection could be raised against the preaching of sermons, and that it were much to be desired that all sermons should give as useful instruction as did the chapters selected from the Apocrypha. Curiously enough Samuel Pepys in his *Diary* for 1659-60 has this entry: (Feb. 5th) 'Church in the afternoon . . . A stranger preached a poor sermon, and so I read over the whole book of the story of Tobit.'

An example of the wholesome and uplifting influence of the Apocrypha among the common people of the mid-seventeenth century is to be found in a noteworthy passage in John Bunyan's remarkable autobiography, *Grace Abounding to the Chief of Sinners*. He describes a period of spiritual despondency which he experienced about the year 1652. 'One day, after I had been so many weeks oppressed and cast down, as I was now quite giving up the Ghost of all my hopes of ever attaining life, that sentence fell with weight upon my spirit, *Look at the generations of old, and see: Did ever any trust in the Lord and was confounded?* At which I was greatly lightned, and encouraged in my Soul; for thus at that very instant, it was expounded to me: *Begin at the beginning* of Genesis, *and read to the end of the* Revelations, *and see if you can find that there was any that ever trusted in the Lord, and was confounded.* So coming home [does this imply that Bunyan had been in Church when this 'sentence fell with weight upon' his spirit?], I presently went to my Bible, to see if I could find that saying, not doubting but to find it presently; for it was so fresh, and with such strength and comfort on my spirit, that I was as if it talked with me.

'Well, I looked, but I found it not; [16] only it abode upon me . . . Thus I continued above a year, and could not find the place; but at last, casting my eye into the *Apocrypha* books, I found it in *Ecclesiasticus*. Ecclus. 2:10.'

It is curious to observe how Bunyan almost apologizes for

16. Alexander Cruden's concordance to the Bible and the Apocrypha had, of course, not yet appeared. Although the first American edition of Cruden (Philadelphia, 1806), like many British editions, contained his separate concordance to the Apocrypha, unfortunately most present-day reprints, though advertised as 'complete,' lack the concordance to the Apocrypha.

finding anything helpful in these writings at all! He is honest
enough, however, to confess that, 'This, at the first, did somewhat daunt me; but because by this time I had got more experience of the love and kindness of God, it troubled me the less;
especially when I considered, that though it was not in those
Texts that we call Holy and Canonical, yet forasmuch as this
sentence was the sum and substance of many of the Promises, it
was my duty to take the comfort of it; and I bless God for that
word, for it was of God to me.' He concludes this moving account with the admission, 'That word doth still, at times, shine
before my face.'[17]

On the Continent, Protestant theologians were also involved
in controversy over the Apocrypha. At the Synod of Dort (1618
-19) Gomarus of Leyden and Diodati of Geneva, along with
other representatives of the Reformed Churches, demanded the
exclusion of several of the Apocryphal books (Esdras, Tobit,
Judith, and Bel and the Dragon) from printed editions of the
Bible. This the Synod refused to do. At the same time members
of the Synod spoke strongly against them and adopted the Belgic Confession of 1561, with its clear demarcation between
canonical and Apocryphal books (quoted above, p. 190). The
new official Bible, which the Synod had decreed, included the
Apocrypha; only, for the consolation of the vanquished, an
offer was made to bestow less pains on them than on the canonical books, and to print them in smaller type with marginal notes
calling attention to each divergence from doctrines taught by
the canonical Scriptures. It was also recommended that they be

17. *Grace Abounding*, section 62ff. Is it too far-fetched to speculate that
if the Apocrypha had not been included in a poor man's Bible in 1652 or had
not been read as Lessons in Church services even in the days of the Common-
wealth, Bunyan might never have overcome his spiritual despondency, and
consequently might never have written his immortal allegory, *Pilgrim's
Progress?*

put at the end of the Bible, after the New Testament and with a space between.

One of the most recent disputes of some consequence over the Apocrypha took place during the first part of the nineteenth century. From its first organization in 1804, the British and Foreign Bible Society in London had been accustomed to give aid to affiliated societies on the Continent which circulated various editions of the Scriptures (chiefly Luther's German translation), all of which contained the books of the Apocrypha. Opposition to this policy arose among some of the auxiliary societies, particularly those at Edinburgh and Glasgow. For more than a decade there was a continual discussion of the subject in the pulpit and press of Great Britain. The Edinburgh Bible Society denounced the Apocrypha as 'replete with instances of vanity, flattery, idle curiosity, affectation of learning, and other blemishes; with frivolous, absurd, false, superstitious, and contradictory statements.'[18] Others, admitting that the Apocrypha were uninspired and were marred with many questionable features, urged that the addition of these books facilitated the circulation of the Scriptures in European countries where people, being accustomed to their presence in most editions, would be suspicious of an edition which lacked what for centuries had been generally included. Lamentably enough, the whole controversy was characterized by unparalleled bitterness, which often degenerated into gross scurrility. Especially disgraceful were several series of pictures caricaturing eminent Scottish divines who had been outspoken on each side of the controversy.[19] After a bitter dissension within the Bible Society itself,

18. *Statement . . . Relative to the Circulation of the Apocrypha* (Edinburgh, 1825), Appendix, p. 8.

19. See [Herbert Pentin], 'The Edinburgh Apocrypha Controversy in Caricature, 1827–28,' *International Journal of Apocrypha*, Series VIII, No. 29 (April 1912), pp. 29–33, and No. 31 (October 1912), pp. 76–78. On the con-

which had passed a succession of mutually contradictory motions, it was finally resolved in 1827 that the fundamental law of the Society forbade its circulating the Apocrypha,[20] and that therefore no persons or societies which circulated the Apocrypha could receive aid from the Society. Several other Bible Societies, including the American Bible Society, which was founded at New York in 1816, followed the decision and practice of the London Society. As a consequence it was not long before commercial publishers, for obvious reasons of economy, likewise ceased including the Apocryphal books in their editions of the Bible, and it soon became difficult to obtain ordinary editions of the Bible with the Apocrypha.

About the middle of the nineteenth century, controversy over the Apocrypha was revived in Germany. The immediate occasion of the resumption of the strife was the offering by an 'Inner Mission' Society in Karlsruhe, in 1851, of prizes for the best works on the character and worth of the Apocrypha. The two monographs which were awarded the first and second prizes exposed the deficiencies of these books and urged that they be. dropped from editions of the Bible. A rash of books, dissertations, pamphlets, and sermons followed. Champions for the re-

troversy in general, see Henry F. Henderson, *The Religious Controversies in Scotland* (Edinburgh, 1905), chapter 6, and the various histories of the British and Foreign Bible Society, such as those by George Browne (Vol. I, [London, 1859], pp. 94–101 and 360ff.) and William Canton (Vol. II [London, 1904], pp. 224ff.).

20. It is a fact, not widely known even in Great Britain, that in the elaborate religious and civil ceremony at the crowning of a King or Queen of the British Empire, the copy of the Bible which the newly invested monarch kisses before signing the coronation oath must contain the books of the Apocrypha. An embarrassing situation occurred at the coronation of Edward VII in 1901 when, at almost the last minute in the preparations for the occasion, the specially bound copy of the Bible provided for the ceremony by the British and Foreign Bible Society was refused and another copy was secured which contained the Apocrypha.

tention of the Apocrypha in published editions of the Scriptures included persons of even the most conservative position theologically (for example, Rudolf Stier and E. W. Hengstenberg). One of the happy consequences of this controversy was that leading scholars on the Continent were led to make exhaustive critical studies of these books, the fruits of which greatly enriched theological and philological literature.

By way of summarizing and classifying various attitudes toward the Apocrypha, it is apparent that the chief difference lies between the position of the Roman Catholic Church and that of the Protestant Churches. At the Council of Trent in the mid-sixteenth century the former enunciated a position in opposition to the Reformers, who had reiterated the primacy of the Hebrew canon of Scripture of the books of the Old Testament. Among the several Protestant Churches today, none of which regards the Apocrypha as the Word of God, various degrees of respect are shown the Apocryphal books. The Church that accords them the greatest degree of consideration is the Anglican or Episcopal Church. As was mentioned earlier, the Lectionary attached to the Prayer Book from the first edition of Edward VI (1549) onward has always contained prescribed and alternative Lessons from the Apocrypha. The latest revision of the Lectionary used by the Anglican Church in Great Britain contains forty-four Lessons from the Apocrypha, and the latest revision of the Lectionary used by the Protestant Episcopal Church in America contains one hundred and ten such Lessons. Furthermore, in the Communion Service of the Anglican and the Episcopal Churches, among the Offertory sentences, which are otherwise all taken from the New Testament or the Psalms and Proverbs, two are taken from the book of Tobit. These have stood in all revisions of the Prayer Book from the first edition to the present. In general the other Protestant Churches pay little heed to the Apocrypha—though Luther, Œcolampadius, the translators of the Geneva Bible, and other leaders of the Reformation approved and/or recommended these books as useful for Christians to read.

XVIII

The Pervasive Influence of the Apocrypha

DOWN THROUGH THE CENTURIES THE BOOKS OF THE APOCRYPHA HAVE LEFT THEIR MARK IN MANY PLACES AND IN MANY MEDIA; NOT ONLY have they inspired homilies, meditations, and liturgical forms, but poets, dramatists, composers, and artists have drawn freely upon them for subject matter. Common proverbs and familiar names are derived from these books. Even the discovery of the New World can be traced in part to the influence of a passage in II Esdras upon Christopher Columbus. In what follows the reader will find a representative selection chosen from a wealth of material and arranged under the headings of 'English Literature,' 'Music,' 'Art,' and 'Miscellaneous.'

A. *English Literature*

In the history of English literature the influence of the Apocrypha is as pronounced as it is pervasive. By allusion to charac-

ters and passages in the Apocrypha and by adoption of plots and
motifs from these books, many authors disclose their dependence upon this ancient body of literature.

The earliest Englishman, according to Bede, to use Scripture
as a basis for poetical composition was Caedmon. In his poetical
paraphrase of Daniel this Anglo-Saxon poet of the seventh century included portions of the Prayer of Azariah and the Song of
the Three Young Men.

Sometime during the ninth or tenth century an unknown
author, using the West-Saxon dialect, turned the story of Judith
into an Old English epic, transforming at the same time the
heroine into a Christian. It is possible that the poem was written
to celebrate the prowess of Æthelflæd, 'The Lady of the Mer-
cians,' who, like the Hebrew Judith, delivered her people from
the fury of heathen Northmen, and re-established their power.
Originally comprising twelve cantos, only the last three (corresponding to the book of Judith 12:10 to 16:1), have been preserved entire. The following quotation of the section depicting
Judith's act of bravery in killing Holofernes will illustrate the
poet's literary art as well as his interest in Holofernes's punishment in the after-life—of which the original story says nothing.

> ... Then did the wavy-haired
> Smite the foeman with flashing sword,
> The hostile-minded, so that his head
> Was half-way sundered, and he lay swooning,
> Dire-wounded and drunken. Not yet was he dead,
> Bereft of his soul; again she smote,
> The valiant virgin, with nerve and vigor,
> The heathen hound, so that his head rolled
> Forth on the floor; the body so foul
> Lay lifeless behind, but the soul sped away,
> Sank beneath the abyss, and there was abased,
> Ever thereafter pinioned with pangs,

Bewound by serpents and bound by torments,
Fastened firm in the flaming of hell,
Since hence he removed. Nor may he hope ever
That he shall evade from that vault of vipers,
But, drowned in darkness, there shall dwell,
Ever for ages without end,
In that black abode, bereft of bliss.[1]

Among the many characters depicted by Chaucer in his immortal *Canterbury Tales*, Holofernes and Judith are included:

But tak kepe for the deeth of Olofern;
Amidde his host he dronke lay a night,
With-inne his tent, large as is a bern,
And yit, for al his pompe and al his might,
Iudith, a womman, as he lay upright,
Sleping, his heed of smoot, and from his tente
Ful prively she stal from every wight,
And with his heed unto hir toun she wente.

('The Monkes Tale,' lines 3757–64).

In 'The Tale of Melibeus' Chaucer refers repeatedly to Jesus the son of Sirach (lines 2185, 2235, etc.), and to Judas Maccabaeus (lines 2848f.).

During the fourteenth and fifteenth centuries a poem called 'The Pistill of Susan' [2] circulated in Scotland. Written in stanzas of thirteen lines and characterized by an unusual combination of alliteration and rime, this piece of early Scottish literature evidently enjoyed more than a small degree of popularity, if we

1. The translation is that of A. S. Cook in his edition, *Judith, an Old English Epic Fragment* (Boston, 1888), p. 11. The passage is the poet's expansion of part of one verse in the original story, namely Judith 13:8a.

2. The word *Pistill* is a corruption of the word *Epistle* and probably points to the time when the story of Susanna was read in church as the Epistle Lesson. In the Sarum Rite and the modern Roman Rite it is appointed for the Saturday after the third Sunday in Lent.

may judge from the fact that five slightly divergent forms of it have come down to us. The author, who is thought to have been a certain Huchown (Hugh) of Ayrshire in west Scotland, adorned the Apocryphal story with many imaginative details. For example, the trees and birds in Joakim's garden, where Susanna was accustomed to stroll, are described at length. A part of the sixth stanza will illustrate this aspect of the poem.

> The palme and the popeler, the peres and the plowine,
> The junipere gentill, ioynying hem bytwene,
>
> . . . .
>
> There were popyniayes prest,
> Nightyngales upon nest,
> Blithe briddes of the best,
> On blosmes to sytte.[3]

Among noteworthy Elizabethan ballads, William Elderton's early production, 'The Constancy of Susanna,' which was licensed by Thomas Colwell in 1562–63, was very popular. The first lines are as follows.

> There dwelt a man in Babylon,
>   Of reputation great by fame;
> He tooke to wife a faire woman,
>   Susanna she was call'd by name;
> A woman faire and vertuous:
>   Lady, lady,
> Why should wee not of her learne thus to lieue godly?

The tune to which the words were set was catchy, and the ballad had a wide sale. A snatch of it is quoted by Shakespeare

---

3. F. J. Amours, *Scottish Alliterative Poems in Riming Stanzas* (The Scottish Text Society, Edinburgh, 1897), pp. 201ff.

in *Twelfth Night*, II, iii, 84, where Sir Toby Belch sings, 'There dwelt a man in Babylon, lady lady!'

How conversant Shakespeare was with the contents of the Bible is a question, like many another question concerned with the Bard of Avon, which has been hotly debated. On the one hand, Sir Sidney Lee argued that the poet's knowledge of the Scriptures was quite superficial, not much more than that which a clever boy would be likely to pick up at church on Sundays. On the other hand, others, such as Thomas Carter and Richmond Noble, have demonstrated a deep and pervasive influence from the Bible (especially the Geneva Version) in his literary works. With respect to the amount of influence which the books of the Apocrypha had on Shakespeare, the fact that two of the poet's daughters have the names of two of the chief heroines of the Apocrypha—Susanna and Judith—may or may not be a mere coincidence. Of greater significance is the fact that more than eighty passages in his plays have been found to reflect more or less clearly allusions to eleven Apocryphal books.[4] Of this number the overwhelming majority come from the book of Ecclesiasticus. Examples of influence from various Apocryphal books are the following. *The Merchant of Venice* contains an unmistakable reference to the climactic scene in the story of Susanna, where Shylock exclaims of Portia:

A Daniel come to judgment! yea, a Daniel!
O wise young Judge, how I do honour thee! (iv. i. 222).

Now, there is nothing in the canonical Book of Daniel to suggest that the Seer ever acted in a judicial capacity; but the denouement of the story of Susanna turns precisely on Daniel's wisdom

4. See Thomas Carter, *Shakespeare and Holy Scripture, with the Version He Used* (London, 1905), and especially Richmond Noble, *Shakespeare's Biblical Knowledge and Use of the Book of Common Prayer* (London, 1935).

in detecting the crime of the two lustful elders. In the same play
the comparison in the frequently quoted lines (IV. i. 184f.):

> The quality of mercy is not strain'd,
> It droppeth as the gentle rain from heaven
> Upon the place beneath . . .

had been anticipated in Ben Sira's similitude many centuries
before: 'Mercy is seasonable in the time of affliction, as clouds
of rain in the time of drought' (Ecclus. 35:20).

Holofernes is the name given to the schoolmaster in *Love's
Labour's Lost*. Moreover, he fills the role of Judas Maccabaeus
in the pageant, 'The Nine Worthies of the World,' which is included in *Love's Labour's Lost*. Still more significantly, in
Lear's speech to Gloucester (IV. vi. 182ff.) the passage,

> We came crying hither:
> Thou know'st the first time that we smell the air,
> We wawle and cry. I will preach to thee: mark.
>
> . . . .
>
> When we are born, we cry that we are come
> To this great stage of fooles . . .

bears a striking resemblance to a verse in the Wisdom of Solomon, which in the Geneva Version reads: 'When I was borne I
received the common aire and fell upon the earth which is of like
nature, crying and weeping at the first, as all others doe' (7:3).

That John Milton was as familiar with the Apocrypha as with
the Old and New Testaments is not to be wondered at, for until
he reached his manhood Bibles without the books of the Apocrypha were practically unknown in England. His indebtedness
to the book of Wisdom in *Paradise Lost* is quite apparent, and
his conception of the archangel Uriel is undoubtedly based

largely on II Esdras. To judge by the number of references in his works to the Apocrypha, it would seem that among the narrative books the stories of Tobit and of the Maccabees attracted him most. [5]

Notable among American literary figures who have drawn upon the books of the Apocrypha is Henry Wadsworth Longfellow. His *New England Tragedies* contains references to I and II Maccabees, and the chief episodes of the stirring Maccabean uprising are included in his poetic dramatization, *Judas Maccabaeus*. Particularly moving in the latter is the opening scene of Act II, depicting the anguish of the Jewish mother whose seven sons were being tortured and killed before her eyes.

THE MOTHER

Four! already four!
Three are still living; nay, they are all living,
Half here, half there. Make haste, Antiochus,
To reunite us; for the sword that cleaves
These miserable bodies makes a door
Through which our souls, impatient of release,
Rush to each other's arms.

FIFTH VOICE (*within*)

Thou hast the power;
Thou doest what thou wilt. Abide awhile,
And thou shalt see the power of God, and how
He will torment thee and thy seed.

THE MOTHER

O hasten;
Why dost thou pause? Thou who hast slain already

---

5. For evidence of Milton's wide knowledge of extra-Biblical religious works, see Grant McColley, 'The Book of Enoch and Paradise Lost,' *Harvard Theological Review*, Vol. XXXI (1938), pp. 21-39, especially footnote 6.

> So many Hebrew women, and hast hung
> Their murdered infants round their necks, slay me;
> For I too am a woman, and these boys
> Are mine. Make haste to slay us all,
> And hang my lifeless babes about my neck.

Were one to ask which of the several Apocryphal books has the honor of having exerted the widest influence in European and American literature, the palm would probably be awarded to the story of Judith. Inspiration from this book has fired the imagination of poets, dramatists, and novelists from the ninth century to the present. A chronological list of such versions in English and in German, brought down to 1921, includes more than one hundred examples.[6] In considering the reasons for this popularity one finds that the Apocryphal story has more than one of the essential characteristics of great literature. It embodies a noble idea, the setting is picturesque, and the characters and action provide contrast, dramatic suspense, and enthusiasm.[7]

B. *Music*

It is widely known that many hymns, both ancient and modern, owe their form and content to notable passages in the Bible. It is less widely known that more than one hymn writer has drawn inspiration, as well as, in some cases, the words them-

6. Edna Purdie, *The Story of Judith in German and English Literature* ('Bibliothèque de la revue de littératur comparée,' Tome xxxix; Paris, 1927), pp. 1–22. To her long list there must be added Thompson Buchanan's historical novel, *Judith Triumphant*, published in 1905 (New York and London).

7. For other examples of the influence of the Apocrypha on literature, see below, pp. 235ff.

selves, from the Apocrypha. For example, the noble hymn of thanksgiving, 'Nun danket alle Gott,' written by Pastor Martin Rinkart about 1636 when the Thirty Years' War was near its end, is dependent upon a passage in Ecclesiasticus. Two stanzas of the hymn, as translated by Catherine Winkworth, are the following (the lines which are particularly close to Ecclesiasticus are italicized):

Now thank we all our God
　With heart and hands and voices,
Who wondrous things hath done,
　In whom His world rejoices;
Who, from our mother's arms,
　Hath blessed us on our way
With countless gifts of love,
　And still is ours today.

O may this bounteous God
　Through all our life be near us,
With ever joyful hearts
　And blessed peace to cheer us;
And keep us in His grace,
　And guide us when perplexed,
And free us from all ills
　In this world and the next.

The passage from Ecclesiasticus follows (for purposes of comparison, the King James Version is quoted, since this was the English version current when Miss Winkworth translated Rinkart's hymn in 1858; still closer is the parallel between Rinkart's German hymn and Luther's translation of the passage in Sirach, which begins 'Nun danket alle Gott'):

Now therefore bless ye the God of all, which only doeth wondrous things every where, which exalteth our days from the womb, and dealeth with us according to his mercy. He grant us joyfulness of heart, and that peace may be in our days in Israel forever: that he would confirm his mercy with us, and deliver us at his time! (50:22–24).

The familiar advent hymn, 'O Come, O Come, Emmanuel,' dating from about the twelfth century and translated by John Mason Neale in the last century, contains an obvious paraphrase of the Wisdom of Solomon (8:1), 'Wisdom reacheth from one end to another mightily: and sweetly doth she order all things' (King James Version). The second stanza of the hymn (which is not always printed in modern hymnals) begins:

> O come, thou Wisdom from on high,
> Who orderest all things mightily.

Less apparent in English but no less real is the influence of Ecclus. 24:20–21 on the Jubilee-Rhythm of St. Bernard of Clairvaux. Edward Caswall's partial translation of this hymn (in 1849) begins:

> Jesus, the very thought of Thee
> With sweetness fills my breast.

This is a Christian application of the words originally applied to Wisdom in Ecclus. 24:19,

> For the remembrance of me [that is, Wisdom] is
> sweeter than honey,
> and my inheritance than the honeycomb.

The dependence is much more striking in Latin. The opening stanza of Bernard's famous hymn is:

> Jesu dulcis memoria
> Dans vera cordis gaudia,

> Sed super mel et omnia
> Eius dulcis praesentia.

With this the Vulgate of Ecclus. 24:27–28 may be compared:

> Spiritus enim meus super mel dulcis,
> Et haereditas mea super mel et favum,
> Memoria mea in generationes saeculorum.

Later in St. Bernard's hymn the words

> Qui te gustant, esuriunt,
> Qui bibunt, adhuc sitiunt

reproduce the thought of the Vulgate of Ecclus. 24:29:

> Qui edunt me adhuc esurient,
> Et qui bibunt me adhuc sitient.

Ideas expressed in several Christmas hymns, including the popular 'It Came Upon the Midnight Clear' and 'Silent Night,' are indirectly indebted to the Apocrypha. In the New Testament accounts of the Nativity, nothing is said of the hour of Jesus' birth. Since, however, the shepherds to whom the angelic chorus appeared were 'keeping watch over their flock by night' (Luke 2:8), it has often been inferred that Mary gave birth to her first-born Son at night-time; the phrase, 'for to you is born this *day* in the city of David a Savior' (2:11), is therefore to be taken in a general sense. The popular and widespread identification of the hour of Jesus' birth as midnight is doubtless traceable indirectly to a remarkable passage in the Wisdom of Solomon. As has been mentioned above (p. 76), the early Church Fathers took Wis. 18:14–16 out of its context, which refers to the destruction of the first-born Egyptians at the time of the Exodus, and applied it to Jesus Christ, the eternal Word of God. The passage is:

> For while gentle silence enveloped all things
> and *night in its swift course was now half gone*,
> thy all-powerful word [logos] leaped from heaven, from the
>   royal throne,
> into the midst of the land that was doomed,
> a stern warrior carrying the sharp sword of thy authentic
>   command,
> and stood and filled all things with death,
> and touched heaven while standing on the earth.

Moreover, the reference to silence in the opening words of this passage in Wisdom came to be united with the reference to peace mentioned in the angelic chorus at Jesus' nativity ('. . . Peace on earth . . .' Luke 2:14). This combination of the ideas of silence and of peace prevailing at the time of Jesus' birth are found, for example, in Milton's hymn, 'On the Morning of Christ's Nativity,'

> No war or battle's sound
> Was heard the world around

> . . . .

> But peaceful was the night
> Wherein the Prince of Light
>   His reign of peace upon the Earth began.

The same combination also appears in the familiar words of one of the most beloved of Christmas carols:

> Silent night, holy night!
> All is calm, all is bright,
> Round yon Virgin Mother and Child!

Holy Infant, so tender and mild,
Sleep in heavenly peace,
Sleep in heavenly peace.

(Joseph Mohr, 1818)

Thus, by a curious, not to say ironical, twist of fortune, a passage which speaks of a stern warrior with a sword filling a doomed land with death has had its share in fixing popular traditions of the time and circumstances of the birth of the Prince of Peace.

These half a dozen examples will serve as representatives of a much greater number of hymns that show some degree of influence from the Apocrypha. Probably most churchgoers would be surprised to learn how many of the hymns they sing Sunday after Sunday have been partially inspired by sentiments from intertestamental literature. In the latest edition of *The Methodist Hymn-Book*, published in London in 1933, one finds forty-three hymns that make some allusion to various books of the Apocrypha.[7] In the previous edition (1904) of the same hymn book there were sixty-nine hymns showing such influence. In both editions it happens that the overwhelming majority of instances involve hymns which were written by Charles Wesley. (By way of explanation of this fact, it will be recalled that Charles Wesley, like his brother John, was ordained as a minister of the Anglican Church, within whose fold he remained all his life, and in which he had been accustomed to the hearing and the reading of the prescribed Lectionary selections from the Apocrypha.) Of all of Charles Wesley's hymns perhaps the best-known is, 'Jesus, Lover of my soul,' the first line of which is a Christian adaptation of an exquisite phrase in Wisdom 11:

7. The information has been compiled by the Rev. J. Henry Martin in the *Subject, Textual and Lineal Indexes to the Methodist Hymn-Book* (London, n.d.).

26, 'Thou sparest all things, for all are Thine, O Sovran Lord, Lover of the soul' (literally translated).

The influence of the books of the Apocrypha can also be traced in many an anthem, cantata, and oratorio. One thinks at once of George Frederick Handel's touchingly beautiful funeral anthem, 'The Ways of Zion do Mourn,' the words of which are derived, in part, from Ecclus. 44:14. This anthem was composed in 1737 for the interment of Queen Caroline in Westminster Abbey, and has often been sung at royal funerals. In 1873 Dr. Samuel Sebastian Wesley chose the same section in Ecclesiasticus as the basis of an anthem to be used at a service of commemoration at Clifton College. Such was his creative resourcefulness that in the following year Dr. Wesley composed a second anthem for the same words, but with a less difficult musical setting.

The comforting and elevating words in Wisdom, so often used at funeral services,

> The souls of the righteous are in the hand of God,
> And there shall no torment touch them.
> In the sight of the unwise they seemed to die,
> . . . But they are in peace (Wis. 3:1ff. King James Version),

have been worthily set to music in an anthem, entitled 'Souls of the Righteous,' by the noted composer, T. Tertius Noble. Another modern composer, John E. West, is responsible for a beautiful musical setting for the words from Baruch 5:8 and 9, beginning, 'The woods and every sweetsmelling tree shall overshadow Israel by the commandment of God.' This composition, entitled 'The Woods and Every Sweetsmelling Tree,' is appropriately designated an anthem for harvest time.

Occasionally a composer, though dealing with a Biblical subject, has also included material from the Apocrypha. Such, for example, is true of John Stainer's well-known cantata entitled 'The Daughter of Jairus.' Though it deals primarily with Jesus' raising of the daughter of Jairus, one of the poignantly beautiful choruses contains the words, 'In the death of a man there is no remedy, neither was there any man known to have return'd from the grave; the breath in our nostrils is as smoke, and a little spark in the moving of our hearts; our bodies shall be turned to ashes, and our spirit shall vanish as the soft air. . . . Come on, let us enjoy the good things of the present. Let no flow'r of the spring pass by us; let us crown ourselves with rosebuds before they be wither'd. . . . This man professeth to have the knowledge of God; He was made to reprove our thoughts; Let us see if His words be true!' As will be observed, for this chorus Stainer has skillfully woven together a cento of phrases and clauses extracted from Wis. 2:1, 2, 3, 6, 7, 8, 13, 14, and 17.

Among oratorios based on the Apocrypha, Handel has supplied several. His *Susanna* may be called the sister oratorio to *Solomon,* for it was composed immediately after that work, in the year 1748. While *Solomon* is famous principally for its splendid series of choruses, the strength of *Susanna* lies much more in the beauty, sometimes dramatic and sometimes idyllic, of its solos. Handel took a certain amount of liberty in expanding the story of Susanna. Thus, the first part of the oratorio includes a series of songs describing the happy married life of Susanna and Joakim. This is interrupted by the sudden departure of Joakim on a journey, and the consequent foreboding of evil by Susanna, who in turn is comforted by the chorus. While in the garden Susanna's maid entertains her mistress by singing the charming cavatina, 'Ask if yon damask rose be sweet.' Their solitude is invaded by the two elders who first tempt Susanna in vain and then bring a false accusation against her. In this scene are especially to be noticed the dramatic trio, 'Away, away,' and Susanna's poignant and celebrated song, 'If guiltless blood be your intent.'

For two other oratorios based on the Apocrypha, Handel secured the co-operation of a Greek scholar and antiquary, the Reverend Thomas Morell, D.D., who wrote the librettos. Furnished with scholarly information, supplied by Morell, in 1746 Handel composed *Judas Maccabaeus*, a masterpiece of dramatic power. The chorus, 'We worship God, and God alone,' is not only a superb example of contrapuntal skill and melodious invention, but one of the grandest confessions of faith ever expressed in music. The famous chorus, 'See, the conquering Hero Comes,' was written originally for the oratorio *Joshua*, but was transferred to *Judas Maccabaeus* on the occasion of the Duke of Cumberland's return from Scotland after his victory at Culloden in 1745.[8] Besides this triumphal chorus, other parts of the oratorio are still sung and loved throughout the musical world, as for example, Judas's solo 'Sound an Alarm,' the duet, 'O Lovely Peace,' and the final 'Hallelujah.' Another oratorio, *Alexander Balus*, which is an historical continuation of *Judas Maccabaeus* and involves the story of the love of the King of Syria for Cleopatra, daughter of Ptolemy, was composed in 1747. In spite of its undeniably fine music, this composition has suffered from neglect and oblivion more completely, perhaps, than any other oratorio of Handel. This neglect is probably in

8. Morell dedicated the libretto (or word-book, as it was called) of *Judas Maccabaeus* to Prince William, Duke of Cumberland, as a 'Faint Portraiture of a Truly Wise, Valiant, and Virtuous Commander.' In fact, according to Morell's memoirs, written about 1764, the whole oratorio 'was designed as a compliment to the Duke of Cumberland upon his returning victorious from Scotland,' the Duke being personified in the Jewish hero. The Duke subsequently made a handsome present to Morell (see Otto Erich Deutsch, *Handel, A Documentary Biography* [New York, c. 1955], pp. 851ff).

great measure due to the uninteresting characters, the shapeless plot, and the artificial poetry of the libretto.[9]

Among the many compositions of Thomas Augustine Arne, Mus. Doc. (1710–78), who was one of the foremost English composers of the eighteenth century, is the oratorio, *Judith, a Sacred Drama*, which is noteworthy as being the first oratorio in which female voices were introduced into the choruses. The libretto, which was written by the dramatist, Isaac Bickerstaffe, follows closely the story as it appears in the Apocryphal book.

Among less well-known oratorios inspired by the Apocrypha are four compositions which were written earlier this century. Sir C. Villiers Stanford's *The Three Holy Children* is based on the Apocryphal Addition to Daniel of this name; some of the words of this scholarly composition are also selected from the Psalms, Isaiah, and Baruch (4:36, 37), and from a hymn to Bel in an Assyrian inscription. Another of the Apocryphal Additions to Daniel is represented in Dr. Walter Stokes's oratorio, *The Idol Bel.* Sir C. Hubert H. Parry's *Judith, or the Regeneration of Manasseh*, treats the exploits of Judith as a historical event in the reign of King Manasseh. Abridging and rearranging the libretto prepared by Dr. Morell for Handel, Abraham Binder in 1917 composed an oratorio on the Maccabees for children, which was first performed at the New York Y.M.H.A. in that year.

There is space to mention only a few operas based upon themes from the Apocrypha. At an early date in operatic history, the story of Judith was discovered to lend itself admirably

9. According to a recent biographer of Handel, Morell was 'a worthy person given to writing execrable poetry' (Newman Flower, *George Frideric Handel, His Personality and His Times* [New York, 1948], p. 316).

to dramatic presentation. An Italian opera based on this story, *Giuditta*, written by Andrea Salvadori with music by Marco da Gagliano, was performed in Florence in 1626. This opera was the source of a *Singspiel* composed in 1635 by Martin Opitz, who has the distinction of being the first to introduce the operatic form into Germany. In both of these productions one observes that the original narrative has been overlaid with so much courtly love-making and gallantry as almost to transform Holofernes and Judith into romantic lovers.

In the following century a still more decided incursion of Italian romance is evident in the opera on Holofernes by Joachim Beccau, published at Hamburg in 1720. Its title, *L'Amor insanguinato*, prepares one for the depiction of Holofernes as the courtier-lover, and one is not surprised that wherever Judith goes, both Jew and pagan are smitten by her beauty. The extent to which this amorous theme is pushed can be seen from Beccau's making even Achior the lover of a princess of Midian!

Much truer to the original, both in spirit and in letter, is the lengthy opera, *The Maccabees*, composed in 1875 by the noted Russian pianist and composer, Anton Rubinstein. The libretto was written by one of his collaborators, Dr. H. S. von Mosenthal. Rubinstein's overwhelming prepossession with the idea of producing huge, unwieldy Biblical and Jewish dramas, half opera, half oratorio (including *The Tower of Babel, Moses, Sulamith* [deals with the Song of Solomon], and *Christus,* was somehow bound up with his anti-Wagnerism, which in turn had been provoked by Wagner's pronounced anti-Semitism.

C. *Art*

During the Renaissance and later not a few famous painters chose subjects from the books of the Apocrypha. At the risk of making a somewhat arbitrary selection from many examples, one observes that of paintings inspired by the Apocrypha those depicting Judith, Tobit, and Susanna figure most frequently among the works of the old masters.

The story of Judith, 'that brave woman who did so manfully,' is interpreted in different ways by different artists. Some painters represent Judith's act in slaying Holofernes as an act of justice; others, as an act of vengeance; others, as an act of murder. The best known paintings of Judith in the principal galleries of Europe and America include the following:

AUSTRIA

Gsell Coll.: — Judith (Varotari)
Vienna Gal.: — Judith with the Head of Holofernes (Veronese)
Judith (Varotari)

FRANCE

Lyons Museum: — Judith (Claude Ziegler)
Marseilles Museum: — Judith and Holofernes (H. Regnault)
Nantes Museum: — Judith and Holofernes (Manfredi)
Paris, The Louvre: — Judith and Holofernes (Vernet)
Paris, Coll. Dannat: — Judith with the Head of Holofernes
(John Metsys)

GERMANY

Berlin Gal: — Judith (Rembrandt)—Judith (Romanino)
Dresden: — Judith with the Head of Holofernes (Varotari)

GREAT BRITAIN

> *Edinburgh, Scottish National Gal.*: — The Deliverance of
> Bethulia (a trio of pictures by William Etty)
> *Hampton Court Palace*: — Judith with the Head of Holofernes
> (four pictures, by C. Allori (?), by Guido (?), and by
> Teniers after P. Veronese, and by a student of C. Allori)
> — Judith with her Attendant (Maratti)

HOLLAND

> *The Hague, Royal Museum*: — Judith with the Head of Holo-
> fernes (P. van Dyck)

ITALY

> *Bologna, Gal. Hercolani*: — Judith and Holofernes (Fontana)
> *Florence, Pitti Palace*: — Judith with the Head of Holofernes
> (C. Allori) — Judith and her Maid (A. Gentileschi)
> *Florence, Uffizi Gal.*: — Holofernes Dead in his Tent (Botti-
> celli) — The Return of Judith to Bethulia (Botticelli)
> — Judith (Mantegna) — Judith (Palma Vecchio)
> *Genoa, Pal. Brignole*: — Judith (Veronese)
> *Naples, San Martino*: — Triumph of Judith (Fa Presto)
> *Reggio, Ch. of the Madonna*: — Judith and Holofernes (Spada)
> *Rome, Capitol*: — Judith (Baldassare)
> *Vatican City, Sistine Chapel*: — Judith with the Head of Holo-
> fernes (Michelangelo)
> *Venice, Academy*: — Judith (Varotari)

RUSSIA

> *Leningrad, The Hermitage*: — Judith (Giorgione)

SPAIN

> *Madrid, Museum*: — Judith and Holofernes (three scenes,
> Tintoretto)

UNITED STATES

Cincinnati, Art Museum: — Judith with the Head of Holofernes (Botticelli)

Detroit, Institute of Arts: — Judith with the Head of Holofernes (Titian)

New York, Metropolitan Museum: — Judith with the Head of Holofernes (Cranach)

Washington, D.C., National Gal.: — Judith with the Head of Holofernes (a drawing, Mantegna) — Judith with the Head of Holofernes (Matteo di Giovanni)

Of all of these and many others, John Ruskin, who referred to the 'million of vile pictures' of Judith (*Mornings in Florence*), considered Botticelli's 'The Return of Judith to Bethulia' to be the only true picture of the vanquisher of Nebuchadnezzar's commander-in-chief. Ruskin continues, 'She is not merely the Jewish Delilah to the Assyrian Samson; but the mightiest, purest, brightest type of high passion in severe womanhood offered to our human memory.'

Paintings inspired by the book of Tobit are the following.

BELGIUM

Antwerp: — The Healing of Tobias (John Metsys)

Opbraekel, near Oudenaarde: — Departure and Return of Tobit (Paelinck)

FRANCE

Besançon: — Tobit Restoring his Father's Sight (Lancrenon)

Montpellier Mus.: — Tobit's Wedding Night (Le Sueur)

Paris, The Louvre: — Tobias Curing his Father (Van Hermessen) — The Angel Leaves Tobit and his Family (Rembrandt, 1637) — The Angel and Tobias (Salvatore Rosa)

Rennes, St. Germain: — Tobias Burying a Hebrew (Serrur)

GERMANY

Berlin Gal.:—The Wife of Tobit with the Goat (Rembrandt)
Dresden:—Tobit Pulling the Fish out of the Water (Domenico)
Freiburg:—Tobias and the Angel (Koninck)
Munich Gal.:—Tobit Recovering his Sight (Jan Victoors)
Stuttgart:—The Archangel and Tobias (Palma Vecchio)

GREAT BRITAIN

Bridgewater Gal.:—Tobias Blessing his Son (Jan Victoors)
Glasgow:—Tobit and the Angel (Rembrandt, 1654)
Hampton Court Palace:—Tobit and the Angel (Schiavone)
—Tobit Restoring his Father's Sight (M. de Vos)
London, Bute Coll.:—Tobit and the Angel (Karel du Jardin)
London, National Gal.:—Tobias and the Angel (Domenichino)

HOLLAND

Amsterdam:—Tobias and the Angel (Van der Neer)
Haarlem Mus.:—History of Tobias (Patinir)
Rotterdam:—Tobias Asleep under the Vine (Weenix)

ITALY

Milan, Ambrosiana:—Holy Family with Tobias and the Angel
(Pitati)
Turin:—Raphael and Tobias (The Pollaioli)
Venice S. Marcellino: — Tobias and the Angel (Titian)

RUSSIA

Leningrad, The Hermitage:—Tobias Healing his Father (Domenico)—Tobit and the Angel (Claude Lorrain)

SPAIN

Seville, La Caridad:—Tobias Burying the Strangled Man (a
sketch, Murillo)

UNITED STATES

>*New York, Metropolitan Museum*:—Tobias and the Angel
>(Ghirlandaio)
>*Washington, D.C., National Gal.*:—Tobias and the Angel (F.
>Lippi)—Tobit Blessing his Son (Puccinelli)

Pictures inspired by the story of Susanna are to be found in the following collections.

AUSTRIA

>*Vienna, Accademia*: —The Chaste Suzanna (Lauri)—Suzanna
>and the Elders (Tintoretto)
>*Gsell Coll.*:—Suzanna at the Bath (Vacarro)

DENMARK

>*Copenhagen*:—Suzanna and the Elders (Jordaens)

FRANCE

>*Lille Mus.*:—Suzanna and the Elders (Jordaens)
>*Paris, The Louvre*:—Suzanna Accused (Ant. Coypel)—Suzanna
>at the Bath (Tintoretto (2) and Santerre)—Suzanna and
>the Elders (Veronese)—The Chaste Suzanna (Vouet and
>Chassériau)

GERMANY

>*Berlin Gal.*:—Suzanna and the Elders (Rembrandt)
>*Cassel*:—Suzanna and the Elders (Douven)
>*Dresden*:—Suzanna (Fa Presto)
>*Munich, Pinakothek*:—Suzanna at the Bath (Domenichino and
>Aldorfer)

GREAT BRITAIN

>*Hampton Court Palace*:—Suzanna and the Elders (Veronese)
>*London, National Gal.*:—Suzanna and the Elders (Guido Reni
>and Lodovico Caracci)

HOLLAND

The Hague:—Suzanna at the Bath (Rembrandt, 1637)

ITALY

Florence, Pitti Pal.:—Suzanna at the Bath (Guercino)
Florence, Uffizi Gal.:—Suzanna and the Elders (Guido Reni)

SPAIN

Madrid, Museum:—Suzanna at the Bath (Guercino)
Madrid, Prado:—Suzanna and the Elders (Tintoretto)

UNITED STATES

Hartford, Connecticut, Wadsworth Athenaeum:—Suzanna and the Elders (Tiepolo, *c.* 1720)
Washington, D.C., National Gal.:—Susanna (Tintoretto, *c.* 1575)

It will be seen from this list that of the various dramatic scenes in the book, the scene of Susanna and the elders has been especially popular with the old masters, containing, as it does, the highest passion and feeling.

Though twentieth-century painters seldom choose subjects from the Apocrypha (so little are these books known today), occasionally one finds examples of the continued influence of these ancient writings. As might have been expected, it is Susanna who, more than any other character in the Apocrypha, has caught the imagination of American painters. In 1926 Arthur P. Spear's 'Susanne and the Elders' was exhibited at the Pennsylvania Academy of the Fine Arts,[10] and during the years

10. *Catalogue of the 121st Annual Exhibition*, The Pennsylvania Academy of the Fine Arts (Philadelphia, 1926).

1929–30 Jules Pascin's painting of 'Susannah and the Elders' was displayed at the Museum of Modern Art in New York.[11] Much less traditional in its treatment of the theme than these two is Thomas Hart Benton's handling of the same subject. His oil tempera, executed in 1938, transfers the locale of the story to mid-Western America of the present century, with the spire of a church showing in the background behind the two elders.[12] Likewise in a definitely modern mood is the picture of 'Tobias and the Angel' by Eugene Berman, painted in 1938. It depicts a scene of two travelers, apparently of Spanish-American ancestry, trudging along a great expanse of what may be the southwestern desert.[13]

Other books of the Apocrypha have likewise provided artists with inspiration. One of the notable paintings inspired by the books of the Maccabees is Raphael's 'Heliodorus Driven from the Temple' (II Macc. 3:1ff.), in the Vatican at Rome. The Church of the Madonna at Verona, Italy, contains a series of scenes from the books of the Maccabees painted by Tiepolo.

Besides paintings, artists in almost every other medium have chosen subjects from the Apocrypha. Were space available to make an inventory, examples could be cited from such widely divergent types of *objets d'art* as mosaics, frescoes, gems, ivories, sarcophagi, metal plaques, terra cottas, stained glass, manuscript illumination, sculpture, and tapestries.

Even in much humbler spheres inspiration from the Apocrypha has exerted its influence on craftsmen working in media

11. *Paintings by Nineteen Living Americans*, The Museum of Modern Art (New York, 1929–30).

12. *A Descriptive Catalogue of the Works of Thomas Hart Benton* (New York, 1939).

13. *Art in Progress, A Survey Prepared for the Fifteenth Anniversary of the Museum of Modern Art* (New York, 1944).

not generally considered to be artistic. For example, during the past centuries in parts of Europe and America such mundane things as cast-iron stoves have displayed scenes and maxims drawn from the Apocrypha. From the sixteenth to the nineteenth centuries, German craftsmen took pride in decorating what would otherwise have been quite commonplace stoves with pictures drawn from the classics, landscapes, saints, royal and patriotic emblems, and the Bible. In addition to subjects taken from the canonical Scriptures, stoves occasionally depicted scenes of Susanna in the garden, Judith in the camp of Holofernes, the binding of Achior by Holofernes, the siege of Bethulia, and Judith with the head of Holofernes.[14]

D. *Miscellaneous*

The influence of the books of the Apocrypha in everyday life is to be seen in the currency of certain names. Besides giving children names of persons in the Old or New Testament (such as David, Daniel, Miriam, and Rebecca; Peter, James, Paul, Mary, and Martha), parents have also chosen names such as Edna, Susanna[15] (or one of its many derivatives, such as Susan, Suzanne, and Sue), Judith (or Judy), Raphael,[16] and Tobias (or Toby) from the Apocrypha.

14. See Henry C. Mercer, *The Bible in Iron, or the Pictured Stoves and Stove Plates of the Pennsylvania Germans* . . . (Doylestown, Pa., 1914), pp. iii, 19, and 75.

15. This name also occurs once in the New Testament of one of the women who ministered to Jesus (Luke 8:3), of whom nothing more is known.

16. Though today probably most people think of it as his family name, Raphael was the given or Christian name of the great Renaissance painter (Raffaello Sanzio da Urbino).

Some of the most common expressions and proverbs come from the Apocrypha. Jesus the son of Sirach is ultimately responsible for the sententious sayings, 'A good name endures for ever' and 'You can't touch pitch without being defiled' (see Ecclus. 41:13 and 13:1). 'Birds of a feather flock together' probably had its origin in the more prosaic statement, 'The birds will resort unto their like; so will truth return unto them that practice in her' (Ecclus. 27:9, King James Version). The phrase, 'a hope full of immortality,' which has often been employed without recognizing that it is a quotation, is derived from Wisdom 3:4. The words, 'Great is Truth, and mighty above all things' (or its Latin form, 'Magna est veritas, et praevalet'), which conclude the Tale of the Three Guardsmen in I Esdras 4:41, have been used frequently as a motto or maxim in a wide variety of situations.

What student of English history, reading the story of the English martyrs, realizes that the well-known dying words of a famous Reformation bishop to his brother martyr were but an adaptation of words found in one of the books of the Apocrypha? Yet so it was. On October 16, 1555, in front of Balliol College, Oxford, Bishops Latimer and Ridley were burned at the stake. When the faggots were being lighted, Latimer spoke to Ridley the famous words, 'Be of good comfort, Master Ridley. Play the man. We shall this day light such a candle, by God's grace, in England, as I trust shall never be put out.' The figure of the candle comes from II Esdras, where God is represented as charging Ezra to rewrite the Old Testament after its fabled destruction, and saying, 'I shall light a candle of understanding in thine heart, which shall not be put out' (14:25).

Another text from the Apocrypha has been utilized more than once in eulogizing the departed. When the Prince Consort died, Queen Victoria had inscribed on the monument at Bal-

moral, which was erected 'To the beloved memory of Albert
the great and good,' the verse in Wisdom (4:13) referring to
Enoch, 'He, being made perfect in a short time, fulfilled a long
time.' [17]

This chapter may be brought to a close by referring to the
remarkable influence which the Second Book of Esdras exerted
on three persons of quite different interests—Christopher Columbus, William Whiston, and John Ruskin.

That a passage from the Apocrypha encouraged Christopher
Columbus in the enterprise which resulted in his discovery of
the New World, is a little-known but quite authentic fact. To
be sure, the verse in the Apocrypha is an erroneous comment
upon the Genesis narrative of creation, and Columbus was in
error in attributing its authority to the 'prophet Ezra' of the Old
Testament, but—for all that—it played a notable part in pushing
back the earth's horizons, both literally and figuratively. The
details are as follows.

Near the beginning of the fifteenth century, Pierre d'Ailly,
that indefatigable scholar and churchman who was Archbishop
of Cambrai and was soon to be appointed cardinal, published
a collection of geographical essays with the title *Ymago Mundi*
(1410). [18] Though denying the existence of the antipodes,
d'Ailly—like most educated men of his day— firmly believed in
the sphericity of the earth. In Chapter VIII of this book, en-

17. In a previous century 'that learned and judicious divine,' Richard
Hooker, had applied this verse to the memory of Edward VI (see his *Ecclesiastical Polity*, IV. xiv. 7).

18. A quarter of a century ago it was re-edited, with comments and French
translation, by Edmund Buron, Archivist of the Canadian Government (Paris,
1930).

titled 'De quantitate terrae habitabilis,' he develops the idea that the habitable earth is of great extent in comparison with the amount covered by water. He argues that only one-seventh of the earth's surface is covered with water and that, therefore, the ocean between the west coast of Europe and the east coast of Asia is 'of no great width' and could be navigated in a few days with a fair wind. As 'proof' for this opinion regarding the proportion of water to land he had no less authority than Ezra 'the prophet,' who had commented on God's work of creation in the following words: 'On the third day thou didst command the waters to be gathered together in the seventh part of the earth; six parts thou didst dry up and keep, so that some of them, being both planted and cultivated, might be of service before thee' (II Esdras 6:42; compare verses 47, 50, and 52).

A copy of d'Ailly's book was in Columbus's library, and nothing is more interesting than to observe the handwritten notations which the explorer entered into the margins of the page on which d'Ailly discusses the implications of the passage in Esdras relating to the relatively small extent of the sea.[19] Obviously he had been thinking about the feasibility of a westward voyage, and d'Ailly's appeal to what was popularly regarded as a quasi-canonical book was bound to exercise much influence upon his reasoning. In fact, it was partly by quoting this verse to the doubting and hesitant sovereigns of his day that Colum-

19. This copy of the *Ymago Mundi* is one of the treasures of the library at Seville, and the page referred to above, with Columbus's voluminous comments which embroider the printed text, is reproduced in facsimile in Part I, Vol. III of the 'Raccolta di documenti e studi pubblicati della R. Commissione columbiana,' namely *Autografi di Cristoforo Colombo*, ed. Cesare de Lollis (Rome, 1892), Ser. C, No. 23, Tav. 70. A plate of this page, slightly reduced in size, is given by Buron, op. cit. facing p. 320.

bus finally secured the necessary financial support for his several voyages.[20]

Among what may be called *curiosa* relating to the books of the Apocrypha was the special interest which the learned and eccentric William Whiston had in II Esdras. The author of more than fifty publications, Whiston today is known chiefly for having prepared what became the standard English translation of the works of the ancient Jewish historian, Flavius Josephus. Because Whiston was 'an English Divine of very uncommon parts, and more uncommon learning, but of a singular and extraordinary character' (so John Nichols characterizes him in his celebrated *Literary Anecdotes*),[21] it will not be inappropriate to relate several details about his life and interests. Born in 1667, Whiston had a flare for mathematics, and in 1703 became Sir Isaac Newton's successor in the Lucasian Professorship of Mathematics at Cambridge University. He published numerous treatises on astronomy, arithmetic, geometry, and kindred subjects, as well as a four-hundred-page *Essay on the Revelation of St. John* (1706) and a series of eight sermons *Upon the Accomplishment of Scripture Prophecies* (1708). In 1711 when Prince Eugene of Savoy was in England, Whiston, believing that some of the prophecies in Revelation had been fulfilled by that General's victory over the Turks in 1697, presented a copy of his *Essay on the Revelation*, with a suitable dedication, to the Prince. The Prince is said to have replied that he did not know that he had the honor of having been known to

---

20. See, among other discussions, Henry Vignand, *The Letter and Chart of Toscanelli* (New York, 1902), pp. 86ff.; John Boyd Thacher, *Christopher Columbus, His Life, His Work, His Remains*, Vol. III (New York, 1904), p. 486; and Samuel Eliot Morison, *Admiral of the Ocean Sea, Life of Christopher Columbus*, Vol. I (Boston, 1942), pp. 123ff.

21. Vol. I (London, 1812), p. 494.

St. John! At the same time, in return for Whiston's well-meaning endeavors, he sent him a present of fifteen guineas. The money was doubtless welcome, for in 1710 Whiston had been dismissed from teaching mathematics at Cambridge because of his Arian leanings. Thereafter he earned a livelihood from free-lance writing and by giving popular lectures[22] on such varied topics as eclipses, comets, earthquakes, and the symbolism of the Tabernacle of Moses and the Temple at Jerusalem. Among certain 'new discoveries' which he had made were that anointing the sick with oil is a Christian duty, that the Tatars are the lost tribes of Israel, and that the millennium would begin in 1766.

It was in connection with his consuming interest in interpreting the signs of the end of the age that he turned his attention to II Esdras. From this book, as well as from various portions of the canonical Scriptures, Whiston drew up 'the several remarkable Tokens, Signs, or Signals which the old Prophecies afford us, as belonging to the very last Times, and to the Restoration of the *Jews*; not fewer in number than ninety-nine, vastly the greatest part of which have been already fulfilled, and are sure Pledges that the rest will be fulfilled in due Time hereafter.'[23] It was particularly in II Esdras 5:1-13, 6:20-24, and 9:1-8 that Whiston found thirty-three of his 'proofs' that the end of the age was at hand. Some of these signs are general enough, and resemble similar predictions in the canonical Scriptures. For example, the 46th and the 65th 'Signals' in his total list are that 'Wickedness should be vastly encreas'd beyond the Measure of

22. These scientific and religious lectures were illustrated with models. Whiston was the first or among the first in London to use models while giving lectures.

23. William Whiston, *Memoirs . . . to which are added, his Lectures on the late remarkable Meteors and Earthquakes, and on the Future Restoration of the Jews,* Part III, 2nd ed. (London, 1753), p. 45.

former Ages' and that 'Incontinency, Vileness, and Wickedness, shall be increased upon the Earth.' Much more specific is Whiston's discussion of the credibility of a curious story regarding a certain Mary Toft, who was popularly and somewhat crudely called 'the rabbit breeder.' In 1726 this poor, illiterate farm woman of Surrey was supposed to have been delivered of a litter of fifteen (or eighteen) rabbits. According to the staid *Dictionary of National Biography*, in whose folios Mary Toft shares space with the most illustrious statesmen, ecclesiastics, and literary figures of Great Britain, the local physicians who examined the woman authenticated her story. The excitement occasioned by the rumor reached such proportions that King George I ordered his own surgeon, Cyriacus Ahlers, as well as Sir Richard Manningham, one of the chief obstetricians of the day, to make a report on the case. The latter promptly satisfied himself that the woman was an imposter seeking notoriety. To the torrent of pamphlets, lampoons, and editorials in newspapers written by those who argued for or against the truth of the tale, Whiston added his impassioned defense—for he was convinced that Mary Toft had fulfilled a prophecy made by Ezra. His indignation was particularly aroused by a pamphlet entitled *The Anatomist Dissected*, published with the nom de plume of Lemuel Gulliver.[24] This merciless satire, from the witty pen of Dean Swift of *Gulliver's Travels* fame, is ostensibly directed at Mr. St. André, the attending physician who attested the confinement (and who failed, Swift complains with

24. The full title page reads, *The Anatomist Dissected; or the man-mid-wife finely brought to bed. Being an examination of the conduct of Mr. St. André touching the late pretended rabbit-bearer.* By Lemuel Gulliver. Surgeon and anatomist to the kings of Lilliput and Balnibarbi, and fellow of the Academy of Sciences in Blefuscu. Westminster: A. Campbell, &c., 1727. See William A. Eddy, 'The Anatomist Dissected—by Lemuel Gulliver,' *Modern Language Notes*, Vol. XLI (1926), pp. 330-331.

characteristic flippancy, to 'smell a rat instead of a rabbit'); but in reality the victims of the ridicule are the Fellows of the Royal Society, whose pedantry in conducting researches in this case is properly lampooned. In one of the curiosities of theological literature, Whiston heatedly defends the veracity of this peasant woman, confessing that, for his part, he finds in 'this wonderful and supernatural Production of *Mary Toft* . . . an eminent Completion of the Prophecy' in II Esdras that at the end of the age 'women shall bring forth monsters' · (5:8)![25]

It is somewhat surprising that John Ruskin, though brought up so strictly as an Evangelical, should have cared as much as he did for the Apocryphal books. In his *Fors Clavigera* there are references and allusions to the book of Wisdom, II Esdras, Tobit, and Bel and the Dragon. To Ecclesiasticus he attributes a 'still more close and practical wisdom' than to the Psalms and Proverbs ('Our Fathers Have Told Us,' *The Bible of Amiens*, 3, 51), and, indeed, speaks of the Bible, including the Apocrypha, as 'a direct message' from God (ibid. 3, 40). Esdras was a favorite of his, and on one occasion he expounded what he regarded as the deepest meaning latent in a text of that book.

It chanced, this morning, as I sat down to finish my preface, that I had, for my introductory reading, the fifth chapter of the second book of Esdras; in which, though often read carefully before, I had never enough noticed the curious verse, 'Blood shall drop out of wood, and the stone shall give his voice, and the people shall be troubled.' Of which verse, so far as I can gather the meaning from the context, and from the rest of the chapter, the intent is, that in the time spoken of by the prophet, which, if not our own, is one exactly corresponding to it, the deadness of men to all noble things shall be so great, that the sap of the trees shall be more truly blood, in God's

25. Op. cit. pp. 119 and 122.

sight, than their hearts' blood; and the silence of men, in praise of all noble things, so great, that the stones shall cry out, in God's hearing, instead of their tongues; and the rattling of the shingle on the beach, and the roar of the rocks driven by the torrent, be truer Te Deum than the thunder of all their choirs. The writings of modern scientific prophets teach us to anticipate a day when even these lower voices shall be also silent; and leaf cease to wave, and stream to murmur, in the grasp of eternal cold. But it may be, that rather out of the mouths of babes and sucklings a better peace may be promised to the redeemed Jerusalem; and the strewn branches, and low-laid stones, remain at rest at the gates of the city, built in unity with itself, and saying with her human voice, 'My King cometh.' [26]

26. Introduction to Ruskin's *Deucalion. Collected Studies of the Lapse of Waves, and Life of Stones*, written in 1875.

APPENDIX I

ALTHOUGH THE VAST MAJORITY OF ORDINARY
EDITIONS OF THE KING JAMES OR SO-CALLED
AUTHORIZED VERSION OF THE BIBLE FOR THE
past two centuries have been issued without the books of the
Apocrypha, the Oxford and Cambridge presses have always
provided a limited number of editions of this version with the
Apocrypha. Likewise, it is possible to secure the books of the
Apocrypha in a separate volume. A convenient edition was
issued in 1952 by Eyre and Spottiswoode in London and by
Harper & Brothers in New York under the title, *The Apocry-
pha, According to the Authorized Version*, with an Introduction
by Robert H. Pfeiffer, of Harvard University and Boston
University.

The King James translators, it must be said, took the least
pains with their work on the books of the Apocrypha. As Scrivener pointed out, 'They were content to leave many a rendering of the Bishops' Bible as they found it, when nearly any
change must have been for the better; even when their prede-

240 INTRODUCTION TO THE APOCRYPHA

cessor sets them a better example they resort to undignified, mean, almost vulgar words and phrases; and on the whole they convey to the reader's mind the painful impression of having disparaged the importance of their own work, or of having imperfectly realised the truth that what is worth doing at all is worth doing well.'[1] Scrivener mentions as colloquial forms such examples as, 'He sticks not' I Esdr. 4:21; 'Cocker thy child' Ecclus. 30:9; and as archaisms, 'brickle' Wisd. 15:13 and 'liberties' I Macc. 10:43.

The seven scholars appointed by King James to work on the revision of the Apocrypha were the following:

John Bois (Boyes), Fellow of St. John's College, Cambridge, and Prebendary of Ely.
William Branthwaite, afterward Master of Gonville and Caius College, Cambridge.
Andrew Downes, Professor of Greek at Cambridge University.
John Duport, afterward Master of Jesus College and four times elected Vice Chancellor of Cambridge University.
Jeremiah Radcliffe, Fellow of Trinity College, Cambridge.
Samuel Ward, afterward Master of Sidney College and Lady Margaret Professor of Divinity, Cambridge University.
William Warde (Ward), Fellow of King's College, Cambridge.

In addition to these seven, Thomas Bilson, afterward Bishop of Winchester, and Miles Smith had charge of the final revision, and prepared the summary of contents at the head of each chapter.

---

1. F. H. A. Scrivener, *The Authorized Edition of the English Bible* (1611) (Cambridge, 1884), pp. 140ff.

Somewhat fuller information is available regarding the preparation of the English Revised Version. Undertaken in 1870 by a group of British and American scholars, this revision of the King James Version was finished in successive stages; the New Testament was published in 1881; the Old Testament in 1885; and the Apocrypha in 1895 (the title page of the Apocrypha indicates that the work of revision was completed the previous year). After the completion of the Revision of the New Testament, it was resolved to divide the New Testament Company into three Committees, to be called the London, Westminster, and Cambridge Committees, for the purpose of beginning the revision of the Apocrypha.

The London Committee, responsible for the book of Ecclesiasticus, was to consist of the following:

Joseph Angus, Principal of Regent's Park College, London.
Edward Bickersteth, Dean of Lichfield.
Charles John Ellicott, Bishop of Gloucester and Bristol.
William Gibson Humphry, Prebendary of St. Paul's Cathedral.
George Moberly, Bishop of Salisbury.
Robert Scott, Dean of Rochester.
Charles John Vaughan, Master of the Temple and later Dean of Llandaff.
Charles Wordsworth, Bishop of St. Andrews.

Of this number, however, Bishop Moberly and Bishop Wordsworth found themselves unable through age and distance from London to attend the meetings of the panel.

The Westminster Committee, which revised the books of Tobit, Judith, and I Maccabees, was to consist of the following:

David Brown, Principal of the Free Church College, Aberdeen.

William Lee, Archdeacon of Dublin.

Samuel Newth, Principal of New College, Hampstead, London.

Edwin Palmer, Archdeacon of Oxford, Christ Church, Oxford.

Frederick Henry Ambrose Scrivener, Prebendary, Hendon Vicarage, London.

George Vance Smith, Principal of Carmarthen Presbyterian College, Wales.

Arthur Penrhyn Stanley, Dean of Westminster.

Richard Chenevix Trench, Archbishop of Dublin.

Of this group, Principal Brown did not take any part in the work, and Archbishop Trench and Dean Stanley worked with the panel only for I Maccabees.

The Cambridge Committee, which was to take the books of Wisdom and II Maccabees, was to consist of the following:

Joseph Williams Blakesley, Dean of Lincoln.

Fenton John Anthony Hort, Hulsean Professor of Divinity, Cambridge University.

Benjamin Hall Kennedy, Canon of Ely and Regius Professor of Greek, Cambridge University.

Joseph Barber Lightfoot, Bishop of Durham.

William Milligan, Professor of Divinity and Biblical Criticism, University of Aberdeen.

William Fiddian Moulton, Master of The Leys School, Cambridge.

Alexander Roberts, Professor of Humanity, University of St. Andrews.

Brooke Foss Westcott, Regius Professor of Divinity, Trinity College, Cambridge.

Of this number Dean Blakesley, Professor Kennedy, and Bishop Lightfoot were compelled for various reasons to withdraw from the work of revision, and Dr. Roberts merely provided notes on various parts of the two books.

After the work of revision of the Old Testament had been completed (1884), the Old Testament Company delegated the following of its members to translate the remaining books of the Apocrypha.

> Robert Lubbock Bensly, Fellow and Hebrew Lecturer, Gonville and Caius College, Cambridge.
> Thomas Kelly Cheyne, Fellow and Hebrew Lecturer, Balliol College, Oxford.
> Joseph Rawson Lumby, Norrisian Professor of Divinity, Cambridge University.
> John James Stewart Perowne, Dean of Peterborough.
> William Robertson Smith, Lord Almoner's Professor of Arabic, Cambridge University.
> William Aldis Wright, Fellow and Bursar of Trinity College, Cambridge.

The Company also invited Frederick Field, Fellow of Trinity College, Cambridge, to assist in the formation of the text.

Drs. Perowne and Cheyne found themselves unable to take part in the work and Dr. Field died before he could render any material assistance. The rest of the Committee revised I and II Esdras, the Additions to Esther, Baruch, the Song of the Three Holy Children, the History of Susanna, Bel and the Dragon, and the Prayer of Manasses.

In view of the division of the work among four separate committees, it is not surprising that the language and style of the Revised Version of the Apocrypha is far from being consistent. For example, in some books the proper names appear in their familiar Old Testament forms, after the Hebrew; while in others, the forms of the King James Version are usually retained, or are but slightly altered, in accordance with the Greek.

The promise by the Revisers, mentioned in their preface, to publish shortly lists of Greek readings—or, in II Esdras, the Latin readings—adopted by the Committees, was never fulfilled. One gets the impression that the energy and perhaps the interest of the original Old and New Testament Companies of Revisers dwindled during the years, and that it was only by a herculean effort on the part of a relatively few that the work was finally accomplished.

In 1913 a group of scholars, under the leadership of R. H. Charles, published at Oxford two massive volumes of *The Apocrypha and Pseudepigrapha of the Old Testament in English*. The translation of most of the books is a fresh rendering, though in several cases the Revised Version was adopted. The introductions, as well as the critical and explanatory notes, contain a mine of information on literary, historical, and critical problems relating to this body of literature.

In 1938 Professor Edgar J. Goodspeed of the University of Chicago published a translation of the Apocrypha in vernacular, American English.

More recently several Jewish scholars, under the leadership of Professor Solomon Zeitlin of Dropsie College for Hebrew and Cognate Learning in Philadelphia, have begun (1950) to issue a series under the title, *Jewish Apocryphal Literature*. Several volumes have been published, each with an English translation of the ancient language text, as well as introduction, notes, and critical apparatus. These volumes are to be welcomed as supplying the point of view of Jewish scholars and the distinctive contribution which they can make in this field of study.

After the publication of the Revised Standard Version of the

Bible in 1952, the Standard Bible Committee was requested by the General Convention of the Protestant Episcopal Church to prepare a revision of the Apocrypha. Consequently in 1953 the National Council of Churches invited and authorized a committee to translate these books. This panel was composed of five members who had served on the Committee that produced the Revised Standard Version, and four additional members. In the following list the new members are designated by an asterisk. (The titles and positions of all members are those at the time of invitation to participate in the work.)

Millar Burrows, Winkley Professor of Biblical Theology, Yale University, New Haven, Connecticut.

Henry Joel Cadbury, Hollis Professor of New Testament, Harvard University, Cambridge, Massachusetts.

Clarence Tucker Craig, Professor of New Testament and Dean of Drew Theological Seminary, Madison, New Jersey.

* Floyd V. Filson, Professor of New Testament Literature and History, McCormick Theological Seminary, Chicago, Illinois.

Frederick C. Grant, Professor of Biblical Theology, Union Theological Seminary, New York City.

* Bruce M. Metzger, Associate Professor of New Testament Language and Literature, Princeton Theological Seminary, Princeton, New Jersey.

* Robert H. Pfeiffer, Lecturer in Semitic Languages and History, and Curator of the Semitic Museum, Harvard University, and Professor of Old Testament, Boston University.

Luther A. Weigle, Sterling Professor of Religious Education and Dean of the Divinity School, Emeritus, Yale University, New Haven, Connecticut.

* Allen P. Wikgren, Associate Professor of New Testament, Federated Theological Faculty, University of Chicago, Chicago, Illinois.

On August 20, 1953, Dean Craig died, and his place was sub-sequently taken by J. Carter Swain, Executive Director, Department of English Bible in the Division of Christian Education, National Council of Churches of Christ in America. The Chairman of the Committee was Dean Luther A. Weigle, who had also served as Chairman of the Old and New Testament committees which produced the entire Revised Standard Version of the Bible. Professor Metzger served as Secretary of the Committee on the Apocrypha.

The procedure of the Committee may be briefly outlined. After the books of the Apocrypha had been allocated to the several members of the Committee, each prepared a translation of the book or books for which he had assumed responsibility. These preliminary drafts were circulated in mimeographed form among the other translators. Meetings of the Committee were held at various times during the years from 1953 to 1956 inclusive, averaging one month or more each year. At these meetings all disputed points were discussed and resolved by voting, and the decisions thus reached were embodied in new drafts which were again circulated. At a subsequent meeting each book was reviewed in the light of written agenda proposed by members of the Committee and of an Advisory Board made up of representatives appointed by denominations which accepted the invitation to review the drafts. In general, the principles of translation which had been followed by the Committee which prepared the Revised Standard Version of the Bible were followed by the Committee on the Apocrypha.[2]

2. For a succinct statement of these principles, reference may be made to two pamphlets prepared by members of the Revision Committee and published by Thomas Nelson and Sons, entitled *An Introduction to the Revised Standard Version of the New Testament* (1946), and *An Introduction to the Revised Standard Version of the Old Testament* (1952).

The Revised Standard Version Apocrypha was published
September 30, 1957, by Thomas Nelson and Sons, New York
and Edinburgh. This is the first translation of the books of the
Apocrypha prepared by a committee of American scholars. [3]

---

3. Besides the several Protestant and Jewish translations of the Apocrypha
mentioned above, it goes without saying that most of these books (but not I
and II Esdras and the Prayer of Manasseh, see above, p. 189) are available also
in Roman Catholic editions of the Bible—although of course not under the
rubric of 'Apocrypha.' The most recent English translation is still currently
under way, being prepared by Members of the Catholic Biblical Association
of America and sponsored by the Episcopal Committtee of the Confraternity
of Christian Doctrine.

APPENDIX II

New Testament Apocrypha

AS WAS INDICATED IN THE OPENING SECTION (ABOVE, PP. 5F.), BESIDES THE FOURTEEN OR FIFTEEN BOOKS WHICH COMPRISE THE APOCRYPHA in the narrow sense of the term, there are many other books which once enjoyed a certain amount of sanctity among either Jews or Christians or both. Some of these which fall into the category of Old Testament pseudepigrapha have already been mentioned; many others belong to the category of New Testament Apocrypha. These were written during the period from the second century to about the eighth or ninth centuries. Taking the canonical books of the New Testament as their models, the unknown authors of these Apocryphal books imitated each of the several literary genres of New Testament documents (Gospels, Acts, Epistles, and Apocalypse), the gospel-type most often and the epistle-type least often.

In general the authors of the New Testament Apocrypha sought to supplement (or occasionally to correct or even to supplant) the canonical books. Because the four Gospels say little of Jesus' infancy, childhood, and early manhood, and are silent altogether regarding his experiences during the three days in the tomb, several Apocryphal gospels were produced to satisfy the pious curiosity of Christians regarding these two periods of Jesus' life. For example, the Protevangelium of James, the Gospel of Thomas, and the Armenian Gospel of the Infancy refer to the early years of his life; the Gospel of Nicodemus (otherwise known as the Acts of Pilate) and the Gospel of Bartholomew refer to his experiences in Hades. Still other gospels were written to support heretical doctrines, such as docetism (the view that Christ only seemed to be human) in the Gospel of the Egyptians, or to minimize the guilt of Pilate, such as the Gospel according to Peter and the Gospel of Nicodemus. In general, these gospels show much less knowledge of Palestinian topography and customs than do the canonical Gospels—which is what one would expect from the much later date of the composition of the Apocryphal documents.

Because the missionary activities of only a few of the Apostles are recorded with any detail in the canonical Acts of the Apostles, certain unknown authors of the second and succeeding centuries thought it necessary to compose many other books of 'Acts,' telling of the work which the rest of the Apostles were reputed to have accomplished. These include such books as the Acts of Andrew, the Acts of Thomas, the Acts of Philip, the Acts of Andrew and Matthias, and others. Furthermore, even Apostles whose work is mentioned in the canonical Book of Acts found admiring authors who wrote of other exploits of their heroes in such Apocryphal works as, for example, the Acts of John, the Acts of Paul, and the Acts of Peter. These 'Acts,' which possess only a most meager historical basis, resemble in some respects the Greco-Roman novels of that period, though replacing the obscenities characteristic of many of these with doctrinal moralizings calculated to provide instruction in Christian piety.

The epistolary form, which is the most difficult of all New Testament literary genres to imitate successfully, is represented by such examples as Paul's Apocryphal Epistle to the Laodiceans, III Corinthians (which was regarded as canonical by the early Syrian and Armenian Churches), the correspondence of Paul and the pagan Roman author, Seneca, and the Epistle of the Apostles (which may also be classified as an Apocalypse).

Apocalypses depicting the future blessings of the redeemed and (with even greater vividness of detail) the future punishments of the damned, betray obvious dependence upon popular traditions of the after-life, reflected in such wide-ranging sources as Homer's *Odyssey*, book XI, Plato's eschatological myths (such as the famous vision of Er in book x of the *Republic*), Vergil's *Aeneid*, book VI, and scenes of mythological persons in the underworld painted by Polygnotus on the walls of the Lesche (club-house) at Delphi (described by Pausanias, book x, §§ 25–31). Among the many Apocryphal apocalypses, especially noteworthy are the Apocalypse of Peter, the Apocalypse of Paul, the Apocalypse of Thomas, and the Apocalypse of Stephen.

An English translation of these documents, as well as of scores of others, with brief introductions and notes may be consulted in Montague Rhodes James's standard volume, *The Apocryphal New Testament* (Oxford, 1924). During the thirty-odd years since the appearance of this volume not a few other Apocryphal books of the New Testament have been discovered. In 1935 H. I. Bell and T. C. Skeat of the British Museum edited *Fragments of an Unknown Gospel*, and in the following year Wilhelm Schubart and Carl Schmidt published at Hamburg the Greek text and a German translation of a substantial portion of the Acts of Paul. The most important single acquisition of new material was made in 1946 when almost fifty Gnostic treatises in Coptic were found near Nag-Hammadi, close to the ancient Chénoboskion, Egypt. Dating chiefly from the third century, these documents preserve not only several Apocryphal treatises hitherto imperfectly transmitted to us, but also many which had been previously unknown even by title (such as the Wisdom of Jesus, the Secret Book of John, the Traditions of Matthias, the Letter of James, and the Apocalypse of Dositheos). Unfortunately disputes as to the legal ownership of this material have contributed to a delay in the publication of these documents, and thus far all that has appeared is the *Evangelium Veritatis*, edited by M. Malinine, H.-C. Puech, and G. Quispel (Zürich, 1956).

Of discoveries made subsequent to 1924 perhaps the most interesting is the Greek papyrus codex mentioned above containing several episodes from the Apocryphal Acts of Paul. It is estimated that the original length of this Apocryphal book was about a third again as long as the canonical Acts of the Apostles; prior to this most recent find only about half of the Acts of Paul was known, which may be read in English translation in James's volume already mentioned. In view of the intrinsic interest of the discovery, and in order to provide a typical specimen of a New Testament Apocryphal book, the episode of 'St. Paul and the Baptized Lion' is given here in the English translation which the present writer made several years ago for the *Princeton Seminary Bulletin* (November 1945).[1]

Before giving the translation of the episode, it will be appro-

---

1. Another English translation, prepared by J. W. B. Barns of Oxford, has been available since 1953 when an appendix containing this portion of the Acts of Paul was added to the fifth printing of James's *Apocryphal New Testament*.

priate to supply some information about the Apocryphal Acts of Paul. The author of this book, so Tertullian informs us (*de Baptismo*, xvii), was a certain presbyter of the Roman province of Asia within Asia Minor, who wrote the book (probably about 180-190) with the avowed intention of doing honor to the Apostle Paul. Although well-intentioned, the author was brought up for trial and, being convicted of composing the apocryphon, was removed from his clerical office. But his book, though condemned by ecclesiastical leaders, achieved great popularity among the laity. Certain episodes, such as the section dealing with 'The Journeys of Paul and Thecla,' exist in a number of Greek manuscripts and in half a dozen ancient versions, thus testifying to their popularity.

In the cycle of tales about Paul in these Acts perhaps the most entertaining is that which concerns the Apostle's encounter with a fierce lion in the amphitheater at Ephesus. Probably the unknown presbyter had read Paul's rhetorical question in the course of the Apostle's argument in I Cor. 15:32, 'What do I gain if, humanly speaking, I fought with wild beasts at Ephesus?' No doubt wishing to supply details of what seemed to be a tantaliz-ingly brief allusion, the author determined to incorporate into his religious romance a thrilling account of Paul's encounter with wild beasts at Ephesus. In doing so, however, this second-century author overlooked evidence, both literary and histor-ical, that prevents one from taking literalistically Paul's rhetor-ical question in I Cor. 15:32. That Paul was speaking figura-tively is shown by his immediately preceding words, '. . . I die every day!' Furthermore, being a Roman citizen Paul could not be forced into the amphitheater as a performer. Moreover, even supposing that Paul, by some miscarriage of justice and in spite of his influential friends at Ephesus (Acts 19:3), had been actually condemned to the wild beasts and had been marvelously rescued, is it conceivable (as Jerome asks in his *de Viris Illustribus*, vii) that such an event should have been totally ignored in the canonical Book of Acts? Paul's allusion in I Cor. 15:32, therefore, is no doubt to be taken as a strong metaphor referring to some plot or attack made by his enemies against his life. Furthermore, the words in II Tim. 4:17, 'So I was rescued from the lion's mouth,' are generally taken by commentators as a figurative expression of deliverance from the direst danger, the exact nature of which the writer does not specify. Because in the context reference is made to Paul's release from his (first) Roman imprisonment, the Greek Fathers understood the expression as a veiled reference to Nero. There is, therefore, no substantial external evidence for the historicity of the following episode of Paul and the lion; the internal evidence can be judged by the reader.

In the following translation, words which must be supplied to complete the sense in English, but which are not present in the Greek, are enclosed in parentheses. A lacuna in the papyrus with a corresponding break in the narrative is indicated by a series of dots. Where it is possible to conjecture with more or less certainty what may have originally stood in the lacuna, the reconstructed word or words are printed in italics. If, for example, the first three letters of the Greek word for slave (δοῦλος) are lacking, the English translation is printed thus 'slave.' The numerals within square brackets indicate the pagination and lineation of the Greek original. It should also be mentioned that the rendering was deliberately cast into an archaic style so as to be congruous with the previously published portions of the Acts of Paul in M. R. James, *The Apocryphal New Testament*.

St. Paul and the Baptized Lion

(The papyrus fragment begins with part of a conversation between a certain Hieronymus, the Roman governor at Ephesus, and the Apostle Paul.)

[Papyrus p. 1] '. . . of God . . . *Do thou* therefore speak, what are the facts *concerning the god whom thou dost proclai*m?' And Paul said un*to him,* '*Do what thou wilt,* for thou hast no powe*r over me except ov*er my body; but thou wilt not *kill* the soul. [5] *Hear* now how thou must be saved and receive thou all *my words* into (thy) heart . . . sun *a*nd earth and stars and principalities and dominions and all the good things in the world for the sake of *mankind* hath he formed . . . *for the us*e of men according . . . [10] . . . being led astray and enslaved utterly . . . by pure gold *and silv*er and precious stones . . . and by adulteries and drunkenness. For watching . . . the women who lead (them) into deceit, they walked through the aforemen*tioned* (sins) and were slain. But now since the Lord wis*heth* [15] us to live in God because of the error which is in the world, and not to die in (our) sins, he saveth (us) through the chaste men who preach that ye should repent and believe *that there is one* God and one Christ Jesus and (that) there is no other. For your gods are *of bronze* and stone and wood, neither are they able to ta*ke* nourishment *n*or [20] see nor hear nor even stand (alone). Do ye lay hold upon the good *choice* and be saved, lest *G*od be wroth *and con*sume you with unquenchable fire and *your* remembrance be lost.'

And when the governor had heard these things . . . *in* the theater with the crowd, he said, 'Men of Eph*esus,* [25] that this man hath spoken well, I know; but still it is not time *now* for you to learn these things. Decide therefore what ye wish.' Some kept saying that he should burn him at the ... and (others), the goldsmiths, kept saying, 'To the wild beasts with the man!' And because a great *uproar* was raised, Hieronymus condemned him to the wild *beasts*, [30] after he had had him scourged. Now, since it was Pentecost, the brethren wept not nor *bowed the kn*ee, but rejoicing they prayed *while standing.*[2]

And *after* six days Hieronymus held a pa*rade* (of wild beasts), so that all who beheld were astounded at the great size of *the wild beasts.* [Papyrus p. 2] While Paul *sat* bound ... he did not shrink away but came ... he heard the creaking of the wagons *and the tumult of those who* were carrying the wild beasts. And *as the lion* [5] ... came to the side door of the sta*dium, beside which* (*door*) *Paul* had been imprisoned, it roared mightily, so that all *the people* shouted, 'The lion!' And then (the lion) roared fiercely and with ra*ge, so that even Paul* left off praying, being afraid.

Now there w*as a certain man*, Diophantus, a freedman of Hieronymus, whose wife *was* a [10] disci*ple* of Paul and night and day would sit beside him, *so that* Diophantus was jealous and urged on the fight with wild beasts. *And* Artemilla, the wife of Hieronymus, earnestly desired to listen to Paul while he was *pray*ing, and she said unto Eubula, the wife of *Dio*phantus, ... '*I wish* to listen unto the prayer (and) the word of him who is to fight with wild beasts.' And she departed and [15] announced (it) unto Paul. And Paul, filled with joy, said, 'Fetc*h her* (in).'

2. In the ancient Church the postures of prayer generally practiced and allowed were four; namely, standing, kneeling, bowing, and prostration. Standing was the custom on the Lord's Day and during the fifty days between Easter and Pentecost because the Church felt that the Saviour's resurrection (ἀνάστασις, literally, 'up-standing') ought to be commemorated even in the posture assumed for prayer.

And, clothed in rather sad-colored garments, she came unto him with Eubula. But when Paul saw her, he sighed and said, 'O woman, thou ruler of this world, the mistress of much gold, the citizen of great luxury, [20] thou who makest a vain display of garments, sit thou upon the ground and forget thy wealth and beauty and ornaments; for these will profit thee nothing unless thou make request of God, who considereth the might of this world as refuse, but giveth freely the marvelous things of the next world. Gold perisheth, wealth is [25] squandered, garments wear out, beauty groweth old, and great cities pass away, and (the) world is (going to be) brought to nought in fire on account of the wickedness of men. Only God remaineth, and the adoption which is given through him, in which it is necessary to be saved. And now, Artemilla, hope thou in God and [30] he will save thee; hope thou in Christ and he will grant thee forgiveness of sins and will place upon thee a crown of freedom, that thou mayest no longer serve idols and the smell of burnt offerings, but (mayest serve) the living God and father of Christ, whose glory is forever and ever. Amen.' And after Artemilla had heard these things, [35] with Eubula she besought Paul that he would straightway baptize her in God.

And on the morrow was the fight with wild beasts. [Papyrus p. 3] And Hieronymus heard from Diophantus that their wives would sit night and day beside Paul, and he was angered not a little at Artemilla and the freedwoman Eubula. And after he had dined, he departed earlier (than usual) that he might quickly accomplish the [5] fight with wild beasts.

And the women said unto Paul, 'Dost thou wish us to bring a blacksmith, that thou mayest be loosed and baptize us in the sea?' And Paul said, 'I do not wish it, for I have a firm trust in God who hath delivered the whole world from fetters.' And Paul cried to God on the Sabbath, while the Lord's Day was approaching, on which Paul was to fight with wild beasts; and he said, [10] 'O my God, Christ Jesus, who hast redeemed me from so many evils, in the presence of Artemilla and Eubula, who are thine own, grant that the fetters may be broken from my hands.' And while Paul was earnestly begging these things, a youth, very beautiful in loveliness, entered; and after the youth had smiled, he loosened Paul's fetters, [15] and immediately he departed. But because of the vision which had been granted to Paul, and the wonderful sign concerning the fetters, his sorrow at fighting with wild beasts fled away, and exulting he leaped as though in paradise. And taking Artemilla he led her out of the narrow and dark place where the prisoners [20] are kept. And when they had passed outside, having escaped the notice of the keepers, and were now in safety, Paul besought his God earnestly saying, 'The gates . . . thy dispensation . . . that Artemilla may be initiated with the seal in the Lord.'[3] And then the locked doors opened wide at the name of [25] God . . . and the guards were weighed down with a deep sleep. And immediately the matron went out, and the blessed Paul (went out) with Eubula, and they were invisible on account of the darkness . . . And a youth resembling . . . the body of Paul, shining not with a lamp but from the sanctity of his body, went before [30] them until they drew nigh to the sea, and the shining one stood opposite . . . And after Paul had prayed, he laid his hand on Artemilla and blessed (?) . . . the water in the name of Christ Jesus, so that the sea rose in great waves; and, seized with a great fear, Artemilla almost fell into a swoon . . . and (Paul) said, 'O thou bright and shining one, help, lest the heathen say [Papyrus p. 4] that Paul,

---

3. Beginning in the second century (in II Clement and Hermas) 'seal' came to be used as a name for Christian baptism (F. J. Dölger, *Sphragis, eine altchristliche Taufbezeichnung in ihren Beziehungen zur profanen und religiösen Kultur des Altertums*, Paderborn, 1911).

the prisoner, fled after he had killed Artemilla.' And after the
youth had smiled again, the matron revived and proceeded to
her home, while now dawn was appearing. But when she (?)
went in, while the guards were sleeping, he (Paul) broke bread
and brought water, [5] drank it with (the) word,[4] (and) sent
her off to Hieronymus, her husband. But he himself (Paul)
prayed. And at dawn there was an outcry from the citizens,
'Let us go to the theater; let us go; let us see him who possesseth
God fight with wild beasts.'

And Hieronymus was himself present, partly because of his
jealousy of his wife, partly also lest he (Paul) should escape;
and [10] he commanded Diophantus and the other slaves to
bring Paul into the stadium. And while he was being dragged
in, he said nothing but kept bowed down and was groaning
aloud because he was being made sport of by the city. And having been led away, he was immediately cast into the stadium,
so that all were angered at Paul's stately seriousness. And when
[15] Artemilla with Eubula had fallen most perilously ill (with
anxiety) lest Paul should perish, Hieronymus was grieved not
a little concerning his wife, but also because it had already been
noised abroad in the city, and (because) he did *not* have his wife
with him. When he had therefore taken his seat, the *chief hunts-
m*an commanded that an exceedingly fierce lion, *caught a little
while* before, [20] be turned loose on him, so that the whole
multitude . . . in order that *Paul* should be killed . . . But *the lion
sprang from* the cage and . . . prayed, and still to th*em* . . . which
[25] was from the brambles . . . and a great amazement seized
all, while he . . . exceedingly. And Paul *kept on making* his
proper work of prayer . . . and gave (his) testimony. *The lion*

---

4. In the Apocryphal Acts the Eucharist is observed with bread and water,
as was usual in early heretical groups whose ascetical tendencies kept them
from the juice of the grape.

looked around *in a circle* and, after showing *it*self entirely, [30] came on the run and *lay down* against Paul's legs, docile as a lamb *and like his serva*nt. And when he had ended his pray*er, as from a drea*m it arose and said unto Paul in a hum*an voice, 'Grace be with t*hee.' And Paul was not affrighted but he like-wise said, *'Grace be with t*hee, lion,' and laid his hand on *it. And the whole multi*tude cried out, 'Away with the enchanter, away with the s*orcerer!' And the lion lo*oked at Paul, and Pau*l at the lion, and Paul perce*ived that this *was the li*on [Papyrus p. 5] which had come (to him) *and had had itself bap*tized. *An*d borne along by faith Paul said, 'Lion, wast thou the one *whic*h I baptized?' [5] And the lion answered and said unto Paul, 'Y*ea*.' And Paul said to him a second time, 'And how wast thou captured?' And the lion said with one voice,[6] 'Even as thou wast, O Paul.'

While Hieronymus was letting loose [5] many wild beasts in order that Paul might be destroyed, and (setting) archers

---

5. We do not possess a clear and entirely unambiguous account of the actual baptism of the lion (referred to by Jerome as 'totam baptizati leonis fabulam,' *de Vir. Illustr.,* vii), but the Epistle of Pelagia, preserved in three Ethiopic manuscripts the oldest of which dates from the fifteenth century, gives the following. While Paul was walking on a mountain, a lion as large as a horse saluted him and said, 'Make me to enter among the mature Christians.' The meaning of this request is not absolutely certain but doubtless it is a periphrasis for baptism. The Epistle continues, 'And Paul took him and made him to enter among the mature Christians. And when he had finished the law of the seventh day, then they bade each other farewell. And again Paul returned to the city' (E. J. Goodspeed's translation in the *American Journal of Semitic Languages and Literatures,* xx, 1904, 100; reprinted in his *The Epistle of Pelagia,* Chicago, 1931, p. 12).

6. The text has what is undoubtedly a scribal error, μιᾷ φωνῇ. The author may have originally written either ἰδίᾳ φωνῇ, 'with his own voice,' or θίᾳ [itacism for θείᾳ] φωνῇ, 'with a divine voice.' In favor of the former is the statement made a bit earlier regarding the lion's speaking with a human voice; in favor of the latter is the tradition preserved by the Christian poet Commodian (c. A.D. 400), '[Deus] leonem populo fecit loqui voce divina' (*Carmen apologeticum,* line 628, ed. Dombart).

against the lion so that that one also might be destroyed, and although the air was clear, a very heavy and exceedingly great (and) violent hailstorm did hurtle from heaven, so that many died and all the rest fled. But it touched neither Paul nor the lion, but the other wild beasts [10] died under the quantity of the hail, (which was so violent) that Hieronymus's ear was struck and torn off, and the multitude cried out while fleeing, 'Save us, O God, save, thou God of the man who fought with wild beasts!' And after Paul had bidden farewell to the lion, which no longer spoke, he went forth from the stadium, went down [15] to the harbor, and embarked in a boat sailing to Macedonia; for there were many passengers, because the city was like to be destroyed. So he also embarked with them as one of those who were fleeing, and the lion went away into the mountain, just as was naural for it (to do).[7]

7. The reader is struck at once by the similarities between this story and that of Androcles (or, more correctly, Androclus), a Roman slave of the first century. He is the hero of a tale which Aulus Gellius (c. A.D. 160) included in his *Noctes Atticae*, v. 14, and which he says he took from the fifth book of Apion's *Aegyptiaca*. (This Apion, a grammarian of the first Christian century, was the one against whom Josephus directed his *Contra Apionem*.) The gist of the story is that Androclus had taken refuge from the cruelties of his master in a cave in Africa, when a lion entered the cave and showed him his swollen paw, from which Androclus extracted a large splinter. The grateful animal subsequently recognized him when he had been captured and thrown to the wild beasts in the circus, and, instead of attacking him, began to caress him. Both Androclus and the lion were then set free. According to Aulus Gellius, Apion said that he was present in the Circus Maximus of Rome and beheld this incident with his own eyes. The conclusion of Apion's yarn is charmingly naïve: 'Afterwards we used to see Androclus with the lion, attached to a slender leash, making the rounds of the shops throughout the city; Androclus was given money, the lion was sprinkled with flowers, and everyone who met them anywhere exclaimed, "This is the lion that was a man's friend, this is the man who was physician to a lion."' The popularity of the tale is evidenced by the use which the anonymous Asian presbyter made of it in the Acts of Paul. (In modern times George Bernard Shaw's play, *Androcles and the Lion*, presents a delightful *réchauffé* of the pagan story in a Christian setting told with a characteristically Shavian twist.)

Then Artemilla and Eubula grieved not a little [20] while they fasted and . . . what might have happened to Paul. But when it was night, *a youth* (?) came . . . visibly into the bed chamber where . . . *one* another *and Hie*ronymus's ear began to mortify. *He came to Eubula . . . an*d Artemilla on account of (their) affliction and said unto them, 'Be not [25] troubled *concerning Paul . . . for in the n*ame of Christ Jesus and in the mi*gh*t *of the Almighty, Paul,* his *servan*t, hath departed into Macedo*nia, that there also* he may fulfill the dispen*sations of the Lord,* but you . . .' *Then* great amazement seized them. *And because Hieronymus was now* wide awake (literally, sober) at night [30] in his pains, *he said,* 'O God, *who didst help* the man who fought with wild beasts, sa*ve thou me through the youth* who in a vision came through *the closed* bed chamber.' But he seeing them in fear . . . great . . . while they were sitting beside . . . the physi*cians* . . . *loud* cry, 'Through the will of Christ Jesus . . . the ear!' And it became whole, as *the you*th had bidden him, (saying), 'Treat thy*self* with honey.'[8]

What is the value of documents such as the Acts of Paul? To call them, as some have done, the 'excluded' books of the New Testament is to suggest circumstances of their circulation and position which are entirely false. To suppose that such Apocryphal books were ejected from their rightful place in the New Testament by a council or an assembly of ecclesiastics is to suppose what, as a matter of cold historical fact, never happened. The most cogent proof that these books are intrinsically on a different plane from the books of the New Testament is afforded merely by reading them side by side with the books of

---

8. Then there follows in the papyrus a narrative entitled 'From Philippi to Corinth,' part of which was known before the discovery of the Greek original through a Coptic translation.

the New Testament and allowing each to make its own impression. Then, in the words of M. R. James, 'it will very quickly be seen that there is no question of anyone's having excluded them from the New Testament: they have done that for themselves.'[9]

Yet the New Testament Apocrypha are important documents in their own way. True enough, as historical sources of information concerning the Apostolic age they are negligible. The permanent value of this body of literature lies in another direction, namely in reflecting the beliefs of their authors and the tastes of their early readers who found profit as well as entertainment in tales of this kind. That is, the New Testament Apocrypha are important historical documents which tell us much, not about the age with which they profess to deal, but about the age which gave them birth. They purport to be reliable accounts of the words and deeds of the Apostles; in reality they set forth under the names of the Apostles certain ideals of Christian life and conceptions of Christian faith current in the second and succeeding centuries. To inculcate these ideas the authors did not hesitate to elaborate marvelous tales, and, in the credulous temper of that age, almost anything was believed. That the tale about Paul and the lion was accepted as true by the common Christian is shown by the use which Hippolytus of Rome made of it early in the third century. Employing an argument *ad hominem* he writes in his *Commentary on Daniel* (iii. 29), 'For if we believe that when Paul was condemned to death, a lion, let loose upon him, fell down and licked his feet, how shall we not believe the things that happened in the case of Daniel?'

Furthermore, representing as they do the lush growth of Christian legend, folklore, and romantic literature, the New

9. *The Apocryphal New Testament*, pp. xif.

Testament Apocrypha are indispensable for the interpretation of contemporary and subsequent Christian art, literature, and dogma. In art, for example, one finds their influence reflected in paintings in the catacombs, bas-reliefs on ancient Christian sarcophagi, mosaics in early basilicas, miniatures in illuminated manuscripts, and stained glass windows in medieval cathedrals. In the field of literature, besides allusions to them in the writings of the Church Fathers, the New Testament Apocrypha exerted a decisive influence on several cycles of miracle and mystery plays in the Middle Ages,[10] on the *Golden Legend* by Jacobus de Voragine (often considered to be the most influential book produced during the Middle Ages), Dante's *Divine Comedy*, and other classics of the world's literature. As regards doctrine, several New Testament Apocrypha contain traditions to which the Roman Catholic Church appeals in support of recently defined dogmas and beliefs regarding the Virgin Mary. Less obvious but no less pervasive is the interaction between certain New Testament Apocrypha and the development of the doctrine of the descent of Christ into Hades, as well as popular beliefs regarding the after-life, the blessings of the redeemed, and the punishments of the damned.

But to give an adequate account of all these topics would require another book!

---

10. It is remarkable that although the Mysteries seldom drew upon the Old Testament Apocrypha, not a few are paraphrases of New Testament Apocrypha. See William Hone, *Ancient Mysteries Described, Especially the English Miracle Plays founded on Apocryphal New Testament Story* . . . (London, n.d.), and Georges Duriez, *Les Apocryphes dans le drame religieux en Allemagne au Moyen Age* (Lille, 1914).

A SELECTED BIBLIOGRAPHY

A. THE HISTORY OF THE INTERTESTAMENTAL PERIOD.

E. SCHÜRER, *A History of the Jewish People in the Time of Jesus Christ*, 5 vols. Edinburgh: T. & T. Clark, 1885–1891.

Though out of date in certain respects, this is still the standard work of reference.

W. O. E. OESTERLEY and T. H. ROBINSON, *A History of Israel*, 2 vols. Oxford: at the Clarendon Press, 1932.

The second part of Volume II covers the intertestamental period.

NORMAN H. SNAITH, *The Jews from Cyrus to Herod*. New York: Abingdon Press, 1956.

A brief and popularly written account.

B. THE APOCRYPHA AS LITERATURE.

W. O. E. OESTERLEY, *An Introduction to the Books of the Apocrypha*. New York: Macmillan Company, 1935.

A general work of reference.

EDGAR J. GOODSPEED, *The Story of the Apocrypha*. Chicago: University of Chicago Press, 1939.

A brief account, with suggestions for study.

C. C. TORREY, *The Apocryphal Literature: A Brief Introduction*. New Haven: Yale University Press, 1945.

A fresh and independent examination of questions of date, authorship, and original language of the Apocrypha and the Pseudepigrapha.

Robert H. Pfeiffer, *History of New Testament Times, with an Introduction to the Apocrypha.* New York: Harper & Brothers, 1949.

The fullest and most scholarly of modern introductions to the Apocrypha (pp. 233–541). Does not deal with II Esdras.

Robert C. Dentan, *The Apocrypha, Bridge of the Testaments.* Greenwich, Connecticut: The Seabury Press, 1954.

A concise guide for the layman.

C. commentaries on the apocrypha.

(not including volumes on single books of the Apocrypha)

Edwin Cone Bissell, *The Apocrypha of the Old Testament, with Historical Introductions, a Revised Translation, and Notes Critical and Explanatory* (being J. P. Lange's 'Commentary on the Holy Scriptures,' Vol. xv). New York: Charles Scribner's Sons, 1886.

Old but still useful.

Henry Wace, editor, *Apocrypha* ('The Speaker's Commentary'), 2 vols. London: John Murray, 1888.

A careful and scholarly work, by eight clergymen of the Anglican Church.

R. H. Charles, editor, *The Apocrypha and Pseudepigrapha in English, with Introductions and Critical and Explanatory Notes to the Several Books,* 2 vols. Oxford: at the Clarendon Press, 1913.

The standard work of reference in the field, written by acknowledged authorities.

Charles Gore, H. L. Goudge, and Alfred Guillaume, *A New Commentary on Holy Scripture, Including the Apocrypha.* New York: Macmillan Company, 1928.

A convenient and concise one-volume commentary.

Bernard Orchard, E. F. Sutcliffe, R. C. Fuller, and R. Russell, editors, *A Catholic Commentary on Holy Scripture.* New York: Thomas Nelson and Sons, 1953.

Written from the Roman Catholic point of view, this one volume commentary regards the Apocryphal books as Holy Scripture. Does not include I Esdras, II Esdras, or the Prayer of Manasseh.

D. THE CANON OF THE OLD TESTAMENT.

H. E. RYLE, *The Canon of the Old Testament,* 2nd edition. New York: Macmillan and Co., 1895.

A scholarly and exhaustive work, in a popular style.

G. WILDEBOER, *The Origin of the Canon of the Old Testament: An Historico-Critical Enquiry.* London: Luzac & Co., 1895.

A detailed study with the citation and discussion of the ancient testimonies.

SOLOMON ZEITLIN, *An Historical Study of the Canonization of the Hebrew Scriptures.* Philadelphia: Jewish Publication Society of America, 1933.

Makes large use of rabbinic sources and reaches some conclusions at variance with those generally held.

GUNNAR ÖSTBORN, *Cult and Canon: A Study in the Canonization of the Old Testament.* Uppsala: A.-B. Lundequistska Bokhandeln, 1950.

Considers the canon from the point of view of the liturgical use of the books.

FLOYD V. FILSON, *Which Books Belong in the Bible?* Philadelphia: Westminster Press, 1957.

A thoughtful study dealing with theological aspects of the canon.

E. RELIGIOUS DEVELOPMENT DURING THE INTERTESTAMENTAL PERIOD.

H. MALDWYN HUGHES, *The Ethics of Jewish Apocryphal Literature.* London: Robert Culley, 1910.

An analysis and synthesis of ethical teaching.

R. H. CHARLES, *Religious Development between the Old and the New Testaments.* New York: Henry Holt, 1914.

A brief and popularly written account.

HENRY J. WICKS, *The Doctrine of God in the Jewish Apocryphal and Apocalyptic Literature.* London: Hunter and Longhurst, 1915.

Deals with the transcendence, the justice, and the grace of God.

NORMAN B. JOHNSON, *Prayer in the Apocrypha and Pseudepigrapha: A Study of the Jewish Concept of God.* Philadelphia: Society of Biblical Literature and Exegesis, 1948.

A collection and analysis of sources pertaining to the devotional life.

H. H. ROWLEY, *The Relevance of Apocalyptic: A Study of Jewish and Christian Apocalypses from Daniel to the Revelation,* revised edition. New York: Harper and Brothers, 1955.

A helpful discussion by a recognized authority.

INDEX

Psalm, the apocryphal 151st, 176
Psalms of Solomon, the, 5, 155f.
Pseudepigrapha, 6
Puccinelli, 227
Purim, 60
Puritans, 195

Quakers, 196 note
Qumran, 31, 80, 156, 177

Raphael, 229, 230 note
Raphael (angel), 34ff.
Razis, 145
Regnault, 223
Rembrandt, 225, 226 (bis), 227, 228
Renaissance painters, 223ff.
Reni, 227, 228
Resurrection, the, 26, 75, 87, 147, 157, 164
Revelation, the Book of, 166
Revised Standard Version, the, 3
Revised Standard Version, translators of the Apocrypha of the, 245f.
Revised Version, translators of the Apocrypha of the, 241ff.
Ridley, Bishop, 23
Rinkart, Martin, 213
Roman Catholic views of the Apocrypha, 6; see also Trent
Romanino, 223
Romans, the Epistle to the, 159f.
Rubinstein, Anton, 222
Ruskin, John, 225, 237

Sadducees, the, 87f., 131, 135, 154f., 157
St. Bernard of Clairvaux, 214f.
St. George, 121f.
Salisbury, ritual of, 40
Salvadori, Andrea, 222
Sarah, 33ff.

Sauer, Christoph, 24
Sayers, Dorothy, 107 note
Schiavone, 226
Scribes, 78f.
Seleucus IV, 130, 141
Septuagint, 9, 178
Serpent Worship, 119f.
Serrur, 225
Shakespeare, 208ff.
Shaw, George Bernard, 261 note
Sheol, 74, 156
Sirach, the Wisdom of Jesus the son of, 77ff.
Simon, 134
Slavic Bible, the first, 194
Slovenian Bible, the first, 184
Solomon, the Wisdom of, 65
Song of the Three Young Men, the, 99ff.
Spada, 224
Spear, A. P., 228
Spenser, Edmund, 122
Stanford, C. Villiers, 221
Stoics, the, 69, 73, 162
Stokes, Walter, 221
Susanna, 107ff., 227f.
Swain, J. Carter, 246
Swedish Bible, the first, 184
Swift, Jonathan, 236f.

Tale of the Three Guardsmen, the, 14ff.
Tammuz, 97
Tertullian, 172, 252
Testament of the Twelve Patriarchs, the, 6
Thirty-nine Articles, the, 191
Thomas Matthew Bible, the, 186
Three Guardsmen, the Tale of the, 14ff.
Tiepolo, 228, 229
Tintoretto, 224, 227 (bis), 228 (bis)
Titian, 225, 226